GRINDSTONE
An island world remembered

By Stanley Norcom

Edited by Norvin Hein,

Advised by
Harold Kendall
Historian of the Village of Clayton
and
Marjorie and Leon Rusho,
Octogenarians of Grindstone Island.

Published by Robert Edwards
1993

Distributed by

River Heritage Book Store
532-534 Riverside Drive
Clayton, N.Y. 13624
315-686-5790
and
The Landing
41 King Street
Gananoque, Ontario K7G 1 ES
613-382-7897

$17.95

For mail order copies
send check to

Robert Edwards, Publisher
541 7th Street
New Cumberland, Pa. 17070
717-774-2955

$22 US or $25 Canadian
includes postage, handling and tax

Copyright © Norvin Hein
1993.

Beyond quotation for use in a review, no part of this book may be re-published without the written permission of the copyright holder.

1st Printing May 1993

Cover:
View across Thurso Bay from its western cliff. Opposite, Webster Point, and, far right, the onetime home of Nettie and Dick McRae.

Contents

Editor's Introduction vii

Chapters

1. Reverie in Thurso Churchyard 1
2. Clayton in 1909 4
3. Crossing to the Island 11
4. A Glimpse of Thurso Village 27
5. Dick and Nettie McRae 33
6. Lew Webster 43
7. Jay Robinson 49
8. Hi Marshall's Store 55
9. Flossie Sturdevant 63
10. Frank Slate 69
11. The North Shore Road and its People 73
12. The Coterie at the Head of the Island 81
13. The Heritage of the Great Quarries 89
14. Davy Black 95
15. Elizabeth Brown 103
16. Charlotte McIntosh 107
17. Emmet and Nellie Dodge 113
18. Fire on the Island: Mort Marshall's House 117
19. Hub Garnsey and his Family 121
20. Life on the Island Farms 127
21. Aboard "the Whistler" 135
22. The End of the Webster Saga 139
23. The Cheese Factory 147
24. The Post Office 153
25. The Shore "Below the Marsh" 157
26. Death on the River 165
27. Canoe Point 169
28. Mary Crouch 173
29. The World Wars and the Rum War 177
30. Bertha and Mabel McRae 181
31. The Church 187
32. My Island Sinks 207

Index 216-219

Maps:
    Homes and Farms of Grindstone Island .... Inside front cover
    The Thurso Village of My Earliest Memory .... Inside back cover
    The Island in its Regional Setting .... Back cover

The Author in 1915
The sharp recollections of this thirteen-year-old make up much of this book.

To the islanders,
who took into their community
long ago
a small boy from Brooklyn

In visions when the night is deep
   Their plaintive faces haunt my sleep.
"Must we now vanish in this night,
   Though you we knew, and you could write?"

Editor's Introduction

Those who travel along the shores of Grindstone Island and look up into its dense crown of trees often imagine that it is the primeval forest of the continent that they see, unchanged since Iroquois used this island as a summer hunting ground. Those who fly over the island see from the air no brown soil turned over by the plough and very few mown fields of grass. In all the island's ten square miles only six homesteads are inhabited in winter and only three, by reason of raising a few beef cattle, are classified as farms. Even the two hundred families who in summer enjoy the river in their cottages on the shore have little notion that the heart of the island was ever a home for anyone or anything but its present abounding game. But a few old residents and a few aged exiles remember an island of half a hundred farms and a thriving community that lived by its own distinctive customs, insulated from the world by a river-moat that was miles wide on every side.

This peopled island of former times is threatened with erasure from human memory. The late Jessie Matthews Newberry has told the story of a few heroic months in island life in her fragile self-published booklets *The Longest Winter* (1989) and, undated, *The Summer After*. But no more will come from her pen, and no comprehensive history of the island has ever been published. The memoir that follows does much to rescue this fascinating community from oblivion. It is a marvellous demonstration of the treasures that lie in aged minds, and of the wonderful preservation of human experience that can occur when the aged exercise their power to write. Stanley Norcom first came to the island with his parents in 1909, as a very small boy. It was a case of love at first sight. Such headlong reactions to the island are not rare, but it is rare when devotion to the island's sights and sounds continues throughout the whole of a long life. Stanley Norcom, retired from his profession of dentistry, was willing and able to work quietly throughout his 80's to create this vivid record of persons and places. Few on the island had any inkling that this writing was going on, but as a very near neighbor on Thurso Bay I found him out, and thereafter gave him no peace. He was compelled to give informal readings and to report constantly on the progress of his work. As years passed his difficulties in keeping house on an inaccessible island increased, and failing eyesight and other ailments finally forced him to retire to his Florida home, taking his unfinished manuscript with him. There he continued to work, and to endure my seasonal greetings in which I accused him annually of sloth and asked whether he had burned his manuscript by mistake or sent it off with the week's trash. Recently he silenced me in a letter saying that his complete manuscript was on its way to me. The rather despairing note mentioned serious new ailments and declared that he had done all he could: "The script is now yours to do with as you like."

And I have done that. In preparing a rather long manuscript for publication I have made economies of space, but I have not changed its spirit. A few of his tales have been omitted. With regret I have shortened his genealogical accounts of the later generations of Grindstone families. Realizing that these "begats" are important to researchers in family history I have deposited a bound volume of the original manuscript in the Flower Public Library in Watertown, New York, where all of Dr. Norcom's information on family trees can be seen in its untouched form.

The time-span covered by these memoirs is wide. Island legends are retold that go back even into the 1870's and he mentions some events of quite recent date. Readers will be happier if they understand from the start, that it is not Dr. Norcom's intention to write a complete chronicle of island history. It is only rarely and casually that he gives accounts of early and very recent times. His serious intention is to sketch the Grindstone people and events of his mature years, from about 1914 to 1960. Even then he does not write as a chronicler. He gives hints about periods and about the sequence of events, but he mentions few dates. His real aim is to present the island's fascinating personalities, utilizing the archive of his own memory.

Readers will discover that Dr. Norcom writes with deep affection for island persons and island places. Sentiment flows strongly in this book—but not sentimentality. He does not sugar-coat these ancestors. He presents them so frankly that the feeling of living persons could be hurt. If wounds should be given, the editor—and the author—regret them very much. Readers are begged to delay reacting to these candid character sketches until all anecdotes have been told. It is a matter of principle with Dr. Norcom to present his first impressions just as they arose in him in moments of first meeting. The same honesty guides him in setting forth his later and deeper impressions of persons, which are often quite different. My local advisors, of the same generation as the author, forbid me to tamper with these pictures of people of long ago. "They're right on the button!" Leon Rusho declared. So I have used the blue pencil lightly, trusting that the descendants of these doughty characters will want to see them "warts and all" and will, like the author, respect them for what they were "in all their oddities and quiddities."

Quite different kinds of readers should find meaning in this book. I mention first the summer people who will be able to understand at last the foundation stones and ruined chimneys that they have noticed in the bushy backlands of their plots. It is a book also for those who are fascinated by the study of small communities—perhaps living themselves in social worlds too big to love, and looking for alternatives. And the diaspora of old Grindstone Island families, now scattered far and wide, will in this book recover knowledge of the very nature of their ancestral home. Last, there is and always has been a circle of sensitive people who respond to the plight of refugees everywhere and to the literature of their homesickness. Exiled by forces not under his control, the author himself writes with nostalgic longing for a well-loved island home. In this he is at one with former island families who left under different compulsions, leaving their hearts behind. The dispersion from Grindstone Island has been like the expulsion of crofters from the Scottish islands in the eighteenth century, even though the tyrants in this case have not been landlords able to make more money by keeping sheep than by keeping people. The "villain" has been the marvellous new efficiency of twentieth century American agriculture, able to supply the world's needs at such low cost that island farmers could no longer make a living from their small and rocky fields. However callous human beings may be, they have a blessed ability to participate in others' sickness of heart. We are willing to turn our thoughts way down upon the Swanee River, or to that old Kentucky home. We may not long to go to either of these places personally, but we feel for those who do. Those who have been able to love Oliver Goldsmith's *Deserted Village* or Edgar Lee Masters' *Spoon River Anthology* will be moved by Stanley Norcom's pained backward look upon a beloved place and its people.

The certainty of this picture of old island life rests on the supportive work of local consultants who are old enough to share the author's memories. Marjorie and Leon Rusho and Harold Kendall, slightly junior members of Stanley Norcom's own generation, have scrutinized these pages and have offered priceless explanations and amplifications and corrections. In the difficult work of turning the author's informal ink sketches into actual maps, these advisors and many other senior persons have given valuable help. I thank Allan M. Jackson, assessor of the town of Clayton, for many maps of the island past and present, for access to the official data of his office and for a helpful continuing correspondence. Ada Bazinett, Milton Carnegie, Donald and Doreen Meeks, Patricia Parker, Peter Rossmassler, Milton Rusho, Erma Slate and Chester Taylor have corrected errors in our early versions. Beverly Pope, graphic designer on the staff of Yale Medical School, used her computer with much skill to draft the finished maps that appear in the covers of this book. Elizabeth Haxall took great pains to share her extensive knowledge of the western shore of Grindstone Island and to make possible my one extensive supplement to Dr. Norcom's text. For clarification of certain historical questions I have used and appreciated the resources of the Flower Public Library of Watertown and the public libraries of Clayton and Gananoque. Many thanks to the latter particularly for access to its useful index to the Gananoque Reporter. For careful readings and valuable literary evaluations and advice I am indebted to Ann Childs, Douglas Cook, Verda Corbin, Alvin Eisenman, John and Aminta Marks, Gertrude Pfeiffer, Joan Rueckert, Eric Zencey, William Vitek, and, last but not least, to my wife Jeanne whose contributions have ranged from consideration of cosmology to the placing of commas.

In illustrating this memoir, pictures were a problem. Few of the islanders of three generations ago were wealthy, photo shops were many difficult miles away, and even snapshots were never common. We are exceptionally grateful, therefore, to Douglas Cook, Ruth Kufchock, Dr. Josephine Murray, Erma Slate, John Webster and my wife for supplements to Stanley Norcom's own modest collection of old photos.

The greatest of all debts is to the Edwards family of New Cumberland, Pennsylvania, who out of nothing but a lifelong love of the Thousand Islands have undertaken the actual production of this book. The immense labor of creating a press-ready computerized text from my untidy pages has been done by Robert D. Edwards, retired acting Director of Vocational Education in the State of Pennsylvania's Department of Education. The Edwards' friend George "Speed" Ebersole, a retired printer and graphic arts instructor, has kindly designed the book and assisted in its printing. Many thanks to Jeff Davis, for technical assistance. Above all, we thank Robert's son, Lloyd Edwards, for producing the actual volume with the cooperation of his students, in his Graphic Arts Shop at the Dauphin County Technical School. To these generous and dedicated persons, including those keen students, our great gratitude.

                                Norvin Hein
                                Professor Emeritus of Comparative Religion
                                Yale University

1.
Reverie in Thurso Churchyard

One afternoon last autumn, I walked among the blue bachelor-buttons and goldenrod that grew among the graves in the Thurso cemetery westward from the church on Grindstone Island. The names on the headstones were Scotch-Irish: McRae, Carnegie, Kelly, Black; French Canadian: Turcotte, Rusho, and Dano. One name seemed everywhere—Garnsey. Almost all in the cemetery had Garnsey in their blood. On the island if anyone stepped on one Garnsey toe there followed an island-wide howl of pain.

And almost all the people who lay here I had known—some intimately. And as I came upon stone after stone bearing the old familiar names, the bygone islanders themselves came to life, as clear and vivid in my mind as if they had died only yesterday. With clarity I could recall the sound of their voices, their odd mannerisms, the way they had looked, the things they had done in their lives. Nowhere in the whole wide world—and I had seen much of it—had I known people quite like them. Not only were these people now gone and for the most part forgotten even on the island, but a way of life unique to the island was gone forever too. It had been a life barely known to the outside world even in the island's heyday, when Grindstone Island sent red granite across the land from New York to Chicago, and when its cheese brought the highest price at the annual auction at Lowville. Even then Grindstone Island was as remote from the world and as mysterious as any island in the South Pacific.

While the broad avenues of the cemetery were well-mowed (the church committee still sees to that), most of the individual graves were scraggly and neglected. Vases of long-wilted flowers stood here and there, pathetic attempts at remembrance. Many of the graves were poorly marked. Other old family monuments however, stood over others with proud elegance, in a lavishness that is not surprising when one remembers that most of these peoples' business in the beginning had been red granite. There were few left to care for these graves— graves of ancestors now so remote in time that they mean little to anyone today. Their children and grandchildren left the island long ago. Some return for the annual homecoming day—a persistent custom, for once the island is in your blood, they say, its call is heard for generations.

In a far corner of the cemetery I saw a tall shaft of polished red granite rising out of a thicket of wild-rose briars and burdock. Even at a distance I could discern the name of Black chiselled on its glassy surface. Beneath that monument lay Davy Black. I had known him well. I could see him clearly, pipe in mouth, with his jutting black beard, and the cap he often wore on his bald head.

Then I came to a monument bearing the name McRae. This family had been as close as kinfolk to me as I grew up on the island. In the grass below was a small marker bearing the name Alexander Richard. In the real world he was Dick. He had died years ago yet there suddenly he stood before me, his disconcerting stare intimidating me as it always had, for he had a glass eye that looked in a slightly different direction and never matched his own pale blue one in color. With his hearty booming voice and an odd speech impediment, I could hear him calling, "C'mon, Tanny, let's go."—for I was always going somewhere with Dick.

He had lost his eye when he was securing a stove-pipe overhead in the Grindstone church and a wire snapped. Apparently Dick felt that the Divinity had not shown a proper appreciation of his services, for he never entered the church again, except for funerals. When I first knew him in 1909, Dick was a big man in his early forties, balding, fair, good-looking with a perfect nose and a close-cropped blond mustache which he would chew in time of stress. He had an impressive display of gold teeth which for this small boy enhanced his appearance. He had the gruff way of most country menfolk, yet with the ladies he could be charming. At the winter dances held in "the Hall" over Hi Marshall's store, his step was as light as a feather. I think my mother was more fond of Dick than she would ever admit. Dick now lay sleeping here amid his wife, daughters, and grandchildren—all of whose lives had been extinguished within my long lifetime, now of ninety years.

Next, my eye was caught by a larger monument inscribed "Hubbard Garnsey." The name of Garnsey was the most common one on the island. The early Garnseys must have had prodigious procreative powers in comparison with fellow islanders, for their

Reverie in Thurso Churchyard

progeny has ever been in strong supply. The man whose name was inscribed on the monument I had never known. But his nephew and namesake Hubbard—born 1859, died 1932—was the man who on a drizzly noonday in 1909 had brought me at the age of seven for the first time from Clayton to Grindstone Island. In a rush I remembered the events of that great day of wondrous journeying from Brooklyn—first the Hudson River steamboat, the "Robert Fulton," and then finally the sleeping car that had rolled through the night across northern New York state from Albany toward Clayton.

2.
Clayton in 1909

I remember that early morning arrival as an event in a vivid dream: the long drawn-out whistle of the locomotive as it rolled down the pastures into Clayton, the slow stop on the long curved dock, the locomotive's high-pitched hissing and panting like a live thing after its long run north from Utica. Quickly the engine detached itself, switched to an adjoining track, and backed out around the curve to disappear for the day. At nine o'clock P.M. it would pull the night train south again across New York. Alongside the line of unmoving Pullman cars, white-coated porters stood beside heaps of unloaded luggage, ready to put it aboard the boats and receive their tips.

Waiting at the dock for the train was a small fleet of steamboats. Always the little "Newsboy" was there with its high hatchet bow, and the new "Thousand Islander" with its odd fantail, and the narrow "New Island Wanderer" and the old side-wheeler, the "St. Lawrence," which could illuminate whole islands with its big searchlight on its evening excursions. All the boats were creaking and groaning as their lines tightened against the dock. The dock itself was a scene of bustle and confusion. There was the rumble of the hand-trucks that carried mail-bags, bundles of newspapers, steamer trunks, bulging suitcases and valises and express packages over the gangways into the shadowy holds of the little steamers. Doctors, business men, clergymen, college professors, all in formal business suits and straw hats, searched about for their luggage, clutching tickets in their hands. The ladies, fashionably dressed in leg-o-mutton sleeves, long skirts, plumed hats and their inevitable veils, waited on the dock and held onto the children in their sailor suits or lacy frocks, and their wide straw hats held tight with rubber chin-bands. All were to board the steamboats for such down-river resorts as Round Island with its huge Hotel Frontenac. The brochure of the Frontenac declared that money was not considered in its construction and equipment. "The paramount wish of its proprietors is to make it first class in every way possible, equal to anything of its kind on the European Continent." This was the tone of the Thousand Islands in 1909: exclusiveness, high fashion, elegance. The Frontenac Hotel was all that its owners declared save in one ominous detail: it was not fireproof.

The little steamers were headed also for exclusive Thousand Island Park down river, with its Columbia Hotel and its fashionable boarding houses such as the Rochester. The boats would go on to Murray Hill Island with its Park Hotel, then on to Grennell Island, to Point Vivian, to Fine View and finally to Alexandria Bay, twelve miles down-river, with its elegant big Crossman and Thousand Island Houses. In this pre-automobile age everyone from afar had to arrive in Clayton, the only waterfront rail-terminus in the area. Alexandria Bay was the Newport of the Thousand Islands region, however. It was, so to speak, where the action was. It was there in the midst of a cluster of island castles and Newport style "cottages" that "high Society" made its stand. Very few of the arrivals on the Clayton railway dock stayed in Clayton. The dateline in the society columns describing social affairs of the region for their readers in the big cities always carried the name of Alexandria Bay, rarely that of Clayton. Perhaps Clayton was overshadowed because the island scenery around Clayton was not as picturesque as that around Alexandria Bay; but more likely, because of short-sightedness on the part of Clayton's leading citizenry. In Clayton there was little to stay for, actually. The village had three undistinguished hotels, the Walton House, the Hubbard House and the Herald House, scattered along Water Street (now renamed Riverside Drive). All three had street-side verandas with rocking-chairs from which visitors could watch the horse-drawn vehicles and little else, for none of these hotels had a view of the river. The lack of a view did not matter much to their type of guests who were typically fishermen, not noted for their aesthetic sensitivity. Provided with guides and baskets for shore dinners, they would soon be off for a day's fishing.

While Clayton had little elegance, it was not entirely devoid of aristocracy. It could boast of a top-crust drawn from all New York society: the Morgans, the Cleveland Dodges, the Whites, the Murrays, the family of J. Walter Wood. They were always met at the morning train by uniformed boatmen and immediately escorted up Water Street to their private dock at the west end of town and from there whisked away in sleek mahogany launches to their rambling homes on the islets of Watch, Papoose, Whiskey, Hickory, and Wild Goose off the head of Grindstone. The Murrays and the Whites and one of the Morgans had their retreats on Grindstone itself. All of them were

Clayton in 1909

determinedly reclusive. Clayton saw little of these wealthy families. Some womenfolk would come to town on fair summer mornings, dressed in deceptively plain blue or white linen frocks and garden-hats, and meander along Water Street in search of some fancied delicacy. Mr. and Mrs. A. L. Williams would greet them in front of their grocery store with unctuous smiles and bows. Mr. Williams always dressed in grey flannels and formal coat. The Williams charged outrageous prices for their produce —charged enough so that in the less prosperous times that were to come they would be able to retire to world travel and even indulge in some minor philanthropies. A little farther along Water Street was the shop of Mr. Gordon Cerow. With his round face resembling a stout Chinese mandarin's he dispensed choice meats—again at outrageous prices and again with sycophantic smiles. Mr. Williams and Mr. Cerow had little competition. The checkout emporiums and their shopping carts were far in the future.

Farther along Water Street past the town's two banks and opposite James Street was a very large and immaculate drug store and ice-cream parlor. Mr. Charles Ellis presided over it with lordly dignity. Without the false smiles and bowings of others along his street, Mr. Ellis quietly greeted the townspeople and summer visitors alike. Mr. Ellis was the town's one true aristocrat, reserved and intelligent, and highly respected. One could say without hesitation that over these years and well into the 1930's, he was Clayton's most distinguished citizen. Although he was on familiar terms with everyone, he did not encourage familiarity. And during all the years he held sway over his store, I never spoke a word with him because he had little to do with dispensing the excellent ice-cream sundaes that were at that time my only interest in Mr. Ellis's establishment.

The entire length of Water Street from the railway dock to the Ellis Block (as the apartment building over the store was called) was aristocratic in its pose. The subservience of the shop-keepers, the formal dress, the small courtesies were all a carry-over from the Edwardian period just ended. This genteel age concluded with the arrival of the automobile. Very soon, Water Street would begin to acquire its present "touristy" atmosphere with more and more souvenir stands, hot-dog counters, and boat-tour hawkers, while uptown, "tourists accommodated" signs appeared, responding to the new motorists' demands. And thus the "genteel age" ended.

But the tin lizzy tourist was nowhere to be seen in the first decade of the 1900's at the time of the arrival of the morning train on the Clayton dock. Quickly, baggage would be trundled over the gangways into the steamboats, and families would be gathered together and put aboard. Lines were cast off and the steamboats one by one would churn away down-river in a blur of soft-coal smoke. And there would be a sudden quiet in Clayton except perhaps for the far-off tinkling of a locomotive bell out back of town or the clop-clop of Joe Pelow's horse, hauling freight up an embankment on the landward side of the tracks. And from its roof-top cupola over the town hall on Water Street, the town clock would ring out its sweet chimes into the morning stillness. Only one boat remained, the little "Yennek," the gasoline-powered ferryboat that would leave later in the morning for Gananoque, Clayton's twin village on the Canadian side of the river. Captain Kenney had named his little boat by spelling his own name backward.

Meanwhile the wide river was empty in front of Clayton. Perhaps a Great Lakes freighter would appear and move slowly by in mid-channel. No one ashore gave it a glance. The long line of Pullman cars would stand all day in the hot sun on the curved track to which they had been switched, and be thoroughly heated up to receive their passengers at 8:30 that night for the run back to New York. The porters would idle about all day on the cars' steps or fish from the deserted railway dock. There was little else for them to do. At one o'clock a mail train would arrive and at six-thirty the day train from New York. This last train was in the charge of Mr. Frank Cole, a genial, grey-haired conductor who as the train rolled down over the meadows back of Clayton would announce to his passengers, "If you will look off to the right, you will have your first view of the beautiful Thousand Islands and the St. Lawrence river." And on a fair afternoon they would see a blue expanse of water studded with rocky wooded islands as far as the eye could see.

The early morning quiet of the railway dock was to be interrupted by one more exciting event—the arrival of the big steamer from Toronto. It would be either the "Toronto," with its two red stacks or the single-stacked "Kingston." Both were multi-decked, paddle-wheeled vessels which had left Toronto the evening before and crossed Lake Ontario with stops at Rochester and Kingston before reaching Clayton. The trip on a stormy night could be a rough one. Passengers who had crossed an angry Atlantic declared that the Lake Ontario crossing could be much worse. The steamer was bound down-river to Alexandria Bay and Prescott, forty miles on, where passengers making

Clayton in 1909

"The Grand Tour of the Great Lakes" would change to a smaller steamer for shooting the famous rapids to Montreal 190 miles away—an exciting day's run.

Even at this early hour, the high upper decks would be lined with passengers, emerging sleepily onto their balconies to watch the activities on the dock below. There would be the thud of heavy lines against the bollards, and a great rush of foaming water as the steamer's paddle wheels reversed to back the vessel slowly into position alongside the dock. It was always the practice of these pilots, like those down on the Hudson, to overshoot their mark and then to find better precision in landing by backing up. Then there would be a clang of bells, the paddle wheels would stop churning, the lines ashore would tighten, and a gangway was rolled out.

Very few got off or boarded these vessels at Clayton and little baggage came ashore. The customs and immigration officials who had appeared with the boat's arrival vanished as the gangway was withdrawn. Then there would be a sudden sharp blast of the ship's whistle, another clang of bells, and a casting off of lines. The paddle wheels would begin to thrash again amid broad whirlpools of bottle-green water as the ship angled slowly away from the railway dock toward midstream to resume its course down the river. Winding its way through the American Channel, it would pass the great Frontenac Hotel, and then the impressive summer palaces of Brooklyn's department store magnates, Mr. Abraham and Mr. Straus, and those of Mr. Browning, the Gillespies, Mr. George Boldt, and Mr. Pullman (whose cars were sitting on the siding in Clayton). Their towers, parapets, and flowered terraces proclaimed them to be the dwellings of the wealthy. Nowhere in this entire region were any of Mr. Abraham's or Mr. Straus's department-store clerks seen, nor Mr. Gillespie's steel workers, nor Mr. Browning's salesmen of men's clothing, nor any blue-collar worker of any kind. With the advent of the automobile, they would come in hordes. But now, the region was lost in a gentle somnolence, the playground of the very rich.

3.
Crossing to the Island

We have almost forgotten the small boy who stood with his father and mother on the Clayton dock. He was looking out on a wide leaden river that seemed formidable in comparison with the small New Jersey lake he had known on previous summer holidays. There was a sudden flurry of excitement in this family group when "Uncle Charley" arrived. Charley Happ had come to meet us on behalf of the Websters, my parents' Brooklyn friends who had invited us to camp with them on what is now known as Webster Point on Grindstone Island. Uncle Charley's wife, "Aunt" Clara, was the sister of Mrs. Webster.

Uncle Charley owned a large cabin launch, the "Clara B." and was a jolly St. Lawrence fishing guide. He had only one "party," a wealthy old bachelor named Scudder ("Old Scudd") who stayed at the Frontenac Hotel and spent all summer fishing with Uncle Charley. Uncle Charley played a horn in the Clayton band. That was his only distinction other than a repute for building fine birdhouses for starlings. Uncle Charley's bird houses were everywhere, perched atop high poles. They even got over to Grindstone Island. Uncle Charley sank badly in my estimation when some years later he borrowed my precious Daisy air rifle to shoot unwelcome birds in his garden, and broke the gun. He never repaired or replaced it—much to my vexation, but undoubtedly much to the relief of everyone else in the neighborhood.

Uncle Charley led us along Water Street to the "Ellis Block," the building in which Mr. Ellis had his store, and then up a staircase to an airy apartment with shining hardwood floors and a high porch overlooking the river. My unforgettable recollection of that apartment was its bright cheerfulness, in such contrast to other gloomy houses I had known in the city. And here we met Aunt Clara Happ, who had prepared breakfast for us. Aunt Clara was a pleasant woman with a warm vibrant voice. I liked her on the spot. Her taste in reading was discriminating. Intellectually, she must have been a very lonely woman in a town like Clayton. After her death I learned that she had played a major role in founding Clayton's public library. To me it is sad that it is not her name that is commemorated in large letters across the facade of the modern library building and that there is no public recognition of her immense contribution to Clayton's cultural life.

At nine o'clock Uncle Lew Webster was to arrive on the mailboat from Grindstone Island. He was to escort us back to the island on the mail boat at noon, after the eleven o'clock mail train had come in. In the meantime the drizzle ended, the sun came out, and the river became a beautiful blue. Off-shore from Clayton, Uncle Charley pointed out Grindstone Island, two miles away. To those who did not know, it seemed to be the great river's northern shore. It ran for miles up and down the river and rose up in green hills, one very high. A very few houses were visible along its shore. The only sign of activity was a small plume of coal smoke drifting from a thin stack tucked among the ledges in the middle of the island. The cheese factory was in operation.

No one on the railway dock that morning had glanced in the island's direction. No boat had left the Clayton docks to go there, and none had come from there to meet the train. The island seemed to be as serene and undisturbed as on the day after creation. It was a land of mystery. When the island was mentioned in Clayton, people would smile knowingly and shake their heads. The islanders, they said, were a rough lot, a bunch best left alone. Yes, there were a few good folk there, but for the most part, the townspeople associated with the islanders only in banking and in buying and selling livestock and hay and grain. The Clayton people had nothing to do with the marketing of the island's major product, cheese. The island's cheese was sent directly to the big cheese center in Lowville. Once in a while a box of Grindstone cheese would appear in the Clayton stores and quickly disappear. It was in great demand.

As for the islanders themselves, they came to Clayton only to see a doctor or to make purchases which were either not available or costly in the island's two stores. They would arrive in Clayton on the mailboat at nine o'clock, attend to their errands and then return to the mailboat to sit in its cabin and chat until the departure of the boat at noon. Such trips were rare events in their simple lives. They were citizens of a secluded commonwealth of their own, itself not inconsiderable in size, that was far separated

Crossing to the Island

from the Thousand Islands' fashionable world. Roughly ten square miles in extent, if Grindstone Island lay in the Scottish Hebrides it might have been the domain of a lord. But no one lorded over Grindstone Island. Not even a deputy sheriff resided there. The islanders lived by their own internal law.

I recall clearly that journey on Hub Garnsey's mailboat to Grindstone Island—the first of many in the years to come. The islanders on the dock on that day or any other would have passed three hours in shopping, visiting doctors and gossiping with friends, and were now waiting watchfully for the departure. When the clock above the town hall (now the Clayton Museum) would be chiming the hour of twelve, Hub would appear with David, his son, age nine, carrying mailbags destined for the island post office in Hi Marshall's store. Then everyone on the dock would clamber aboard the mailboat and young David would cast off the lines and jump into the boat while Hub, amidships, cranked the big gasoline engine. There would be a sudden explosion, a burst of fumes from the motor's petcocks. They would be hastily closed while young David rushed to the steering wheel. Then Hub threw the motor into gear and the boat would leave for Grindstone instantly and woe to any islander arriving on the dock five minutes later.

Not more than twenty-five feet long, the wooden boat was unbelievably small for the hauling it did. The passengers sat on board seats along the sides of the boat with bags and boxes about their feet while the engine pounded and shivered. The trip across was a social occasion. Everyone aboard knew one another intimately and almost all were related in some degree. The talk was usually sheer gossip, lively and good-natured but with sly innuendos and earthy humor about the island's latest scandals. Sometimes the talk would turn serious, with questions about the sick child in a mother's arms, or about what the doctor had told a worried islander after the morning's consultation. But usually the river crossing was a convivial occasion, rarely inhibited by the presence of strangers such as ourselves or the occasional traveling salesman bound for the island stores. Always on board, I remember, was a pale elderly woman with gold spectacles —chilly and aloof and intimidating to children. When rare occasions demanded a response she would offer complete banalities or only a wan Cheshire-cat smile. This was Mrs. Ratchford. No one seemed to know very much about her other than that she came from Brooklyn. Brooklyn was our home also, but that coincidence never created much rapport between us down through the years. Apparently she went to Clayton every day on the mailboat simply for something to do. When the boat landed on

Grindstone, she would promptly pick up her string-bag and disappear in the direction of an ugly house of a type more usually found in a Brooklyn suburb. Bleak as its owner, the house stood on a rocky treeless knoll and could be seen for miles around from the river. One spring in the thirties, Mrs. Ratchford was no longer on the mailboat and we were told that she had died. It was an event in a familiar pattern, one of many such winter deaths that would follow down the years.

I remember well the unfamiliar accents of the people sitting around me on that first trip across the river—the emphatic explosive sounds of their voices as they talked, the exaggerated "R's" and "O's", the flattened "A's" in their speech. Their diction was totally Anglo-Saxon, however, untinged by any foreign brogue.

The mailboat was heavily loaded. Our trunks were perched precariously on a small deck at the stern. There were barrels of kerosene there also, and mowing machine parts, boxes of freight for the island stores, spools of barbed-wire, and a crate of cheeping baby chicks. Fortunately the river was quiet. But on days when a strong southwest wind was blowing down the river, wallowing in the troughs of the waves for two miles could be very disconcerting. When the winds were "squealing," as the natives would say, then the oncoming waves would lift their heads like green-hooded cobras and lunge toward the boat with a mighty slap. When particularly vicious waves sloshed over the gunwales, the islanders would laugh nervously and clutch at the boards beneath them as the boat rolled heavily on its side. But there was no deep anxiety. The mailboat had always come through and in summer it always would. Autumn, spring and winter were another story. But those months do not concern us now. In summer, the days were usually fair and the air soft and clear, full of sunshine sparkling on blue water.

My first meeting on that day of slowly clearing skies was not with the St. Lawrence at its best. But Uncle Lew Webster was reassuring as he stood before us with his customary jovial smile, wearing his business suit and Panama hat as if a moment before he had just left Wall Street. He was in old familiar territory. He had come across the border to Clayton from around Forfar in Canada as a penniless youth, it was said, and had gotten a job in one of the two Clayton banks. Then he had married the president's daughter, Gertrude Reese. Still in the best Horatio Alger tradition, he soon carried her off to the great city, New York, and, a shrewd trader, he had prospered on the New York

Crossing to the Island

Stock Exchange. Not long ago, with the same shrewd perception, he had bought the McRae farm on Grindstone Island, one of the most beautiful properties on the river. It was to it we were now going. Lew Webster, or "Uncle Lew" as I had learned to call him, was the most personable man I have ever known, and possibly one of the most unscrupulous.

Now as Hub's little boat chugged through the waves, half-way across the river it passed Calumet Island on which stood a Norman castle, a red-granite pile with conical towers, shadowed archways, stone balustrades and terraces and gay flower beds, all surrounded by green lawns that ran to the river's edge. The castle appropriately belonged to a king. The king was Charles G. Emery and his kingdom was tobacco. Mr. Emery also owned many of the islands off Grindstone's north shore, and for many years these islands lay untouched in primeval loveliness through his protection. Then, just before the second World War, Mr. Emery died. "For Sale" signs now appeared on the islands. One by one these lovely wild islands fell to purchasers whose ego would compel them to build ugly cottages sited as conspicuously as possible on points and headlands—and much of the islands' pristine loveliness would be gone forever.

Mr. Emery was rarely in residence on Calumet in the early 1900's. The island's only inhabitant was usually its caretaker Mr. Ivey, who lived in a small wooden cottage tucked away at one side. I never saw Mr. Ivey. Like much else about this fairy-tale palace, he was invisible. The Grindstone mailboat sometimes stopped to drop off supplies. They seemed to be picked up by invisible hands. The boat usually passed by quite close to the mysterious island and I would often imagine a maiden leaning from one of the upper casements talking to a plumed prince on the ramparts below. I doubt that any of the island passengers were similarly intrigued. Fairy tales to them were an alien land. This island with knights and golden ladies, that should have been gay with flying pennants, was nothing of the sort. It was a dead place, alone and lonely. After Mr. Emery's death, the castle stood unkempt for years, unattended and ignored. Not many villages in America have a shining Norman castle on their doorstep and one would have thought that the village of Clayton, dependent for its very livelihood on tourism, would have cherished such a treasure. Instead the village taxed it heavily and permitted the castle to be vandalized and to be destroyed eventually by fire.

The mailboat wallowed on beyond Calumet and soon entered Aunt Jane's Bay, the principal harbor on the south shore of Grindstone Island. For a small boy from Brooklyn, to arrive at the granite public dock in Aunt Jane's bay on a day in June in that first decade of the century, was to arrive in Paradise. Here, out of the wind of the open river, a wonderful peace lay over the land. The stillness was broken only by the songs of meadowlarks on the upland pastures above the dock. Green meadows, weathered barns and one or two farms could be seen on this upland. Shining woods capped the hills that bordered the bay. From a rocky ledge southward from this dock, (called the town dock), a long row of tall hemlocks hung far out over the river. Suddenly with a scream a kingfisher would plunge headlong from these hemlocks into the river and then fly upward again into the trees. Beyond the hemlocks, the land to the south rose to a pasture and to the promontory on which stood Mrs. Ratchford's house. Still further south, far out on the river, one might see a Great Lakes freighter slowly disappearing behind Calumet Island and then reappearing on the other side. Ashore, the air was heavy with the smell of sweet clover and the roadside was abloom with wild roses, daisies, buttercups, and wild geraniums.

A narrow dirt road—the South Shore Road went from the town dock up a steep river bank and continued westward along the south shore of the island past pastures and farmlands. Just at the top of the rise, another road branched off sharply from it to the right and ran northward. This was the great thoroughfare of the island, the Cross-Island Road that ran from shore to shore, from Aunt Jane's Bay to a cove shielded by McRae Point on the island's north side. Just short of that cove lay the tiny village of Thurso, metropolis of the island. There Hub would deposit his mailbags and freight, at Hi Marshall's store. On this particular day, he would go further, turning eastward from the village square to deliver us and our trunks at the McRae farm where the Websters were encamped.

As soon as the mailboat had tied up at the dock, passengers scrambled to pick up their purchases and climb out of the boat. There was always help for the elderly. The heavy cargo—the crates, the barrels, the mailbags (there were always two)—were unloaded from the boat with everyone lending a hand. Usually some farmer's wagon was waiting nearby to pick up urgent freight such as a new mowing-machine part, or freight for a home not reachable via the mailwagon's regular route. Quickly such drivers would load and vanish over the embankment. Sometimes boxes and parcels would be forgotten aboard the boat or be mistakenly switched. Nobody worried. They could be picked up the next day at the dock or exchanged at the cheese-factory the next morning. But it was always wise to write one's name on one's purchases.

Those who were going across the island with Hub waited patiently on the dock, exchanging gossip until all the freight and mail-bags had been hoisted onto the wagon and stowed behind the cross-seats up forward. Young David Garnsey in the meantime had climbed up the bank to a shed from which he led the harnessed horse that had hauled the mail wagon across from Thurso that morning. He led the horse down to the dock and hitched it between the shafts of the loaded wagon. It was all a very leisurely business, carrying the Grindstone Island mail. There was no hurry. There would be a delay while Hub stuffed small mail pouches into a row of mailboxes at the roadside at the foot of the slope—pouches destined for the few farms that lay westward along the south shore road which Hub did not traverse. A leather pouch with brass fasteners was always given directly to a waiting Scotsman, Davy Atherton, who had been exchanging amenities with the islanders. He would take the leather pouch around the southern headland to Boscobel Island. There the Johnson family from Washington lived, in their gracious two-storeyed white house, with upper and lower verandas suggestive of the south. I was to get to know the Athertons and the Johnsons well and to love them all. Since the south side of Grindstone in those days was as remote as the antipodes for a small boy living on the north shore, to my deep regret I never got to know the Athertons until their last years. In my maturity I came to appreciate these kindly intelligent people.

The mail wagon leaves for Thurso, David Garnsey at the reins.

Grindstone tongues could be malicious, but over years I heard no one report anything but the best about these families. They came faithfully to the church in Thurso. The Johnson family I came to know very quickly, since daughters were involved. The good times we all had together remain among my happiest memories.

By now the horse was hitched to the wagon and all was ready for the cross-island journey. The mailwagon was always crowded with chatting passengers. Often one or two would sit behind the freight on the rear end, dangling their legs over the edge. Most sat on the cross-seats up front, as many as four abreast. Young David Garnsey, who was about my own age, took little part in the merriment aboard the wagon. When spoken to he replied in monosyllables, contributing only reticent grunts to the friendly hubbub. It was impossible to "be friends" with David. Nowadays he would be recognized, I think, as autistic.

The ride across the island began with a stiff pull up the westward rise from the town dock. To spare the horses some passengers walked this first stretch of road. As the wagon was reaching the top of the hill one could see at left a white house where lived Bob Garnsey, Hub Garnsey's eldest son who would years later succeed him as carrier of the mail.

Now the wagon turned sharply right into the Cross-Island Road and into a wilderness of thickets and high rock ledges. The sun had finally come out. The clear air was full of bird-song, the drone of insects, and the sweet fragrance of blossoming trees. In the first stretches of the road the mail wagon passed only one mail box, at the lane of Elmer Dano, who lived far back from the road in a small white house on the border of the marsh at the head of Aunt Jane's Bay. Sometimes Elmer's wife, a tall blonde woman, would come to the road to converse briefly with Hub, perhaps about some package she had ordered from Clayton. The Danos belonged to a family almost as numerous on the island as the Garnseys. The wagon wound on through the narrow passes between the ledges, emerging now and then into secluded meadows and plunging again into wild rocky defiles. A certain stretch of road was filled with the strong scent of sweet fern, rare in these parts. The ferns grew there for years until the town widened the road. Then they vanished—another victim of progress.

The grating of the iron-rimmed wagon-wheels on the gravel road is a sharp memory

Crossing to the Island

with me, and the clop of the horse's hooves, and the horsey smell of the draft animal that drifted back across the wagon. The flat voices of the islanders were sharp and clear in the stillness, framed in the pervasive whisper of the leaves of the popple trees by the roadside, and in the chatter of disturbed red squirrels as they vanished into the treetops with a flick of their bushy tails.

Finally the mail wagon came to the center of the island and to a narrow pass through the island's highest rock ledges. They were crested by green pines bent to the northeast, away from the prevailing southwesterly winds. This central ridge of rocks and trees ran the length of the island.

Here at the half-way point, the Cross-Island Road intersected with its east-west counterpart, the Baseline Road. Sometimes called the Middle Road, it divides the island quite evenly into northern and southern halves. In the time of the island's first settlement it had been a convenient measuring line from which, on each side, farms were laid out that ran to the river in very long rectangles. From the crossing, the Baseline Road ran eastward as a well-kept way, climbing a steep hill and passing between wooded ledges to rich meadows across which it went to the foot of the island. A mile or so along this road on the south side stood the cheese factory, for fifty years the economic hub of the island. The island's farmers brought their milk there from all over the island early each morning. The portion of the Baseline Road that ran westward from the crossroad was less used. It ran ultimately to the old Flynn farm at the head of the island. After crossing over wooded ledges it ran through magnificent virgin forest to pass through a rickety pasture gate and emerge at last beside Flynn Bay. The farmhouses of Grindstone Island were almost never built on the Baseline Road, however, but rather on the shore. The river, for all its treachery, carried people and cargo much more smoothly than long earthen lanes, and to much more varied destinations. At the crossing with the Baseline Road several lonely mailboxes stood, into which, leaning far out from the wagon, Hub stuffed mail-bags destined for the unseen farms far off on the eastern part of the island.

Just north of the intersection in a grove of oak and maple trees a white one-room schoolhouse stood, with its privies in the rear. This was the island's Upper (i.e. up-river) School, built in 1885 when the opening of great quarries caused a burgeoning of the island's population. Since 1840 there had been a Lower School, its latest building erected in 1880, on the Baseline Road near its end at the foot of the island. The many happenings in island life that centered on these schools were forever beyond my observation, as a summer person. When I saw the schools in late June they were already empty—and so they would remain in my experience and in my memoirs.

In the yard of the Upper School and very close to the road was a well with a tall iron pump, and now Hub stopped to water his horse. It drank deeply with slow deliberate drafts from a tub beneath the spout. The water had an excellent reputation. Some islanders drove long distances to haul it to their homes in large milk-cans. It was never tested to my knowledge, but typhoid fever never made any incursion into Grindstone. Clayton had periodic outbreaks of that scourge through ignoring hygienic principles in laying out its water system. In some earlier decade of its history the island had known cholera, and one winter in the 1930's there was a deadly outbreak of diphtheria at a time when ice floes made the river crossing almost impossible. Mrs. Newberry's heroic tale of that epidemic stands almost alone as literature by the islanders. Their suffering received nationwide publicity at the time. But for the most part the Grindstone Islanders have been a healthy lot.

After the horse had been watered Hub drove on through a rocky pass and soon came to a carefully fenced meadow which lay like a fertile island between the high ledges, and in the middle of it there lay an immaculate vegetable garden planted in rich black soil. Beyond the meadow, set snug against a high rock cliff on the right, stood a tall green house. An amplitude of "ginger-bread" supported its roof peak and a small side-porch. There in the distance stood a large woman, shading her eyes to see who was on the mail wagon today. Beside her stood a very fat little girl about my own age. The little girl was Korleen Rouse. The woman, in her forties, was Lizzie Rouse, her mother. Beside a pasture gate alongside the road, stood an old old man, "Uncle" Joe Rouse, leaning on a cane and waiting for the mail as he always did. In his eighties, he had sired Korleen and while there were many jokes about the old man, none cast any doubt on the actuality of his parenthood. Bent double with arthritis, he lifted up to Hub a gnarled face with a stubbled jaw and close-set faded eyes. Uncle Joe undoubtedly had little reason to celebrate life. As I recall the Rouse's circumstances it seems clear that they were poor. While they were in some ways a comic family, one had to respect them for their independence and the scrupulous neatness of their place.

Crossing to the Island

Uncle Joe always had business to discuss with Hub, for the little family was totally dependent on him for their needs. The fact that he was very deaf shut the old man off from the world about him. The cane he carried gave him a false air of menace. No one on the island seemed to like him. In his prime, he had been a ship's carpenter. He still did odd jobs of carpentry very beautifully. He had built his own house with the same sturdiness and precision he would have applied to building a ship. The house could have been stood on end, people said, with no damage of any sort.

Slowly, Uncle Joe hobbled to his mailbox where Hub had reined in his horse. He twisted his wry neck upward to see what the mail wagon had brought. There was a brief exchange of shouts punctuated with "Eh?" and "How's that?" The talk went on until Uncle Joe was satisfied as to the business in question. Then he turned away without any amenities whatever. Hub drove on, passing the Rouse's cow—an ill-tempered beast with a crumpled horn. It grazed on the roadside for want of pasture on the small Rouse place. Like the Rouses themselves, their cow was a "character"—given on occasion to unexpected mad pursuit of a passerby on foot, but always stopping just short of giving the "coup de grace." It was never known to injure anything but pride.

The mail wagon now followed the road around a blind "S" curve past a final spur of rock and entered a straight course running north across rolling farmland. It passed on the right the original McRae homestead, a long-deserted log cabin standing on a knoll. Then came two farmhouses, directly opposite each other on either side of the road— the Tom McRae house on the right, and the George McCarthy house on the left. Tom McRae's great red barn in a hollow just south of the house was the largest on the island.

Tom McRae, a brother of Dick McRae whom we have already mentioned, was a no-nonsense, taciturn moustached man with eyes of pure ice. As I was to learn later he was a fiercely compulsive worker, shrewd and prosperous, and thrifty to the point of miserliness—totally unlike his brother. Far too busy in the fields in June, neither he nor his shy young son Jimmy were ever on hand to greet the mail. Tom's wife, Deed, and his daughters Jessie, Bessie and Mary were ever bustling about, either in the house, or out back scrubbing and polishing the milk cans that stood on a platform. It was usually the bright gold-spectacled Mary, an odd quizzical girl, who would run out to the mail wagon flashing a white apron, to talk a moment if the occasion required. But

21

as a rule the Tom McRae family were far too busy to indulge in the frivolous business of visiting. So, after stuffing their mailbag into their roadside box, Hub drove on.

Young Jimmy McRae, like David Garnsey, was reticent. But unlike David whose sullen face was never livened by a smile, Jimmy when spoken to would smile enigmatically and offer a pleasantry or two. The islanders described him as "odd." His family never attended that hub of island society, the Methodist church in Thurso. His humorless father never, to my knowledge, went to any meeting public or private, on or off the island. Jimmy never went to the Saturday night ice-cream socials on the church lawn, nor to the Sunday School picnics at Potters' beach, nor any other event at which the islanders gathered for their good times. Though Jimmy was of my own age, I doubt that I exchanged more than ten words with him in all the years we were together on the island. There was no opportunity for more. Jimmy slaved continually for his father without protest. When the family finally broke up in the late forties, Jimmy went to work for the railroad over on the mainland, and was eventually killed by a train. I feel an immense pity for this unfortunate lad. Even in death, he seems an outcast, for his grave lies off at the farthest limit of the cemetery in a tangle of weeds—but at his mother's feet.

The George McCarthy place across the road from the Tom McRae's offered a very different picture in all respects. Here was a long, low ranch-house of a cheerful yellow accented with brown trim, with a narrow veranda across its front, and dormer windows. George McCarthy, a tall, lanky Irishman, invariably came out to the gate to greet the mail wagon with a smile—an intelligent, kindly man, always eager to pass the time of day. On that first trip with the mail across the island, I remember seeing on the McCarthy veranda in the distance a thin willowy figure in a gay red and yellow kimono, George's wife. She had contracted tuberculosis, that other scourge of the time, slower than typhoid in its course but just as deadly. I never saw her again: She would die within months. The islanders always remembered her as a gracious, artistic woman, who told imaginative fairy tales and made pretty pictures for her little boy Lowell who was exactly my own age.

George McCarthy never remarried. He lived quietly alone and reared his son to become an amiable normal boy much like his father. He sent Lowell to high school in Dexter in the care of an aunt, and later to Syracuse University where Lowell was to study medicine—all in sharpest contrast to the father-son relation across the road. While I was always very friendly with Lowell, I saw little of him in those summer months because Lowell was always working hard on his father's farm. But we met frequently in the Thurso store, and there, with a conspiratorial air, he would tell me confidential tales of his life in Syracuse—of wild drinking parties and of visiting brothels, and other escapades many of which were fantasy, I'm sure. It was the beginning of the Jazz Age when it was always Three O'clock in the Morning and teenagers were indeed dancing the whole night through. At least so it was in the stories we read, which created a dream world in which many of us liked to dwell. Actually, for most teen-agers of the time, it was an age of incredible innocence.

Probably it was a lack of self-discipline rather than debauchery that made Lowell fail to complete his work at medical school. He continued his studies in the field of education, however, and eventually became superintendent of schools downstate at Maybrook. He said that he found the crooked politics in that community intolerable and quit to join a textbook publishing house in Toronto. There he married, acquired a family, became successful and highly respected, and returned in summers to the island, always lean and lanky with a pleasant smile, and much loved like his father. After Lowell left the island, George McCarthy lived on alone, farming as usual, always the same amiable, smiling, clean-looking, decent person. One spring in the forties when I arrived on the island, George wasn't at his gate to greet the mail as usual. He had died of a heart attack the winter before.

Now over an hour out of Clayton, the mail cart drove downhill into a deep shady vale below the McRae and McCarthy farms, and then crossed a small iron bridge over a sluggish stream buried deep in witch hazel and willows. Coming down from the left, the brook originates from a boiling spring a mile or so away, hidden in deep lonely woods. To the right, it disappeared in the farthest inland extension of the great upper marsh, the cat-tail wilderness that sundered the northern half of Grindstone Island into two realms of human habitation. The region to the west is almost urban by reason of having the village of Thurso as its center. The other is wildly rural country, always spoken of as "Below the Marsh."

Climbing up again on the far side of the brook, the mail wagon swung around a final rock ledge, and then rolled on to a green plateau where for the first time a church spire could be seen far ahead, rising above the trees. On this last lap, set far back from the road on the right, a final farmhouse was seen. It was the prosperous Will Cummings place. Since this farm was too near the post office to be entitled to a mailbox, one frequently saw the Cummings—Will and Addy his wife—at that great gathering place. Will was an elderly man who was heavy-set but good-looking and dignified, with an aristrocratic mustache. In full evening dress, he could have been taken for a diplomat, but when he opened his mouth, his amiable talk punctuated with vacuous "yes-sir" and "no-sir," he became a simple farmer. His wife Addy, invariably neat, was a stout dark-haired woman with even white teeth and a milk-white skin dotted with freckles, and a large very round face lighted by small black eyes. She had a wide Cheshire-cat grin that did not put one at ease but falsely suggested hypocrisy. They had an adopted daughter Nelly, whose real parentage was much discussed. By this time Nelly had married Emmet Dodge, a youngish island "wise guy" who had served as school teacher at intervals on the island and was given to instructing the islanders beyond their wish to be instructed. Emmet was soon to take over his father-in law's farm, while Will and Addy would retire and move into a house northward on the same road beyond the Thurso village square. They kept their retirement house as neat and trim as they had kept their farm, with a carefully-cut lawn rolling downward toward the road under a spreading maple tree which was full of color in the autumn. The Cummings never encouraged intimacy, I am sure more by default than through overt inhospitality. But I was often to pass their village house a little curious about them, and looking through their open front door into the dim interior, wondering whether a large rounded shape in the shadowed room was Addy's ample figure, bending over in a flowered skirt, or their winter stove with such a flowered cloth thrown over it. If the figure didn't move, I knew it wasn't Addy, and I did not wave.

About an hour and a quarter after leaving Clayton, the mail wagon was pulling abreast of the first house of the village of Thurso. It was a rambling white house on the right —the home of the Hub Garnsey family. The yard was full of ragweed and burdock. Much of it was bare, worn by the feet of Hubs' many children. Hub did not even glance at his own house as we passed. Then almost at once, the mail cart arrived at its major destination, the intersection of the Cross-Island Road with the North Shore Road. We were in the village of Thurso. At left stood the white-steepled church surrounded by its lawn, and on the right Hi Marshall's store. It was a drab two-storied structure bearing a sign, "Grindstone, New York. Post Office." Two large display windows, with a main door between them, faced the road. A porch roof sheltered a high platform that ran across the front of the building, and there a cluster of people with eager faces waited for the mail wagon. We pulled in alongside the platform, which then became an unloading dock. Several big canvas mail bags went off with a thud and next, as on every other day, a large crate of fresh bread from a bakery in Clayton. (Few islanders baked their own bread.) A barrel or two were rolled off and placed, with miscellaneous boxes of freight, on a pavement at the side of the store. There was a commotion of pulling and hauling around these pieces of baggage, and small talk continued also for some time among those for whom the arrival of the mail was a social occasion.

Grindstone Island store and post office

During the considerable wait, the Norcom family, bound for a destination beyond the crossroad, sat high in the mail wagon and looked up and down the well-used roads that radiated out in four directions. Our first orientation to the village may be useful for present readers as well.

25

4.
A Glimpse of Thurso Village

Thurso presented itself to its visitors as a settlement of about twenty residences, all of them more or less visible from our vantage point in that day of fewer trees. Right at the center, of course, stood the most important public institutions of the island—the post office, the store and the church. (Those that were elsewhere—the two schools and the cheese factory—we have already noticed.) This intersection was the center of the village in the sense that it was the crux of human comings and goings and the place of most common resort. But it did not comprise a geometric center, around which the homes had sprung up in balanced fashion on all sides. Buildings gave way to farms and fields to the south and west of this center almost immediately. Beyond the church and parsonage at our west lay nothing more urban, in those days, than the truck farm of the Turcotte family; and on the north side of the North Shore Road visibility ended with the cemetery, the terminus not only of the villagers but of the village. Between it and the crossroad lay only two house sites—that of the little home of Mrs. Packard, and the boxlike house on the northwest corner of the square in which the Ben Garnsey family lived in 1909. This family was soon to disappear from the island and leave with me only a memory of the loud shout "Kenneth!" with which Mrs. Garnsey, a tall and hearty woman, used to summon home one of her many roaming children. Aside from this home or two there was nothing on the northside of the road but open meadows and a clear view of gem-like islands in a marvelous panorama running to the Canadian shore five miles away and to distant hills on the Canadian mainland.

The village homes were concentrated, actually, on the two country "blocks" that ran north and east from the crossroads, being the final sections of the Cross-Island Road and the North Shore Road respectively, both about to be stopped by water. The Cross-Island Road runs into the river at McRae's Cove. Beyond lies only Leek Island Channel and Leek Island itself, a Canadian island sometimes called Thwartway. The

North Shore Road as it runs eastward is very soon is blocked by the unbridgeable Upper Marsh, beyond which no shore road has ever been made.

The factor that created this asymmetrical pattern of village residence was Thurso Bay itself, deep and large, that is and has been the real center of the village. From the village square it could be seen in 1909, even though today it is blocked from one's sight and consciousness by dense forest growth. The two residential streets just mentioned actually embrace, even now, the unseen Thurso Bay. The shores of the bay a century ago were the scene of great commercial quarrying operations that left their mark not only on the rocks but on the locating of homes, which were clustered about the quarries. Before the quarries there was no village. Thurso was granite-born, and originally granite-fed, and even today it is granite-centered.

The persons living on these two streets will be receiving our attention again and again. At this stage we shall only point out, with the help of the map inside the back cover, just where the actors in our drama lived. We begin with the west side of the street that runs north from the crossroad. Beyond the home of Ben Garnsey, already noticed, there is a deep swale, and as the road begins to rise again one's eye encounters the well-kept homestead in which Will and Addy Cummings would soon retire from farming. Beyond it, a little higher, lay the ugly green house that would long be know to me as the home of the Turcotte family. They were the island's market gardeners. Jessie Carnegie's neat yellow house came next, that Jessie Carnegie as a widow would live in for many years. Then came another tidy home, that of Harry and Maggie Gordon. An open field followed, and then the row of homes ended with "Uncle Hub" Garnsey's place, the original farmstead that had included all the land that lay round about, in the days before the coming of the quarries. Behind Uncle Hub's barn the fields sloped westward to the river, ending in a sand beach and shallow water much favored by small children. Beyond the beach a virtual sea opened up, miles wide and miles long, a stretch of open water beloved of yachtsmen and called by them "the Wide Waters."

On the east side of that final section of the Cross-Island Road the first house, beginning from the square, was that of Mort Marshall. (He was not related to Hi Marshall the storekeeper). Mort Marshall was a professional fishing guide, a ponderous man of jovial mannerisms whose hearty talk was somehow not convincing. In the early years of my life on the island there was a Mrs. Marshall, occasionally seen flitting about on

A Glimpse of Thurso Village

the veranda in a gay kimono, but she was an invalid whom I was never to know because her life was short. Tales about Mort himself must wait.

Northward from Mort Marshall's place the road dipped sharply as we have noticed. There was a strip of forest on its eastern side, and then, as the road rose again, a row of six old houses was seen, the onetime homes of granite-cutters who worked in a quarry to the east, on the border of the bay. A strike had ended the quarrying forever in 1896, and in 1909 the first four of the six houses were already derelict, with sagging porches and gaping windows. The two northernmost houses in this line were still occupied, however, by former employees of the quarry—the first by Davy Black, former paymaster of the quarry. We shall hear much of him. In the last house in the row lived Sid Chase, who had come over from Canada to work in the nearby quarry and stayed on after its closing. A trim picket fence surrounded his attractive retirement home and its immaculate flower garden. Tall lean and temperate, Sid Chase was neat in his person and in his housekeeping. His house was the last on the eastern side of the street.

Bringing our attention back to the village square we look eastward now into the easternmost section of the North Shore Road, noticing first the homes on the north side. We pass over, of course, Mort Marshall's house. East of it there was a small apple orchard, and then a place that was to be immeasurably important to the Norcoms. It was the home of the Alfred Dorr family. We had no inkling, in that first visit, that in three or four years it would be ours, and that in my case it would be my summer home for three quarters of a century! Directly to the east of it stood the neat house of Claude Hutchinson, and then a rambling building surrounded by apple trees where Charlotte McIntosh lived. She—and Elizabeth Brown who lived on the opposite side of the street—were widows left behind by the dying quarries, eking out a retirement in a place of little cost. Beyond Mrs. McIntosh on an outcropping stood the easternmost structure on the street, empty and ghostly—the abandoned three-story boarding house of the quarry workers. With its broken windows and fallen doors it was a deliciously creepy place for children to explore, with long dark corridors, bordered on each side by tiny empty rooms. Floors everywhere were sagging, half-buried under fallen plaster and broken glass. Everywhere on ceilings walls, window-frames and floors were the crumbling nests of mud wasps. On the lowest floor were the remains of a kitchen and dining hall. Not a trace of their original equipment remained—only rubbish. When one thought of the roistering young quarrymen who once made these still corridors ring with loud laughter and drunken shouts, the present silence was awesome, a grim reminder even to a small boy of the evanescence of life. It was always good to emerge from these dark recesses onto the sunny rock ledges where bird songs gave reassurance that life was going on as usual.

Crossing the road to the south side and accounting for the houses from east to west, we encounter first the house of the just-mentioned Mother Brown. About her we shall have much to say. The home of the family of Will Sturdevant lay westward, and of them there is a tale to tell. The neatly-painted house of Will Pettit followed, and then the blacksmith shop and home of Frank Slate, whose exploits will be notable. In the westernmost of the freestanding residences on this side of the street lived old Phronie Slate, an untidy spinster who would soon move downriver to a house along the shore. Finishing our round we come back to the store and post office on the village square. We notice that it has, in the rear, a large apartment—the residence of Hi Marshall the storekeeper and his wife Eliza and their daughter Mary, aged seven.

The mail wagon's deliveries at the village center have all been made, the small talk finished. The horse is champing, and the Norcoms are still to be taken onward to the McRae farm that is their final destination. The driver seats himself, makes a click of the tongue and flaps the reins. We turn the corner slowly and roll down the shaded avenue.

Such was the village of Thurso when I first knew it as a child. We shall become further acquainted with these village-dwellers in the course of the telling of our island story. All of them are dead now. Most lie in the island cemetery, but we shall try to make them live. If they could return in actuality they would rue the ruin of many a loving creation of their hands, but they might miss most of all the open lands and open views that could formerly be seen from the village on every side. Gleams of the shining river do not come through the dense foliage now to delight the eye of those who walk these roads, and in place of the roadside pastures that allowed far views into Canada and southward to the Base Line ridges, there are walls of trees. Of the houses that were theirs only a few are standing now, saved by having fallen into the hands of summer people. The Hutchinson house and house of Mrs. McIntosh have survived. Mrs. Brown's house has been reduced to a shed. Thurso's living community of year-round residents has scattered afar like milkweed floss borne away by the winds. The Slate house alone is still a Slate house—the home of Buck Slate, the only resident of the street in winter. The other houses have collapsed. There is no store. Of the blooming village that I saw from the mail wagon on that eventful June day in 1909, only the church remains essentially the same.

The village houses all behind now, the mail wagon soon came up against a closed gate. Young David Garnsey leaped off and opened it. Hub drove through and turned sharply left into a lane that ran northward down a long slope. The river lay ahead with distant islands in view and, nearby, a wooded headland. This was the point, now called Webster Point, on which we were to pitch our tents and spend a vacation lasting until Labor Day. In the foreground stood the McRae farmhouse with its outbuildings, and a big barn, and beyond it a strip of sand that extended to the headland. Hub deposited us and our baggage beside the house. We had arrived.

My principle recollection of that first day is of the wondrous smell of sweet clover and of the songs of the larks and song sparrows as Hub drove us down past the lush hayfields of the Dick McRae farm. I recall nothing of our establishing our camp alongside the Websters. However, one clear memory survives because it involved injustice. My mother had brought some boxes of strawberries from Clayton and had placed them on some nearby stumps of trees. Suddenly in mid-afternoon my mother discovered that the boxes had been noticeably depleted. Called to account for the missing berries, I protested my innocence with tears and anger. I had no idea as to what had become of the berries. All I knew was that I had not eaten them and it was unfair to say I had. My protests were received with the usual skepticism. "Well, those berries certainly didn't walk off by themselves!," my mother exclaimed with sharp asperity. "Very strange indeed!"

Sometime later, I happened to glance up into the trees and to my astonishment, here and there in the crotches above were bright red objects, the missing strawberries. I lost no time in pointing them out to my mother and for once experienced a triumph over my mother's incredulity. Red squirrels who were forever chirping and leaping about through the pines and hemlocks around the camp had put them there.

5.
Dick and Nettie McRae

My dearest memories of those early years are of the McRaes. Their farm stood on a cove off to the left as one entered Thurso Bay by water. It included Webster Point which was attached by a little isthmus to the main part of the farm. That promontory, almost an island, lay directly opposite the McRae house across the cove. It was there on the point that we and the Websters had pitched our tents.

It was with the McRaes, therefore, that we were to have our first intimate acquaintance with local people. Other islanders were to follow whom I would love and respect. But none were so significant in my island life as the members of this unusual family who were to become like "blood" relatives.

A big blond man with a bluff hearty way, Dick McRae was unforgettable. His full name was Alexander Richard McRae. His initials spelled ARM and the letters were tattooed on his forearm. Somewhere I have read that when a person's initials spell a word, that person is destined to prosper. Dick confirmed the truth of this observation, for he was the most affluent of all the islanders with the exception perhaps of Hi Marshall.

He became the idol of young Bill Webster and me—so much so that Bill declared that when he died, he wanted to be buried beside Dick in the local cemetery. In a strange way, Dick was very likable—not in the jolly back-slapping way of most people who charm. Actually, he was inclined to be taciturn and given to moody silences. His voice was loud and he could be harsh. When something had gone wrong, his glass eye was intimidating as he stared at you, chewing his mustache. He was vehement when he felt strongly about something. It was said—though I never saw it—that he had rare fits of violent temper that could verge on madness. But usually, especially in the presence of the women of his family, he said little and left the talking to his wife—who often said a great deal! In company he could be gallant and charming with the ladies. In his gruff way he was the life of the party at shore-dinners and other social excursions. There was something about Dick—a rewarding twinkle in his good blue eye, a faint smile or nod of approval—which made us boys his slaves. Dick had an odd speech impediment. For my first name, Stanley, he always called me "Tanny" and he called my dentist father, "Dot."

Dick had two daughters: Bertha, who was twice my age of seven when I arrived on the island, and Mabel, who was five years older than I. Bertha, unlike her quiet, domestically inclined sister, was outspoken, often rebellious and the more dominant of the two girls. Bertha was ever a champion of justice and as she grew older, she took pride in a candor that was sometimes rash. On occasion she jumped to mistaken conclusions. In temperament she was much like her father, given at times to moodiness and at other times to gay conviviality. I liked Bertha and I know that she liked me.

I recall well our first adventure together. It was a drizzly gray morning not long after I had arrived on Grindstone when Bertha and I decided to take a small boat Dick called "the Dinghy" and go fishing. Bertha said it was a perfect day for fishing. As the older of the two of us, Bertha as usual took the initiative, launching the boat and taking the oars, while I sat in the stern, trailing a stout handline to which was attached a shiny "Skinner spoon." For a boy of seven and a girl of fourteen it was an adventure!

Bertha rowed us out of the cove in front of the McRae house and on around Webster Point, where the water dropped off abruptly into green depths. We soon passed a massive knob of rock on the right and entered the "gut," a narrow passage between the knob and Sorrows Isle—a name later to be changed to Jolly Isle. Suddenly I felt a gentle tug on my hand-line. I began to pull in the line. It came easily. When its end came close to the boat to our astonishment we saw a huge fish, surprisingly passive. Suddenly the fish realized its danger, and with a mighty lunge it dove. Slowly, I pulled it back to the surface and again it dove. After repeated attempts to free itself, the fish finally tired. Its struggles became weak as we brought it alongside the boat. Bertha and I looked at one another, uncertain as to what next to do. We decided to run our boat onto the rocky shore of Jolly Isle, very near, and haul our fish onto the land, not exactly in the best of sporting tradition. Somehow we managed the feat and the fish lay gasping and flapping on the stones. The next step was to dispatch it and this we did by hitting it with rocks, again in a most unsportsmanlike manner. Quickly it was lifeless. We put it in the dinghy and rowed home, our fishing done for the day (and I don't think we ever fished together again).

When we reached the McRae dock, Dick was there, selling gas to some Canadian customers. "See what we got!" Bertha called up to him out of the dinghy. Dick looked down into the bottom of the boat where the fish lay. Others looked over his shoulder. He was incredulous. "You younguns never could have landed that fish alone!" He exclaimed. "Who gave it to you?" "Yes, we did land it, Papa," said Bertha, suddenly angry. "Nobody gave it to us. We caught and landed it ourselves." I spoke up. "Yes, and we had to drag it ashore and we hit it with rocks."

With these convincing details, everybody finally believed us. The big fish was cleaned and put into a drum in the McRae backyard and smoked for several hours. Then it was stuffed and baked, and a celebration was declared. A table was set up on the lawn and everyone around—the Websters, ourselves, and the McRae family—sat down to participate in the outdoor feast, an island feast not too different from one in the South Pacific, I'm sure, except that the fish was a Great Northern Pike. It weighed eight pounds.

The McRae farmhouse was once a log cabin, said to be the oldest on the island. It had been a typical pioneer cabin of the region. The original part of the house was long and low, with an attic from which two dormer windows protruded over a veranda that ran the length of the house. Then a large two-storied wing was added at right angles to the old house, and the entire building was clapboarded. At once it became like most of the other northern New York farmhouses—box-like, ugly and bleak. In this region, the lovely neo-classic phase was unknown that followed the log cabins in the building of farmhouses farther south.

The old part of the McRae farmhouse consisted of a large uncarpeted room that served as kitchen and everyday dining area. Partitions at one side concealed a sink, and a hand-pump that drew water from a cistern. Against the back wall was a wood-burning range, with a hot water reservoir that was later supplemented by a New Perfection kerosene stove. There was an icebox, filled daily with ice from the icehouse out by the barn. From the veranda the room was entered by a center door. To the right, as you entered, was the entrance to another room that originally must have been a bedroom, but was now the small McRae store, with counters and shelves laden with candies, canned foods and cigarettes. These cigarettes sold well to Canadians and were a significant source of the McRae income. The store always had a pleasant smell of spicy candy. A door for customers opened out onto the front porch, where a swinging seat hung and visitors could rest. Stairs ascended from the kitchen to an attic, originally a bedroom but now used for storage.

Nearby, a stairwell descended into the cellar. This stair was the scene of a minor catastrophe, a "downfall" literally as well as figuratively, that happened to me one summer years later when I was living in the McRae farmhouse. It was always cool in the stairwell and there were shelves along the side walls, a convenient place to set foods. All but two of the top steps of the stairs had rotted and fallen away. Only the supports of the missing steps remained on each side, jagged with projecting nails. It was rhubarb time and with a large kettle of the freshly stewed stuff I put my foot on one of the remaining steps and reached out to put the kettle on one of the shelves to cool. Suddenly the step gave way. I plunged headfirst downward between the two supports, the nails tearing at me and my clothes as I fell into the cellar. The kettle of rhubarb followed. Instead of the broken neck I might have suffered, I was hauled up out of the cellar with two broken ribs, many bruises and a plastering of hot stewed rhubarb. It was one more cherished tale about "the old place," as Dick called it after he had moved to another farm not far away.

As one entered the old kitchen from the porch there was a doorway to the left and a step upward into the "new" part of the house and then into the dining room. It was a large bleak room with chairs and a massive rectangular dining table of golden oak which was spread for festive occasions. I cannot recall ever having eaten at this table. But then I rarely ate meals at the McRaes. There was the usual china closet, and a strange piece of furniture called a "secretary," a tall narrow bookcase which was attached to a desk —an extraordinarily unlovely creation which was offered for years in Sears Roebuck catalogues.

Off this "formal" dining room was the parlor, with a large Brussels carpet on the floor and a nondescript chair or two covered with velvet. On the wall was a greatly enlarged tinted photograph of Dick ploughing a sloping field, with the river, the marsh, and

Dick and Nettie McRae

Black's Hill in the background. The slightly blurred picture had a wonderful rhythm and movement which gave it an appeal rarely found in professional photographs of the period. This picture hangs today, I think, in a later family farmhouse that Dick's grandchildren now occupy in summer. The McRae parlor's major feature was an Esley pump organ. It was replaced later by a La Farge piano. Both were essentially ornamental in function. I can't recall anyone ever playing these instruments. In fact, I can't recall anyone ever being in this parlor. It too seems to have been ornamental.

The McRae house had—and still has—one of the loveliest locations on the river. In front, a trim lawn runs to the river bank where large oaks and willows leaned outward to spread a leafy canopy over the shore. Wild roses bloomed among the rocks. There was a large mass of fragrant catnip along the well-worn path which led from the house to the base of the dock. To the right of the path on a ledge stood two large gasoline tanks. Beyond, a long dock led straight out into the bay. Up at the house at its west end, a large bush of lilacs stood against its west wall, shading the porch and its swinging seat on hot summer afternoons. One never wearied of the view from this porch. A mile away across the water to the northwest lay Leek Island with its high ledges and ragged pines among which the sun set in June, often in cloud billows of red and gold. The great bald promontory of the Forsyth Quarry on the far side of Thurso Bay, reached northward toward Leek, limiting the view to the west. Directly across our own little cove lay Webster Point, with its high rock bluff and its gnarled pines at the west end, and its evergreen crown running eastward. But Thurso Bay lay in front of the McRae's house like a lake, serene and blue. All day in summer the house was filled with the sound of little waves splashing among the boulders under the bank at the shore. In June the wind was heavy with the scent of clover drifting in from open fields that surrounded the house on several sides.

At the back of the old wing of the house was a shed on whose inside walls were hung old coats, bits of harness and the like. In the yard next to the door of the shed there were stools and wash basins, and benches with pads. In a far end of the shed stood a cream-separator. At first it had been a Sharples. The affluent Sharples family owned Netley Island a mile or so down river, and were gas customers of Dick. Later Dick replaced the Sharples separator with a De Laval which had been made in a factory down-state in Poughkeepsie close by the New York Central tracks. Long after Dick was gone, whenever I saw this factory from a train I was seized with a wistful longing for the old shed and Dick.

Beyond the shed was a yard with a high rack for airing milk cans in the sunshine. In that ample yard there were also chicken houses, scattered apple trees, a pig sty, a rhubarb patch, a kitchen garden, and to one side at the end of a well-worn path, the "back house." All around were hay fields, rising southward to what the McRaes called "outback." In the east Black's Hill loomed up beyond the marsh that bounded the McRae farm. To the west of the McRae house lay a hayfield that extended to the embankment of a long dock from which granite was once loaded onto schooners in Thurso Bay. Except for a few hedge rows and the trees around Thurso Bay, the lands around the McRae farm house were open on every side. The McRaes had little privacy. The neighbors could always observe the flutter of white aprons as the McRae womenfolk went about their work. Their trips to the privy were embarrassingly visible from the dome behind our house across Thurso Bay.

I remember vividly one summer morning, not long after we had first arrived on Grindstone, when my father and I walked over from the Point with our little two-quart enameled pail to replenish our supply of milk. We came upon Dick in the back shed shaving with a straight razor—an operation that always has an irresistible allure for the beholder. His face was hidden in a mass of white lather as he studied himself with deep intensity in the wavy mirror that hung upon the clapboards before him. It was no little tribute to his skill that he was able to carry on a lively conversation while he shaved, and now his talk was becoming vehement. He was reminiscing on a subject very dear to his heart: the rough life he had known as a young man sailing on the schooners up on the Great Lakes. One of these schooners now lay beached on rocks off Moneysunk, an island near Gananoque. It was an old weathered hulk called the "Britten" of Bowmanville. Already I had rowed over to explore it and had swung on the lines that still dangled from its leaning masts. And always I had imagined Dick swaggering along its slanted decks, balancing himself as the ship rolled with the toppling waves. I took deeply to heart the perils Dick had faced on those stormy seas, so very steep and treacherous. It wasn't until I had been on Grindstone Island for some time that I learned that Dick, leaving early employment in the quarries, had sailed the lakes for exactly one season. "Yeah! Those were the days," he boomed, "They didn't have any conveniences on those boats, I can tell you." We listened breathless as he went on, his razor never missing a stroke. "These young fellows today, they don't know what hard living is."

He paused, his razor lifted, "By God, in those days, when you had to go, damn-it you didn't have some fancy water closet to sit on!" Dick's mouth was a red gash in the white lather. "In those days when you had to go, even in a gale of wind you had to climb out on the old jib boom and let her fly!" Again there was a pause for dramatic effect while Dick gave us time to appreciate this precarious situation. It certainly seemed dangerous to me. Dick went on: "Yes, by God, many's the time I've sat out on that old jib boom with the wind a "squeakin" and the seas acomin' head on..."

At this moment, Bertha opened the kitchen door to pass through the shed with a freshly washed milk pail to be set on the rack in the sun out behind the house. She stopped abruptly in her tracks and stared at her father. Already she had a prim schoolmarmish way of speaking. "Why, Papa!" she exclaimed, "What on earth were you doing out there?" Dick's jaw dropped and his glass eye almost popped out of his head. "Doin'?" He stared at Bertha as though she had suddenly gone daft. There was an explosion of lather. "Doin? Doin' my bithness, that's what!" he boomed. Bertha uttered a meek "oh" and ran on quickly through the shed into the yard with her pail, her fair cheeks red with confusion while Dick finished his shave.

Dick had a white motorboat called "the Whistler," an odd boat with a square, outward-slanting stern and a fixed top, with a curtain that rolled down the sides. It had a four-cylinder Barber engine amidships. Someone in Clayton had built several of these boats. Will Cummings had one identical with Dick's except that it had a green scalloped fringe around the edge of the top which enhanced the boat's romantic name, "Arawanna." I can't recall the Cummings ever taking their boat out of Thurso Bay. Hi Marshall's boat was the "Wah Wah." It differed from the others in being larger and having a V-shaped stern. It too had a top. He and Will Cummings shared a large boathouse on the west shore of Thurso Bay. Joe Turcotte had a boat, too, the "Ada T." It was like Dick's and Will's except that it had no top at all, probably because it was easier that way to load the vegetables which the Turcottes grew and peddled at the head of Grindstone. He kept it in a small shed alongside the Cummings' boathouse.

The motors of all these boats—and others that came and went—gave out very distinct sounds. One could recognize whose boat was on the river by its "putt-putt," even when it was far away behind distant islands. One always knew when Joe Turcotte was leaving Thurso Bay for his morning rounds up at the "head" of the island, and when we heard the "WahWah" start up, we would wonder what was taking Hi Marshall to Gananoque or Clayton. The sound of Hi Marshall's boat starting up late at night was always sinister. It meant that someone had been taken ill. In such emergencies, people invariably called on the obliging Hi rather than on Dick. It was a long way down to the McRae place from the crossroads in Thurso, and Dick had the reputation of being grumpy about granting favors.

Yet there were times when Dick would be generous and accommodating. I recall one fine morning soon after we had set up camp on the Point when my mother and I joined Dick on a shopping trip to Gananoque, the Canadian town whose spires and towers rose above the intervening islands as in a Constable painting. Our shopping completed, we returned to the boat and started home. Instead of taking the course we had followed on the way over, Dick set off in an entirely different direction. We came to a maze of strange islands, the Admiralty Group, and entered the "Wanderer's Channel," a reach of the river that contributed much to the Thousand Island's reputation for beauty. My mother, always anxious on the river, became even more nervous as she wondered where this strange man was taking us. The little "Whistler" continued steadily on its way westward. Dick said nothing but I saw the twinkle in his eye and he was biting his mustache to conceal a smile. Then suddenly, Dick turned abruptly left from the Wanderer's Channel to enter a small passage between two islands. On our right, the rock cliffs rose high, and then suddenly we came to a cleft and through it we entered a tiny cove, completely hidden, that curved inland. At the far end in deep woods stood a natural rock-pulpit. Dick had brought us to the celebrated Half-Moon Bay which on Sunday afternoons in July and August is filled with boats gathered to attend worship services. My mother now realized that Dick was paying us a tribute—a rare tribute indeed, for I never knew him to go out of his way again to take any island visitor sightseeing. The river and its islands were too old a story for him.

Dick did not take us ashore to show us, atop the high cliff, the great potholes which had been ground out ages ago by the glacier. The glacier had smoothed many of the rock ledges on Grindstone, and dropped gravel in great moraines such as those at Black's Hill and Canoe Point on the island. I was to discover these glacial relics later for myself.

Nettie E. McRae! Dick's wife! The name brings back a flood of memories both pleasant and not so pleasant. Short and dumpy, she had a tight mouth, drawn down at the corners in a manner that expressed a perennial dissatisfaction with the world at large. She had a short indented nose which had been broken in childhood. I never saw a picture of the Soviet statesman Molotov without being reminded of Mrs. McRae. They could have been twins. Nettie was the daughter of Jim Rattray of Clayton, who ran a ferry from Clayton to Gananoque and, by stopping at the island, became Grindstone's first mail carrier.

She had a sharp tongue. No one was immune. I recall that first summer when she spoke to us of the Turcottes who had just moved into the old Uncle Hub Garnsey house on McRae's Cove. She described the Turcottes as fiends incarnate, horned monsters. And so when my father took me fishing along the shore in front of the house of these horrendous people, we would slink by in our boat, talking in whispers lest the terrible Turcottes should come forth brandishing pitchforks and spitting hideous invectives. We did not see any of them there. The industrious family were too busy working in their vegetable gardens. Later when we tremulously approached their house to buy the vegetables they grew, we found them quite friendly and obliging.

If some island customer for any reason postponed a little long the paying of his bill at the gasoline dock, Mrs. McRae lost no time in declaring him to be "a miserable good-for-nothing who ought to be run off the island." And she would belabor the matter until Dick was convinced too that the offender was a reprobate. Then suddenly some morning at the cheese factory he would explode in anger before the other islanders as he waited his turn to unload his milk at the weighing platform. This would lead to intense ill feeling all around. Everyone knew the source of the invective and everyone agreed that "old Net made the cannon balls and Dick fired them." Nettie McRae was Grindstone's Lady MacBeth, even though her murderous impulses were directed against peoples' character rather than their lives. It is not surprising that she was heartily resented in many quarters of the island.

Nettie McRae's sharp tongue quickly turned mellifluous when affluent summer people and Canadians came to the store. Demur behind the counter, she spoke in dulcet tones of her "to-mah-toes" and "rahs-berries" as she waited on her customers. But in the back shed among the milk pails, minutes later, when her customers were gone, so was her gentility: "Did you see that brazen little hussy, the shorts she had on? High enough to show her you-know-what!" She would give the milk pail a shove; "A little whore, that's all she is."

Of course, Mrs. McRae considered her family to be superior to the others on the island. The McRaes indeed were above many of them. In time they sent Bertha to a teacher's college in Cortland— and they were one of the few island families with such a distinction. The McRae house was scrupulously orderly and clean. Their girls were always neatly dressed. The milk pails were ever being scrubbed, and Dick's milk, unlike that of some of the other farmers, was never sent back home from the cheese factory for being "gassy"—that is, turned sour.

Mrs. McRae worked hard. Night and morning she was in the barn with Dick, milking by hand the eight or nine cows. She baked bread—oddly shaped loaves with very high rounded tops, always identical, week after week, year in and year out. And the McRaes were kind to their animals. There were always cats and a dog around. A favorite cat was called Spiffy. The dogs, a succession of three as I recall, were always named Laddie. And their horses were much loved and petted.

Mrs. McRae was always impressed by wealth or a show of it, and I think Dick was too. Nowhere was their gullibility more evident than in their deference toward their landlord Lew Webster, who had bought their farm a few years before. Why the McRae sons Tom and Dick had ever let the farm fall into other hands is a mystery that I do not understand to this day.

6.
Lew Webster

With every move Lew Webster exuded big-money. He had made money on the stock market and he saw no reason why he shouldn't make more. He could be pompous. He would come over the sand-split from the Point and walking about in portly manner, point with his expensive cigar exactly where he was going to build his boathouse, the possible location of a golf course, or where a canal could be dug through the sand-spit to make the Point an island. He had big plans for building a summer house on the Point, and a dozen other grandiose schemes. He spoke of long conversations he had had with Cleveland Dodge or someone of the Morgan family on the night-train coming up from New York the night before. He had talked with them of the plans he had for the farm on Grindstone. He described how Mr. Morgan, who had a farm and a large summer home at the head of the island, had listened with polite interest. That Lew Webster had hobnobbed with these wealthy men impressed the McRaes still more. He exuded bigness.

Even the Clayton people were impressed when they saw him walking down Water Street, waving his cigar magnanimously in response to the greeting of shopkeepers who were sweeping their sidewalks. They remembered him as the young fellow who had come from Canada, almost a barefoot lad. He had been shrewd and sturdy and good-looking, with a curly head of black hair, and twinkling slate-green eyes. An ingratiating way had gotten him that job at the Clayton Bank. His charm also won the president's daughter, Gertrude Reese. And soon he had taken her to New York and Big Business. Old man Reese was reputed to have been churlish, his only distinction his firm rejection of tobacco king Charles Emery's offer to buy up Clayton's waterfront and create an attractive park along the river's edge. Half a century of continued ugliness along Clayton's priceless river front has been the only monument to this stubborn curmudgeon.

Now, Lew Webster habitually walked along Water Street with his brother-in-law, Charlie Happ, who carried his expensive bags and felt it was a privilege to do so. Lew's farewell wave to Mr. Morgan or Mr. Dodge at the far end of town as they went on to the Morgan private docks was not lost on the townfolk either. The Clayton people knew the smell of big money when it was in the air.

Mrs. Webster's elegance and condescending ways did nothing to diminish the royal image her husband conveyed. Mrs. McRae noted every detail of Mrs. Webster's stylish apparel and discussed it with the girls. "Those diamonds didn't come from Woolworth's," she noted. "She must have paid a pretty penny for those shoes she wore to Clayton the other day. And that handbag she carried cost plenty, too." In these observations her voice carried a perceptible sneer. The McRaes knew the Websters' background all too well. "She needn't put on airs. Old man Reese was nothing to be proud of—the meanest old rat in Clayton. And what was Lew Webster when he came to Clayton! He didn't have a pot to do you-know-what in!"

The McRaes vaccillated in their feelings about the Websters. It was a love-hate relationship. While on the one hand they secretly regarded them with derision, on the other hand, they held them in awed respect. Lew Webster had become royalty by sheer chance. But now he was lord of the fief, and they acted accordingly. They obeyed the Websters' every beck and call. Lew Webster s wish was their command. If he wanted to go to Clayton to catch the Sunday night train back to New York, Dick would take him there in the "Whistler," and he would gladly meet him on arrival on the early train on Saturday morning. Dick would grumble privately about it, but he never balked. Dick kept the farm in perfect order, painting, repairing, building fences, and clearing the land. On one occasion, when the barn had to be shingled, Lew Webster with hammer and nails joined Dick on the roof. In his easy jovial way, Lew made it a merry occasion. Everyone gathered around to celebrate the event and to commemorate it with photographs. But there was no doubt as to who was master of all he surveyed.

Lew Webster liked to roll and putt a golf ball around a well-mowed area on the Point where it flattened out to meet the sandbar. The little golfcourse he had made there was to be the beginning of a golden age of development. He then built a privy at the foot of the slope that dropped down from the campsite. It had nothing of the golden age about it, but with complete faith in wonders expected to come, Mrs. Webster named it the "work of art."

The McRaes had a genuine affection for little Walter Llewellyn Webster, the Webster's small offspring, one year old at the time I came to the island. He was called Llewellyn by his mother, and Bill by his father and by me. As he matured the McRaes understandably idolized him, for the little boy had inherited all his father's charm. He had his father's calculating instincts and he made the most of his assets by making a show of winning smiles and appealing ways that sent the McRaes into raptures. Ganymede had fallen amongst them.

Of course, this small paragon with his Buster Brown haircut and velvet suits was thoroughly detested by me. Jealousy had lifted its ugly head. I was tall and ungainly for my age. I am sure, in retrospect, that I was spoiled and not very lovable. To the McRae's I was a young nonentity. Even at the age of seven, I was aware of Mrs. McRae's disdain. In contrast to her adulation of the smiling immaculate little Fauntleroy, she somehow made me feel dirty. And I was aware that Mrs. McRae regarded my parents, too, as nobodies. Compared with the elegant haughty Mrs. Webster, my mother was deceptively plain and frugal. Although as a girl she had moved in Brooklyn's highest society in its then fashionable "Eastern District" and her uncle had been Brooklyn's last mayor, she was totally without affectation. My father was quietly reserved and unassuming, too. He never made mention of the prominent people he numbered among his patients in Brooklyn. My parents were democratic and friendly with all the islanders. This did not sit well with Mrs. McRae either.

Children are more aware of the nuances of feeling among their elders than we realize. I was not happy with the fact that the McRaes seemed to regard my parents as people of small consequence. I felt ashamed of my parents' unaffected ways. I didn't want them to be regarded as nonentities by the McRaes or anybody else. I wanted my mother to wear smart clothes like "Aunty Web," with her fringes and beaded khaki Indian-squaw dress, instead of the plain skirt and blouse my mother wore. I wanted my father to smoke expensive cigars and walk about with genial ponderous importance like "Uncle Lew." I wanted my father to talk big like Uncle Lew—about a possible trip to Europe, or the purchase of an automobile—about something that would impress the McRaes. I resented the fact that my parents had not the slightest interest in impressing the McRaes or anyone else.

I was not amiss in my understanding of Mrs. McRae's scorn because she often tried to "pump" me about my family's intimate affairs. She asked endless personal questions about our circumstances: Did my father own our house in Brooklyn? Were my mother's teeth false? I was always smart enough to know what she was up to and I lied lavishly if not skillfully when I thought fictions would increase my parent's prestige. The poor woman must have been really confused.

Mrs. McRae mistook my parent's modesty for subservience. She took liberties not only with me but with them, in ways she would never have dreamed of otherwise. Moreover, she enjoyed making trouble for trouble's sake. I remember vividly an occasion when she created a rift between the Websters and my family which was slow to heal.

It was two or three years after our arrival on Grindstone. The Websters were not camping on the Point that summer, but we were camping there again at their warm invitation, this time alone and on their tent platforms. On a lovely September afternoon just before we were to return to the City, Dick and Nettie McRae came across the little strip of beach that connected the Point with the farm. We saw them coming. It was rare for the McRaes to pay social calls and my parents were pleased to have them come. Their pleasure was short-lived. Mrs. McRae lost no time in dropping her bombshell. She told us that because of my family's occupation of the Point, the Websters had lost an opportunity to rent the campsite all summer for the enormous sum of $200 a month. To Mrs. McRae's disappointment, my father did not seem to be disturbed. He said he would have been glad to surrender the campsite if Lew Webster had informed him of the situation. We were leaving the Point in a day or two. He said it was an issue between himself and Lew Webster alone, and he would talk the matter over with Lew when he got back to New York. And thus he dismissed the McRaes without the ado they had expected and they departed abruptly. To be fair about it all, I doubt if Dick had much of a part in this confrontation. Mrs. McRae was capable of working him up to a fierce indignation, but on this occasion he seemed to be there only to give moral support. The root of it all lay in a strain of restless anger that pervaded Nettie McRae's nature. Of course, back in New York, the Websters stoutly denied the McRae assertion. But suspicions remained, and for years there was a chill between the Websters and ourselves that Mrs. McRae had caused.

The Websters never camped on the Point again. And no one else ever camped there either, let alone paid for the privilege. Very shortly after the McRaes' visit, we bought a summer place of our own in circumstances that will be told later.

Mrs. McRae was not entirely the island Gorgon I may have implied. When she could be diverted from her obsession with human faults, she could hold her own in merry company on picnics, and especially on excursions to the mainland which broke the island's oppressive monotony. And she could be kind. If someone were ill, she would send one of the girls with a bowl of nutritious soup, even if she had damned the afflicted to hell-and-gone the day before. And she would send generous covered dishes of food to the church suppers, and sometimes she even attended them. But "Old Net" definitely was not the island's angel of mercy. Eliza Marshall, of whom we shall hear later, had that role on Grindstone.

It was very pleasant on a warm summer afternoon to sit in the swing at one end of the McRaes' veranda and watch life on the dock. It was especially busy on Sunday afternoons. Grown-ups from Gananoque would stroll up to the store with their children to purchase candy, cookies and cigarettes. I recall well the Sampson's cabin cruiser and their aloof elderly nursemaid herding the Sampson children up to the store for sweets. Other prominent visitors from Gananoque included the Parmenters and the Bullocks. And even jovial old

McRaes' Store, c.1912

Willy Britten, Gananoque's customs officer, came over sometimes for a friendly visit. From islands down river came beautifully varnished boats with polished brass fittings. But the elegant boats from Leek Island seldom came, except to bring the Kipp children over to the annual Grindstone Sunday School picnic, for which the Kipps generously provided ice cream and cake. Will Garnsey, the Kipps' boatman, was not friendly with the McRaes. Mrs. McRae undoubtledly had "talked" and her talk had reached his ears.

7.
Jay Robinson

I was sitting on the McRae's veranda one Sunday afternoon when the river out front lay like glass. The hour was late, the shadows were lengthening. The shimmering river was deserted. Only a few gulls were wheeling before the cliffs on the Point across the cove. The air was still. There wasn't even the faraway putt-putt of a motor boat. Out in the tranquil bay, a fish would jump with a splash and then there would be silence. From within the house came the cheerful sounds of preparation for supper.

Suddenly, beyond the Point, I saw a skiff rowed by a solitary oarsman going up-river, midway in its passage of Leek Island. This was unusual. At this hour, one did not often see westbound skiffs in the middle of the Leek Island Channel. Beyond Leek Island were the "Wide Waters," an unbroken expanse of river running far to the westward for many miles. I watched the lone oarsman rowing steadily with measured strokes. Then I saw him drop the oars and stand up unsteadily in his boat. He took a faltering step or two toward its stern and paused. Suddenly he began to flail his arms about wildly and I could hear him shouting. With heavy blows he began to pound the empty stern seat of the boat. After a moment the shouting stopped. The man quit his pounding and returned to his seat. Without a sound he resumed his rowing, trailing behind a long straight silver scar on the blue river. Little waves like writhing serpents rolled shoreward from his boat in the fading light. Suddenly, as the little skiff went past Leek Island's south-shore cove, the man stopped rowing again, stood up in his boat as before and flailed his arms, then toppled toward the stern and resumed his furious pounding on the stern seat. Angry shouts rang out loud and clear across the river on the still air. Then once more the strange business ceased and the man resumed his rowing. Five minutes later, when he was almost out of sight, he repeated the whole crazy performance again. Then he was gone.

I went into the kitchen and reported what I had seen to the McRae family, who were sitting down to supper. "Yea-uh!" Dick grunted. "That was old Jay Robinson. He's on a drunk again." "The old fool thinks he's beating up that relative of his wife's out there in the boat with him," Mrs. McRae broke in. "He's got the idea he got cheated out of her estate when she died. It's a wonder he didn't fall out of that boat and drown himself. Too bad he doesn't, that miserable piss-ant!"

Satisfied, I went back across the sand bar to our camp on the Point and had my own supper. Scolded for being late, I forgot about Jay Robinson for a while. Our tents and their platforms stood in a thick grove of pines and hemlocks on a sort of saddle that lay in the middle of the Point, which would have been an island if a sand bar had not run from our camp to the McRae farm. On the east side of this sandy isthmus lay a sea of dense marsh grasses, the beginning of the upper marsh. On its west lay the subsidiary cove of Thurso Bay, now called Webster's Cove by some, on which the McRae house fronted. The waters of the cove were sparkly and clear with little waves coming in from the Leek Island Channel and forever slapping on its beach. Where the isthmus joined the Point there was a little grassy swale under a granite ledge, and a mound blanketed with blue marsh-flag and vervain. And beneath this mound lay the body of an unknown woman. Davy Black and Sid Chace had found her body floating in the river, and had given it burial there. Whether she had been murdered or was a suicide or had simply fallen into the river by mishap, I never heard. For some reason, I never remembered to ask Davy or Sid about it. The little mound remained for years. It finally melted into the soil and I doubt if any trace of it remains beneath the brush that has overgrown it. And I am probably the only living person now who knows of its existence.

From our tents on the point, our path to the McRae farm ran down a grassy hill, and before it reached the sand bar it crossed a little meadow. To the west lay the mysterious little mound. In the east, hidden beneath one of the rock ledges that made up the Point, stood "the Work of Art." Nearby on the little meadow stood a small weathered building called the Shanty. It had been built by the Cooks from Gananoque, who, according to the McRaes, had been very rough customers given to fishing out-of-season, to use of illegal nets, and other infamous practices. Dick's cattle, grazing, kept the whole area clean and park-like.

During our second summer on the Point the shanty at the foot of the grassy hill was the scene of a debacle for which I was wholly responsible. Happily for me, the event was so catastrophically distracting that I escaped the punishment I deserved. It was all an outcome of my father's decision to use the space of the empty shanty to build a rowboat. He had made it of cypress planking, and now, completed, it lay upside down on wooden horses, ready for painting. The boat filled the little building. There was almost no room to squeeze by as one walked around it.

The boat was unlike anything seen on the river before or since. My father had patterned it after the rowboats we had used on the sheltered New Jersey lake where we had spent previous summers. Flat-bottomed and shallow, with a pointed bow and square stern, it was completely unseaworthy in the great open reaches of the St. Lawrence. The islanders called it "Sharpie." The sharpie now lay upside down on its wooden supports inside the shanty, ready for painting. My father had chosen an oil paint (there was no other kind in those days) named "Forest Green" and a full can of the stuff stood opened on the boat's upturned bottom with a long mixing stick protruding from it. My father had been working under the boat and he was coming out from under it. As luck would have it, I stood in his way, blocking the narrow passage between boat and shanty wall. Never the most patient of men he called sharply to me, "Get out of the way!" I jumped guiltily and as I did so my arm caught the mixing stick, which in turn upset the can of paint. At that instant my father's head was emerging directly below. As he rose slowly, his hair was deluged in a mass of slimy green. Green rivulets ran in streamers down his face. He looked like Neptune rising from the waves. In an instant I vanished from the scene. My father, entirely preoccupied, forgot me as he dashed up hill to the camp in search of soap and water. It was hours before he was presentable again. For weeks thereafter, my father's hair was tinged with forest green and for years afterward, when searching for old rags we never failed to pull out from the pile a rag with a smear of green on it.

Our camp and the Websters' covered a considerable area on the wooded saddle of the Point. Anyone who approached it from any direction encountered a maze of stakes, guy ropes and lines about the tents, to say nothing of fish lines strung between the trees for drying. Camp chairs, buckets, tree stumps and such obstacles were everywhere. This tangle was the scene, one wild night, of an alarm that had the women of the camp frozen with fear in their respective tents and my father crouched outside, clutching a revolver. My father was the only man on the Point. "Uncle Lew" Webster was in New York City, trading on the Stock Exchange. "Aunty Web" and little Llewellyn were alone in their sleeping tent and Mrs. Webster's sister Grace Ackert with her small son Harow were in the guest tent. Outside in the blackness, some enraged person was floundering about, filling the air with obscenities. He would stumble over one guy-rope after another and send each tent into shaking convulsions that threatened to bring it to total collapse, Then there would be renewed cursing as he staggered in another direction, falling and recovering as he floundered. It seemed that if he kept on, he might bring the entire camp down. His loud voice became hoarse and more and more threatening as he encountered yet other impediments, one after another. We wondered what sort of demented wretch had come into our midst, probably armed with a bludgeon and ready to lay everything flat. Just as the suspense was becoming intolerable, suddenly all became quiet. The hoarse voice was reduced to angry muttering as it faded away down the hill and on across the beach toward the McRaes. The trill of the marsh frogs rose again from below the hill, and the camp returned to its usual silence, that continued for the rest of the night.

With daylight, everyone emerged to find out what had happened. Who was this Grendel who had come up out of the fen in the dead of night with such awful threats and foul invective? We had not the remotest idea. Perhaps the McRaes would know. Grendel had obviously gone in their direction. We would go over later to the farm and find out. On the way my father and I paused to make sure the stranger had not damaged the Sharpie, which was now completed and, painted its forest green, lay on the little beach at the foot of the Point. To our surprise we found an old skiff hauled up beside it. An oar lay in it, smashed. My father was studying the skiff for clues about its ownership when suddenly we were aware of a man behind us, carrying an oar. He was unshaven and unkempt and his clothes were torn. He had a dyed mustache and under his slouch hat his eyes were bleary. His manner was mild, almost apologetic. His glance was directed before him, and with great effort he concentrated on each of his steps as he approached. The man was obviously "under the influence." Carefully he put down the oar and held out a dirty hand to my father which my father did not take. My father was sure that this man had been our disruptive visitor of the night before and he was irked. Oblivious, the man reached into his coat pocket and pulled out a flask of cloudy whiskey. With great effort, he withdrew the cork and offered the flask to my father. "Have a drink," he insisted. My father declined. Whereupon the man raised the flask to his lips and took a long swig of the yellow liquor himself. I could smell its rank odor from where I stood behind my father. The man filled his mouth and swished the liquor about with obvious relish. Then to our astonishment, he regurgitated it all back into the flask. Again, he looked at my father. "C'mon, have a li'l drink," he repeated, holding the flask out again. My father was no more inclined to accept than previously. He engaged briefly for a moment in small talk. Not a word was said about the night before and we quickly went on our way.

Over at the McRaes, we heard the complete story. The man was Jay Robinson. In his youth "the iron man" of the island, a person of fabulous strength, he had in later life become tragically feeble before the power of the bottle. That night, drunk as usual, he had been battling his imaginary enemy out on the river and had broken an oar. Seeking help he had landed on the Point, and headed for the McRaes. He had gotten fouled up in our encampment which he had not known to be there. In the tangle he became desperate but finally reached the McRaes. The McRaes knew who it was and did not let him in. After threshing about on the veranda, shouting and pounding on the door in vain, he went on to the village. "A dod-damned nuisance, that's all he is," Dick grumbled. "No one in their right mind would help that miserable thing," Mrs. McRae joined in.

Not long after, Jay Robinson married a respectable woman from Canada and took her and a ready-made family of girls to his farm below the marsh. There, people said, she had laid down the law to Jay. "They say she's a tartar—a holy terror," Mrs. McRae said with smug satisfaction. "She's not taking any nonsense from that miserable drunk." That Jay had been reformed was certainly true. We saw nothing of Jay from then on. Sly stories were built up all over the island about Mrs. Robinson's reign of terror and Jay's complete submission to domesticity. The stories were apocryphal. No one who is alive today can confirm or deny them.

Years later, Mrs. Robinson, as a widow, moved into the house the Claude Hutchinsons had occupied when we first arrived—the green house above and behind our small acre. There she lived quietly, raised her family of pleasant girls to adulthood and finally saw them married and off the island. She lived on alone as long as she was able. When sometimes I called on her I always found her gentle and amiable. Her granddaughter, Doreen Meeks, with her husband, Don, still own the house and come there on summer

weekends from their house in Clayton Center. The Meeks are the kindest and mo
thoughtful of neighbors.

8.
Hi Marshall's Store

The tall plain building facing the church on the crossroads in Thurso was known to everyone around as The Store. It was a true emporium. It had everything under the sun in its dark recesses. The little McRae store with its cigarettes, candy, soft drinks and some canned goods offered little competition, and for Canadians it was only a way stop. Leaving their boats at the McRae dock, they would go on up the hill to see what the big store had to offer—much to Mrs. McRae's irritation. She was never pleased to see the "Cannucks" when they returned loaded with purchases. Her dulcet voice was strained when they asked for cold soft drinks after their long hot walk. She would fulminate against Hi Marshall, calling him "that miserable little runt up on the hill." When salesmen installed the same displays in each store, "old Net" would charge that that miserable little runt was stealing her ideas.

Hi Marshall was a short blue-jowled man, quiet and unobtrusive. He always seemed preoccupied as he attended to his affairs. There was a persistent lump in his lower jaw. One would in time discover it to be a large quid of tobacco, when he paused to spit into whatever container he had at hand for that purpose.

Hi was one of the most decent and obliging men I have ever known. It was always Hi to whom people went in time of trouble — for credit, for loans, for whatever help they needed. It was always to Hi that they turned when someone was acutely ill and needed a doctor. That was usually in the middle of a black night with wind and rain. Then a white face would appear at the Marshall back door. Hi would dress, and one would see lanterns throwing their long shadows through the woods, as he and the newcomer would go down to his boathouse. Then one heard the sputters of his boat as it left the boathouse and headed out of Thurso Bay. Its yellow stern light, like a will-o'-the-wisp, would disappear into the formidable darkness beyond the bay and one would hear the "Wah Wah" cross the channel toward Gananoque, three treacherous miles away.

And after an hour or so, the red and green bow lights would appear around the foot of Leek Island, and Hi's boat would enter Thurso Bay and dock, and shadowy figures bearing lanterns would leave the boathouse and walk quickly through the woods to the road. There Dr. Davis (or Dr. Bird), carrying a valise, would climb into a waiting milkwagon and be driven off to some distant bedside. An hour or so later, the little party would return and Hi's "Wah Wah" would putt-putt out into the night again to take the doctor home. And Hi would get five dollars for his efforts! The next morning we would hear, when we went to the post office, who had been treated, and why.

I recall no one ever dying on these occasions. The islanders usually died during the long winters when the island was hemmed in by ice and pneumonia prevailed. In the actual depth of midwinter, things were not so bad. Then one could drive to the mainland on the frozen river, even though there were always risks. It was in the early spring and late fall, when the river was full of ice floes, and crossing the river was almost impossible, that the sick were truly in peril. Without telephone service, the islanders were even beyond advice. It was then that the ill grew worse and died.

In summer, when someone died, the departure from this "vale of tears" was almost always by drowning. Then one would see a little cluster of boats around a spot on the river where the unfortunate one had disappeared. The men were engaged in the grim business of grappling for the body. Hi was always the first to help on these occasions and Dick was there too. Death brought forth democracy on Grindstone as elsewhere.

Hi was an avid Republican. Politics was all that I ever knew him to grow heated about. His adversary was Davy Black, an equally ardent Democrat. Mr. Black, a bearded Scotsman who lived in the village, was a man of great composure even when he was inebriated—as he often was in the first three or four years of my life on Grindstone. Everyone, even the children, always called him Mr. Black, so impressive was this dignity of his. Many were the arguments I heard between Hi and Mr. Black in the store. Without raising his voice and gesturing with his pipe before him, Mr. Black would puncture Hi's heated polemic with a sharp well-directed word. And Hi would respond with a "But gracious sakes alive, Davy, you should know better than that!" Then Mr. Black, with a strongly burred Scotch accent would reply, "Harumph, mon, ye dinna know what you're talking aboot." And the debate would go on, interspersed with "gracious-sakes" and "gee whittakers," the most vulgar of Hi's expletives.

Hi Marshall's Store

Even when used in its most proper context, the word "bitch" always shocks. And so does "bastard." To describe the thoroughly decent Hi as a bastard seems gratuitous yet that is what he was in the exact sense of the word. His father was Ed Marshall and with his short bowed legs and long body, there was no doubt that Hi was a Marshall. His half brother Fred, a Clayton boatman, had exactly that build, as did his half sister Mrs. Will Farrell, and many of his distant cousins.

I seldom saw Hi Marshall's father, Ed Marshall. He had a rambling farm house and a large farm on the South Shore Road not far west of the town dock where the mail boat landed. The south side of Grindstone was remote, unfamiliar territory for me in those days. Hi was known to have been born in 1870, but no one seemed to know who Hi's mother was, except that she was not Ed Marshall's wife. Hi was reared by Janet Johnson, a widow who lived near the Marshalls and was known as Aunt Jane. This Aunt Jane Johnson may have been his mother. Aunt Jane Johnson and her sister Mary had once lived at the very foot of Grindstone on its north side. They had no known children, however.

His mother or not, Aunt Jane Johnson deserves great credit for having reared the young Hi to be the thrifty, industrious and thoroughly decent man he became! That legitimacy can be less honorable than bastardy was shown at the time of Ed Marshall's death when Hi's only child Mary laid claim to a grandchild's share of old Ed's estate. It was Hi's half brother Fred who succeeded in disqualifying her because her father Hi could not be proved to be Ed Marshall's son. Fred was heartily despised about Clayton as having been greedy and mean in this matter.

As a young man, Hi worked at odd jobs such as carpentry. Sober and thrifty, he was able to buy the Thurso store in 1900. And then he married Eliza, one of the Delaney girls from the remote farm at the foot of the island where Aunt Jane had once lived. Together they prospered.

Eliza Marshall was a handsome woman with an oval face, dark eyes, heavy brows, and iron-gray hair flowing back from her forehead in natural marcelled waves. Her smile was quick and her kindness infinite. She had great dignity. Not possessed of any of the overblown finery of the period, she could nevertheless have stepped out of a Gainsborough portrait. One could say that Eliza Marshall was the one true aristocrat the island had produced within remembered time. Quite unexpectedly one learned that she was a graduate nurse. With her warm gracious manner and authoritative ways in time of illness, she was for Grindstone Island a gift sent straight from Heaven. Always, for the ill, she was quietly able and effective. Her cool hand on a fevered brow was unbelievably healing. At first one might wonder what a woman of Eliza's poise and intelligence had seen in "that miserable little runt" Hi Marshall. Then one realized that on an island where the young men were given to drinking and roistering as only the Scotch-Irish can, Eliza Delaney had found Hiram Marshall's kindness and honest decency appealing.

Hiram Marshall

Eliza was fond of company. She had a lively Irish sense of humor that made her wonderfully convivial on picnics when Hi occasionally took us in his "Wah Wah" to parks down river. The Marshalls' living quarters behind the store were often full of guests, usually some of Eliza's own family or school friends. Theirs was a jolly household. It was always fun to stop and cross the lawn to visit with them on the little veranda at the rear of the store on its north side. Years later, Hi and Eliza bought old Mort Marshall's place across the road and they filled that house in summer with members of her family. Eliza was seldom in the store. Only when it would overflow with Canadians on a buying spree would she appear to wait on them, pleasant and helpful.

The Marshall store bore a sign above its porch "1888." Gregg Burgess had run it for twelve years before Hi bought it. From the front platform one entered the store through a central door. The display windows on each side were full of dust and spider webs and with hit-or-miss displays of perfume bottles, Ingersol dollar watches, men's work-shirts, pots and pans, and any novelty which might appeal to Canadians as well as to the islanders. There were posters praising Sweet Caporal, Lucky Strike, Camel and Murad cigarettes and ads for Velvet, Bull Durham, and Patterson's Cut Plug tobacco.

Hi Marshall's Store

The cavernous dark interior of the store would be called dirty by the more fastidious today. As one entered, one immediately faced a large stove in front of which a bench stood. A first impression was that the store was jammed with merchandise. And it certainly was. On the left was a worn counter at whose inner end stood a red coffee-grinder with two big wheels for turning it, and beside it there were large tin boxes of tea and coffee. Behind the counter shelves reached to the ceiling, and on them there were rows and rows of shoeboxes and bolts of flowered cloth. On lower shelves there were endless cartons of cigarettes. It was here that the Canadians met temptation and found it irresistible. This left counter was all the more fascinating because at its rear was the post-office wicket, set in a partition, filled with tiers of inset cubicles for mail. Behind this was Hi's office—a very dark cubbyhole containing a safe and a desk.

On the floor at the rear, in front of a counter, sat large tin cannisters with hinged glass tops through which one could see fig newtons and soda crackers and such cookies as Mary Ann's. Nearby were small red-and-yellow cardboard barrels of gingersnaps. An array of shovels, pitchforks, bucksaws, milk pails—farm hardware, in short—mixed in with men's clothing and rain gear, was displayed across the back wall.

On the right side of the store as you entered, the wall behind a counter was lined with shelves of canned goods and dry cereals. In front of the stove there was always a large crate that arrived every day with the mail. It was jammed with loaves of bread from the Clayton bakery, wrapped in blue waxed paper. This Clayton product was inferior in taste to the bread one could buy in Gananoque. Nevertheless the crate emptied quickly in the course of an afternoon and one had to come to the store early to be sure of a loaf.

A doorway at the back of the store led into the Marshalls' living quarters. It was a sacrosanct portal which no one ever dreamed of entering except on special invitation. Another doorway led into a south-side shed where stood drums of kerosene, or coal oil as the islanders called it. When some farm boy carrying a five-gallon can descended from a wagon and entered the shed, Hi would go through the door, insert a long-shafted pump into a drum of kerosene and fill the can. The New Perfection stoves which had just come into use in the island's kitchens were thirsty for such oil. Inside the shed a stairway led up to the floor above, a huge room containing a piano and a few stray chairs. This was known as "the Hall." It was in this hall that the islanders held their winter dances. Here Dick had won his reputation for lightness of foot.

The edible contents of Hi's store, by today's nutritional standards, were dreadfully deficient. There wasn't a fresh vegetable or a bit of fruit in the place. To compensate, however, there was a cabinet filled with bottles of cod liver oil, Charles H. Fletcher's Castoria, Sloan's Linament, Lydia Pinkham's Compound, castor oil, tincture of larkspur, worm mixtures, whooping-cough and ordinary cough syrups, and there were the inevitable Carter's Little Liver Pills. The island animals were not neglected. For them, there was an assortment of tinctures and ointments, not least among these, Glover's Mange Cure and "Fly-dose." The odor of this last, dabbed on a herd of bovine quadrupeds, could be smelled a mile away on a down-wind. It discouraged not only flies, but bipeds too. These horrendous foul-smelling veterinary mixtures were recommended heartily by some islanders for stubborn human afflictions also, that were resistant to ordinary measures. The worse they smelled and the more they smarted, the more effective they were believed to be.

The post office of course displayed the usual rogues' gallery of posters bearing photos, finger prints, and descriptions of assorted crooks and gangsters wanted by the Secret Service (the FBI was yet to come). Recollection of this display of criminal characters came to me one day in my teens when I was in the Grand Central railway terminal in New York City. That terminal always turned my thoughts to the north country. It was from there that we left for my beloved Grindstone Island—an island that, as far as I was concerned, remained forever in perpetual summer.

In the endless underground passages of the terminal there were a number of small curtained booths in which one could take a seat before a camera, deposit a quarter, and in five minutes emerge with a small photo which invariably emphasized the more unsavory aspects of one's features. In fact, these photos bore a strong resemblance to the rogues' gallery photographs I had seen in the island post office. Suddenly, I decided to have my picture taken by one of these machines. I obtained full-face and profile photographs of myself that were quite effective for my purpose. I then impressed a couple of finger prints on a sheet of paper, mounted the photos, and typed up a typical Secret Service notice about ghastly crimes I had committed. I put the notice in a blank envelope and sent it to Hi Marshall. I was sure I had pulled off a hilarious joke that would be thoroughly enjoyed on the island.

There was no reply. The months passed. At last it was late June and I was on the island again. Discreetly, I brought up the matter of the poster, expecting to see Hi convulsed with laughter as he remembered my stunt. Instead, he looked reproachful. He spat into a nearby can, shook his head. "You shouldn't have done that," he said. "It gave me a terrible shock. I thought you were in deep trouble." I always tended to accuse Hi as lacking a sense of humor. But in candid retrospect, whose sense of humor was lacking in this instance is a question. What I expected to come of this silly business is unclear to me now.

Flossie Sturdevant

9.
Flossie Sturdevant

Hi Marshall's store prospered enough to support a full-time clerk—Flossie Sturdevant. She was a tall slender brown-haired young woman, in her early twenties, and she could have stepped straight out of a sketch by Charles Dana Gibson. With an air of aloofness she carried her head high. Her manner was always impersonal. What one most remembered about her was her fair, rose-petal complexion. Flossie had the perfect Victorian "hectic flush."

With a chronic cough and a hollow chest, everyone was certain that Flossie was a victim of that scourge of the period, tuberculosis, and was destined for an early grave. The sunless dreary interior of the store and the long hours that she worked and the dust that she breathed as she swept the store out each morning—all made poor Flossie's fate seem more certain. Flossie had a drooping mouth that enhanced the aura of genteel melancholy that lay about her and supported the morbid fascination of watching one so young and fair who is about to die. She had an air of high seriousness that appealed to me immensely as I grew into adolescence, a time when one is always absorbed in sweet sad thoughts of love and death and reflections on the meaning of life. Flossie gave great promise of high serious talk with me about such things—promise that could never be fulfilled in the store where she was forever preoccupied with customers and always discreetly impersonal. But I was sure she could be a Candida to my Marchbanks if we were once free of the gloomy environs of the Marshall emporium.

After much calculating thought, I finally decided to ask Flossie to go for a ride in my canoe some Sunday afternoon. With the proper hesitation, she accepted, and we embarked on Thurso Bay on a golden summer day when the river lay like glass. With Flossie propped up on cushions in front of me and trailing a lily-white hand in the sliding water, I paddled out to the mouth of the bay where in the distance we could see boats coming and going at the busy McRae dock. My long awaited hour had arrived for talking alone with the wistful Flossie. But, alas, I discovered slowly that Flossie was not in the least interested in the meaning of life and the sweet mysteries of love and death. In fact, Flossie didn't seem interested in anything. To each of the pensive musings I would offer with high seriousness, Flossie would reply with languorous indifference or not at all. As she sank back farther into the cushions, I could see that she was becoming more and more bored. Her glance turned toward the McRae dock and suddenly she came to life. "Let's go into the McRaes. There's something I want to talk to Bertha about."

Flossie Sturdevant

I paddled quickly into the McRaes and there I left Flossie. I think that we were both relieved that the ride had ended. It was not too far for her to walk alone up the McRae lane to the village and her own home and I knew that Flossie wouldn't mind. And that was the end of my aspirations for serious and lofty conversation with Flossie. Actually, Flossie was a very simple country girl, fastidious and sensitive, who looked lovely and pensive and poetic. She bore no blame for not being Candida. And I learned at last that she had already played a role in a grim unscheduled drama on the very day we had arrived on Grindstone. She didn't care to play in another.

Flossie lived alone with her mother, Sarah, in a large weathered house—one of the row on the south side of the road that ran eastward from the store. The Sturdevant place was always neat and trim, the lawn carefully mowed. Like her house, Sarah Sturdevant was always neat and trim, too—a plain angular woman, severely good-looking in the manner of a headmistress of a boarding school. There certainly was nothing frivolous about her. As with Flossie, her outstanding trait was gentility—absolute and complete. Even a small share in the racy ebullience that characterized so many of the islanders might have been a saving grace.

Flossie Sturdevant

But a cruel event had overtaken Sarah and Flossie on that very day in late June, 1909, when Hub took us for the first time past their house in Thurso. It was an event that left the two women utterly bereft and I'm sure, quite bitter. For in the small hours of that morning, Will Sturdevant, Flossie's father, had left Grindstone Island never to return. He had been the island's customs-officer—a pleasant man in his forties, easygoing and well-liked.

When the islanders discovered that his boat was missing, they were mystified. Will had vanished without a trace. The river, always ready to exploit the missteps of those who sail it, had actually been tranquil under a starry sky throughout all the preceding night. If the river held the secret of Will Sturdevant's disappearance, it was not apparent. Nor was there any hint of foul play. Will had always been a respected, home-loving man, sober and, they said, honest as the day. The mystery deepened.

That noon, someone came from Gananoque to say that Will Sturdevant's boat was tied up at the railway dock over there, abandoned. Then someone said that a man with a young woman had purchased railway tickets at the station on the wharf and had left at midnight on the shuttle train that went out to the Junction to connect with the big westbound express that stopped there at one in the morning. Then at mail-time at the Marshall store one of the farmers from the foot of the island announced that one of old Ben Calhoun's daughters was missing—the plain one with a shriveled arm. Now there was no doubt. Will Sturdevant had eloped with this girl and taken her away to an unknown land in the west. This strange affair remained a mystery to island people for many years. No one understood how the crippled girl, living on a lonely distant farm, had caught Will's fancy. Nor why he had abandoned his family and everything he owned to run away with her.

Long after, I heard at least a partial resolution of these questions from Mr. Davy Black. Not different from anyone else who was born on Grindstone, Will Sturdevant was never able to forget the Island. That he must have been very homesick for it and craved news of it is betrayed by the fact that, by some means or another, he kept in touch. An islander named Alec Robinson knew where Will Sturdevant now lived. Alec Robinson had become a ship's officer, sailing the Great Lakes. It must have been twenty years after Will's elopement that Robinson's ship was docked in Duluth harbor. At last he had a chance to visit Will. Will Sturdevant had a farm far out in the countryside some miles from Duluth, where he lived under an assumed name. It was a considerable journey, and as the taxi Alec had rented drove on, it began to snow heavily. At dusk, he and the driver found themselves floundering in a blizzard. The traveling became more and more difficult as night set in. It became bitterly cold as only a winter night in Minnesota can be and finally the taxi stalled and could go no farther. The driver knew that they were by now not far from their destination and he left on foot for help. Before long, he returned with a horse and wagon, driven by a young man of about twenty, who expressed great surprise when Robinson told him his destination. That anyone would battle such a storm on a freezing night in November to see his father seemed strange indeed to the young man. At first he was suspicious but as they rode on he became more friendly. And then Alec Robinson realized that this was the infant that the Calhoun girl was carrying when she and Will Sturdevant fled Grindstone Island. By a quirk of fate, the young wagon driver was Will Sturdevant's son.

Little was ever told about the young man or his mother other than that the boy was decent, that there were other children, their farm modest, and the work there had been very hard. But we do know that Will Sturdevant embraced Alec Robinson with great emotion and that the two men sat up the entire night talking. Will was pathetically eager to hear all about the island, longing to know every detail with a hungry appetite that only a long absence could whet. At dawn when it came time for Alec to leave to rejoin his ship, Will Sturdevant wept. And that was the last that anyone heard of Will Sturdevant and his Minnesota family.

Whether Sarah Sturdevant or Flossie ever heard about this strange visit remains a matter of conjecture. They lived on alone together visited in summers only by Flossie's sister Lilla, who always arrived in a flurry of self-assurance, a worldly business woman from some far place such as Fulton or Oswego. I never exchanged a word with Lilla, and I never came to know Flossie or her mother very well. Had not Flossie worked in the store and the two women been seen in church on Sunday mornings, so unobtrusive were they that I never would have known they were on the island.

Mrs. Sturdevant died sometime during the thirties, and as always seemed to be the case, in winter when I was not there. Before World War II broke out, Flossie left the store and the island, to work for the rest of her days in a bank in Fulton. She never married and she never had a beau that I knew of. I am sure that she died a virgin—which was

Flossie Sturdevant

more than one could say of most of the other girls with whom she grew up. And for one who had been deemed to be moribund in those early decades of the century, she did very well. For she lived on beyond the age of eighty, dying in the 1970's. By that time all those who had predicted her early demise, less fortunate, were long gone to their respective rewards. Yet I feel a twinge even now for this lovely girl who by one blow of fate was deprived of both a father and a husband.

10.
Frank Slate

The Slates lived in Thurso just east of the store. Their unpainted house was plain, and they themselves were plain. Grace Slate, the mother of the family, was particularly plain with her dull printed dresses, her pale gray eyes and pale skin and oval face. But plainness of personality was by no means the characteristic of Frank, the patriarch of the Slate family in his later years. He was a testy man, square-jawed and squint-eyed, cocky and confident. He enjoyed his reputation for flamboyance and his status as a community "character." Frequently he made his neighbors victims of practical jokes, enjoying their discomfort immensely and expressing his delight in a whinnying sort of laugh. A taste for controversy and a capacity for meanness on occasion made him less than popular with some. He had a surface geniality, however, that made him popular with me in my younger years.

Frank never farmed. As a young man he worked in the shipyard of his father Sylvester "Van" Slate, down the shore, and later he served as boatman for summer people, or went out to do odd jobs from his boathouse at the head of Thurso Bay. And he always stood ready to shoe horses in a shed beside his house in the village.

One of those odd jobs gave Frank a high reputation with the island people and with me. I held him in awe—a hero, because he had done an impossible feat. He had moved our house from its original site on the North Shore Road. He had taken it up over a seemingly impassable rock and had set it down on a shelf of granite above the waters of Thurso Bay. He had made it a riverside home.

I have told of how the summering Norcoms quit Webster's Point in 1913 and of how we bought a lot of our own at the head of Thurso Bay. The property included a cliff frontage on Thurso Bay, a bald knob of granite rising up behind it, and, beyond the dome toward the south, a fine garden plot and a house on the street, the former home of the Albert Dorr family. My father dreamed of moving the house over the dome to a ledge at the top of the cliff, giving it a splendid view down the bay and quick access to the river. Even on an island well-versed in titanic haulage, all consultants declared the move impossible. Only one islander thought otherwise: Frank Slate. He was cocky enough to declare that he could move the house and furthermore, to state his fee—a hundred and fifty dollars. "If you think you can do it, go ahead!" my father said. In the late autumn, despite the jeers of all about him, Frank tackled the undertaking. From the Slate shipyard below the marsh he brought great timbers over the ice and hauled them up over the cliff with chains. He built a monumental structure of cribs, placed great timbers underneath the house, jacked the house high in the air, slid it across the dome on a greased track, dropped it on the level area atop the cliff, and the job was done. Not only I, but even the islanders, were awed. Thereafter, tossing his head and spitting tobacco juice, Frank would often say, "B'Jeezus, sonny, I told 'em I'd do it!" His conceit was justified.

Frank had an abiding interest in harness racing and drew his son Howard into that fascination as well. In the winter months we would read in the Clayton newspaper, *The St. Lawrence,* of their horses' winnings on the ice in the races in Clayton's upper bay, and in the summer we would hear of their exploits at fairs far back in the mainland. Frank kept his horses pastured in fields around Thurso, and in passing through I would often pause to stroke their muzzles.

Until my middle teens I felt affection and a kind of hero worship for Frank. Then came an unhappy disillusionment that was, I suppose, inevitable with a man of his temperament. It involved injustice, which I have never been able to take lightly. One day Frank confronted me and his manner was threatening: "B'Jeezus Sonny, don't ye let me catch you boys ridin' my horses again or I'll blister ye. I know what ye were up to and that goes for Bill Webster too. Ye keep offen those horses!"

I had never ridden a horse in all my life, on the island or off, and I told him so. He refused to believe me. "Now I'm tellin' ye again, Sonny. Ye keep offen those horses. I'm warnin' ye!"

I hated his nasty use of the word "Sonny" and suddenly I hated him too. I never

Frank Slate

recovered the respect I had once felt for him. My feelings were not soothed when, years later, he assaulted me with another accusation. In Thurso Bay there had been an old flat-bottomed scow which I regarded as abandoned, lying alongside the old Chicago Quarry's jetty. Exploring the scow one day I found on its bottom, half buried in silt, an anchor that I could use very handily on my sailboat. I exercised salvage rights and secured it, used it for a year or so, lost it among some rocks on the river bottom, and then forgot about it. I did not know that Frank Slate owned the old scow until one day when I met him on the road. He stopped me and he was testy. He took his pipe from his mouth and he said, "Sonny, ye wouldn't happen to know anything about an anchor that was in that scow down in the bay, now, would ye." His tone implied that I did indeed know all about it.

Frank Slate

Remembering his accusation about his horses, I was angered by this new confrontation. In retrospect, it seems that I should have stood up to him, told him I did not know the scow was his, and reminded him of the laws of salvage— none of which he would have accepted. At the moment, wisdom suggested that I lie to him: "I don't know what you are talking about!" "Sonny, I don't like being lied to!" he said, and walked off. I don't think I ever talked with him again. His scow continued to rot away and eventually disappeared.

Grace Slate was a patient wife to a temperamental husband, a kind presence and a good citizen of the community. I remember her unusual rolling walk, quiet and sure, as she traversed the roads of Thurso. She was faithful at church, a vigorous member of the Ladies' Aid, and a devoted mother to the three Slate children. Daughter Ellen married Ed Turcotte and joined him in an effort to be the successor to Hi Marshall in running the island store. Ellen died early, of a combination of heart trouble and overwork. Son

Howard married a mainland girl and spent his life off the island. Son Harry, born about 1902, married the widowed Aleitha Calhoun and with her ran a fine island farm, acquired under interesting circumstances.

About the time of the first World War a German named Wendell Wapler in his late thirties, appeared on the island. No one knew how or why. He was a colorless person of few talents who kept very much to himself. His lack of facility in English had much to do with his isolated life. At first he worked as a farmhand, Then a good farm was put up for sale on the North Shore Road west of the cemetery, and to everyone's surprise he was able to buy it. There he settled down to farm alone, getting no attention and asking for none. One saw him occasionally in the store, that was all. The Slates however were kind to him and he responded to their kindness. Their friendship grew as the years passed. Then Wendell died—and surprised all by leaving his entire farm to Harry Slate. It was the old fairy story retold, in which kindness to the ugly is richly rewarded. Harry and Leitha moved to their new inheritance, ran it as long as they lived, and left it to their daughter Erma who lives on it to this day.

11.
The North Shore Road and its People

The shore west of Thurso rises up from the river to a tableland and to dwellings that enjoy fine views of Leek Island and Seven Pines and of the Wide Waters. The first mile or so of the North Shore Road is the residence of Thurso's only suburbanites, intimate participants in the village life because their only road to the outer world takes them first to Thurso. A survey of the Thurso community is not complete without attention to these outlying homes, so closely tied to the village.

Mrs. Packard

On the north side of the road near the cemetery, we have already noticed the little white house of Mrs. Packard, still within the village limits as we have defined them. Emma Packard was the sister of Horace Kelly, operator of the Chicago Quarry. The cottage had been erected for her by the island's extraordinary builder Emmet Dodge, and in consequence the ridge of its roof sagged visibly, and there was evidence of constant patching of a gap between roof and chimney. She was a gregarious and affable person, always present at quilting bees and church socials. She was buxom in figure, particularly broad in derriere. Yet according to island gossip those same ample curves had, long ago, been the enduring fascination of the stony old Clayton banker, Robert Grant. Mrs. Packard's coiffure was a unique composite of colors: strands that were jet black mingled with some that were rust-red, and others of an unusual yellow. The composite did not agree well with the flat white of a heavily-powdered face. Her smile revealed an even row of perfect white teeth that would drop en masse, however, at critical moments in her animated conversation.

Mrs. Packard was a collector of <u>objet d'art</u>. Her house was filled with gewgaws of the Victorian age—bead-tasseled table covers, a china closet filled with bric-a-brac, an antimacassored sofa and chairs, a platform rocking chair, and a flowered carpet on which lay, near the front door, a large seashell with "Florida" printed on it in gold letters. There is a story, to be told later, of an incident in her life as a collector.

A daughter of Mrs. Packard was a beautician in Syracuse. A granddaughter, Betty Kinney, would inherit through her grandmother the site of the Chicago Quarry and build a summer cottage on the rock fill along the east shore of Thurso Bay.

The Turcottes

These were the neighbors that Nettie McRae described so generously as "the terrible Turcottes." Ourselves, we found them to be most amiable when we dropped in to buy vegetables and stayed to chat with Joe's wife Clara and her aged father Chauncy Fowler. Their house was bleak and bare and totally without amenities. At the time of our first meeting they were living temporarily in the old Hub Garnsey house at the end of the Cross-Island Road, but very soon they moved to a house of their own a hundred yards southward along the same road. The land that they tilled lay, however, a half mile away along the North Shore Road, opposite the cemetery.

Joe Turcotte, patriarch of the family, had come over from Gananoque as a young man to work in the quarries. When they closed he stayed in Thurso, creating a new livelihood for his family as a truck farmer raising vegetables for summer people. He conformed to local stereotypes about the nature of French Canadians: ruddy, taciturn, stubborn, bristly-moustached, and above all totally sunk in work. One never found him at home and at ease. He bore the burden of being not only a dairyman like other island farmers, but a truck gardener and retailer of produce as well. Constantly, he had to move cattle and crops back and forth between his land and his homestead. Every morning and evening the Turcottes drove their cattle, for milking, from their fields to their barn in the village, stirring up a great cloud of dust.

Charlie Matthews, the next owner of the Turcotte properties, would eliminate this onerous trudge by picking up the Turcotte house from the village and setting it down in the Turcotte fields. That was the Grindstone Island way with houses, but Joe Turcotte continued to wear out shoe leather to the end of his life.

Out on the farm there were always acres of vegetables to be tended. The Turcotte children did not escape this yoke. They were a family truly French Canadian in size: Clara, Aleatha, Ada, Irwin, Verna, Ellen and Ed. Every morning the Turcottes hauled the best of their produce to their boathouse on Thurso Bay, washed it, put it in baskets and then aboard their open motorboat, "the Ada T." Shortly the village would hear the distinctive chuff-chuff of the motor as Joe Turcotte left to peddle his choice greens to the wealthy people "up at the Head of the Island." At noon he would return home and to the endless work of cultivation in the truck patch.

About 1940 the Turcotte elders passed away. Later generations have known their farm as the place of David and Hildred Garnsey, or of Bob and Gloria Rusho, or simply as the post office, for this is where the flag last flew for postal service on the island.

Daughter Clara married Bob Garnsey, Hub Garnsey's oldest son, and settled with him on a farm near the town dock on the south shore. Leitha, a bright student, married Will Pettit the captain of the Standard Oil supply boat, and settled in Clayton to raise a well-educated family of professional people. Ada, a girl of rather aloof demeanor, eventually married Ernest McFadden who worked on Grennell Island. Irwin married Jesie McRae, daughter of Tom McRae, and served as boatman for Cleveland Dodge of Arabella Island off the head of Grindstone. The amiable Verna finished high school, married a farmer and raised a family on a mainland farm upriver from Clayton. It was Ed, the youngest, who married Frank Slate's daughter Ellen and tried to keep the island store and post office going after the death of Hi Marshall. Ellen died early and Ed moved to Clayton and became a fishing guide. No one continued the work of the truck farm, which was taken over by the universal green strangulation of the land.

The Potters and their Farms

Westward from the cemetery and the Turcotte acres lay the two Potter farms, Albert's farm on the southern side of the road and Orlando Potter's on the north. The Potters of Grindstone Island sprang from a Dr. Potter of Gananoque who on retirement from his practice moved to the island. By inheritance from him each of his two sons, Albert and Orlando, became proprietors of two-hundred-acre farms.

The story of the southern farm is short. Al Potter married Hattie Kittle of a south-shore farming family. Walter, one of their two sons, returned to the island with his wife Eva to help run the farm in Al's later years but neither Al nor this unhappy son were notable farmers. A daughter of Al and Hattie became the wife of Harry Kendall of Aunt Jane's Bay and the mother of Harold Kendall, foremost student of the history of the area and a collaborator in the production of this book. On Al's death his family moved to Clayton.

Northward from Albert Potter's farm a lane descended gently from the North Shore Road to the homestead of Al's brother Orlando. Passing a beach on the left visitors came to a lovely level headland, set above smooth granite ledges that bordered the shore below. On this headland stood a low green rambling house, looking out over the Wide Waters — the Orlando Potter place. With an ancestral background of doctors and lawyers, and a tradition of high education, the Orlando Potters were universally recognized as belonging to the highest level of island aristocracy. My mother and Mrs. Potter were friends and my mother would often walk up to the Potter place to visit. Mrs. Potter was a diminutive old lady with dark hair, untinged by grey. She was highly intelligent and well-read, and of cultivated tastes. Their well-kept house was furnished with beautiful antiques. I always liked to go there with my mother and while she and Mrs. Potter visited, I would wander about the place guided by Mr. Potter, a gentle reserved old man with a grandfatherly white beard and, always, an old straw hat.

Orlando Potter had a wide reputation on the island as a skillful fisherman. On one of my visits to their place, he proved it beyond all doubt. My mother and I had gone to see the Potters on the afternoon before, and suddenly old Mr. Potter had said to me: "If you will come up here about ten o'clock tomorrow morning, we'll go fishing. How would you like that?" Delighted, I accepted this rare invitation and the next morning, I was Johnny-on-the-spot at the Potter farm. The old man led me down to the river where a skiff was beached and we pushed it into the water and climbed in over the bow. Mr. Potter insisted on taking the oars. At the time he was in his eighties but he rowed vigorously with short chopping strokes. He handed me a trolling line, wound on a reel and fitted with a "Skinner spoon." These spoons were made in those days in a little Skinner factory in Clayton and were exceedingly popular among fisherman. The "spoon" consisted of a shining metal leaf which rotated as it was drawn through the water. Behind it was a small sheaf of red feathers, concealing hooks. The spoons were used only for trolling. They snarled hopelessly in casting.

Old Mr. Potter headed straight out into the Wide Waters and to a cluster of rocks known as the Tripod Shoals. As we circled them I could see, down in the deep green water, the sinister shadowy triad of boulders. And then suddenly the line I held tightened and jerked violently. We had caught our fish. Hand over hand, I hauled in the line until we could see our catch—a large Great Northern Pike. The fish writhed and struggled, spreading its red fringed gills, shaking its head violently to rid itself of the deadly hooks. Old Mr. Potter reached for his gaff and deftly caught the fish's jaw. Quickly he lifted it into the boat and stilled its flapping. Then, to my astonishment, he turned the boat about at once and rowed home. Our fishing excursion was ended. We had been on the river no more than half an hour. The old man had demonstrated his mysterious skill—mysterious, for try as I would alone afterward, doing exactly as he had done or so I thought, I never was able to catch another fish on Tripod Shoals; and the old man never took me out again. He died soon after.

I remember well the last time I saw Mrs. Potter. It was a September afternoon of burnished gold, and, the summer ended, we were about to return to Brooklyn. Mrs. Potter stood in the doorway beside her kitchen garden and in the small plaintive voice of an old lady, she bade my mother and me good-bye. And as we walked off along the lane, a most delicious fragrance of stewing tomato ketchup that had filled the kitchen, followed us far along the way. It has followed me, in my recollection of the Potters, for fifty years.

After Mrs. Potters death, the Potter house was shuttered, then pillaged of its antique furniture, and finally allowed to fall into complete ruin along with its large barns. Nothing remains. The farm has returned to scrub-land.

Between the main shore and the point on which the Orlando Potter house stood there was and is a crescent beach of white sand. It curved southward to a bluff on which a magnificent grove of hardwoods stood. The panorama here was one admired by artists and much photographed. The sandstrip was known as Potters' Beach and in the first sixty years of the century solitude prevailed on the beach and in the grove, save on the occasion of school picnics or church outings. Now the boating explosion has turned it into a Coney Island. The beach on its southern side ended in a steep gravelly bluff that was constantly being eroded by rains, and fragments of its edges kept tumbling down to the beach below. It was here that Bob Grant, president of Clayton's bank at the time, once brought me to search for Indian relics. The plateau above the bank, he told me, must once have been an Indian encampment. With its beach, and its direct access to the Wide Waters to the west, it must have been an ideal campsite. Bob had found many artifacts in the fallen gravel and along the top of the bank—arrowheads, shards of pottery, and clay ornaments of all sorts. While our search together that day was not very productive I came home nevertheless with one or two pieces of broken pottery, beaded along their edges, and a couple of arrowheads. On subsequent visits alone I found nothing, and I lost interest. Indian culture has not been one of my hobbies.

Returning to the main road and going west, one passed Wendell Wapler's former farm, and its farmhouse very near the river. We have related how it became the home of Harry Slate and his family.

In the sociology of Grindstone Island the western line fence of this Slate farm was a boundary of high significance. Beyond lay the Murray estate belonging to the wealthy Murray family of New York and Boston. Beyond it to the west and south lay a dozen other imposing summer homes that, with the Murrays', comprised a very distinctive community having an origin and status very different from that of the general island population. The Thurso peoples' tie with them lay in the farm managers, grounds keepers and boatmen of these estates.

The farm manager of the Murrays was John Garnsey. He was an amiable but simple-minded fellow of stammering speech. His wife Carrie was a sister of Frank Slate— a true Slate in her high cheek bones and square jaw. John and Carrie had two sons, Thornton and Garland Garnsey. As they grew up they went deep into the Slate family specialty of management of swift horses. Like their Uncle Frank and cousins Harry and Howard they seemed to have harness racing in their blood. Garland Garnsey and his son Glen, in particular, were the winner of many laurels and achieved national status in harness racing.

It was for another activity, however, that John and Carrie were more talked about locally. Carrie carried on a very intimate relationship with Harry Cook, a river boatman from Gananoque. Her husband John seemed to be happy with this intimacy, and the three of them, together, came as a group to all picnics and church suppers. Harry was Carrie's first cousin, and cousinly affection may have been the heart of the matter. Island gossip saw a _menage a trois_. Harry Cook was a highly respected boatman for wealthy summer families. Quiet and highly intelligent, he was the very opposite of the voluble and vacuous John. He was a short, dark, pleasant man, clean shaven and scrupulously neat. Nettie McRae, of course, would have had me believe that he came of a family of notorious river outlaws. I make no pronouncement, myself, on any of these allegations.

12.
The Coterie at the Head of the Island

With the Garnseys of the Murray farm my account of the people of the North Shore Road ends. To go westward in my descriptions is to attempt to cross a continental divide, very difficult for me because few people and little information crossed that line. For those who lived eastward from the Murray farm all normal travel was to Thurso Village and its post office, store, church, and quarries. Quite otherwise, those who have lived to the west have relied instead on waterways and on the shops and facilities of the mainland shores, which they could reach easily by swift boats. The merchandise available at Hi Marshal's store had no special appeal to them and the service of the Thurso post office was not essential. On very special occasions head-of-the-island people attended the Thurso church. They valued the skill of the river-wise men of Thurso and employed them as their uniformed boatmen, but those faithful retainers did not gossip in Thurso about their employers' private lives. The other island people had very little knowledge of the personalities at the head of the island. I myself had no contacts with them—and without contacts I gained no memories, and without memories, no ability to write character sketches of the kind that appear elsewhere in these memoirs. I can, however, name the families who summered on that lovely western coast, and describe where they lived in the period between the two great wars.

The people "up at the head" differed from most other residents of the island in the fact that they had not come to Grindstone to farm or to cut granite or otherwise make their living there. They brought their incomes with them from the eastern cities—incomes that were not subject to the ups and downs of the internal economy of the island. From their first arrival they were a summer colony, and serenely they remained such throughout a century during which the island underwent depopulation, and then repopulation and became in its entirety the summer land that the head of the island had been from the start. Grindstone's history as a vacation land began in the 1870's with a great explosion in publicity that occurred in the year 1872. It set in motion for the first time the massive summer migrations to the Thousand Islands that transformed them from the wild retreat of sportsmen to the fashionable resort of the elite of American business and industry. The precipitating event was an annual convention of the Editors and Publishers Association of the State of New York, which had ventured to hold its meeting that year in the out-of-the-way city of Watertown. A host of professional journalists, several hundred strong, assembled in June in that city. The presence of editors and reporters from many outside states made the meeting an event of national importance. Wishing to please their guests with regional attractions the local hospitality committee took the entire assembly by special train and boat, with bands and bunting, on a day-long excursion to see the Thousand Islands. The bands played well, it was a perfect June day, and the host of writers was spellbound—but not to the extent of becoming speechless. When they got home the great urban newspapers blossomed with accounts of the incomparable beauty of the Saint Lawrence River and its quiet islands. A northward surge of visitors began that has never stopped. Clayton had become the prime railhead for these reconnaissances, and Grindstone Island lay opposite, and its western shore was shaded by great trees and cooled by unfailing summer breezes. Visitors saw, and they bought, and they built.

First on that particular island scene was a group of friends from New York City who knew each other through shared associations of one sort or another with J. P. Morgan and Company. Though many of them bore the surname Morgan they were not close relatives of the financier, but were either personal friends, or executives in the Morgan firm. One after the other they were caught up in the spell of the St. Lawrence, acquired plots, and joined in the formation of a distinctive summer colony.

The banker Harry Alexander Murray was prominent among these founders, and Henry Sheldon Leavitt and his wife Martha, and William Fellowes Morgan, warehouse magnate, and his brothers James Hewitt Morgan and Lewis Henry Morgan. Relatives and friends were drawn in. When the families began to vacation on the shores together, Cupid did his work among the young, and new summer homes were built for many newlyweds. By 1914 the western shore and offshore islands were occupied by an intimate community tied together by old family friendships, shared fun, and a bewildering network of intermarriages.

The Coterie at the Head of the Island

The locations of their homes can be described best in terms of where they lie in three lines: the north-south line of the western coast of Grindstone, the east-west line of a string of small islands that lie immediately offshore, and, a third line, parallel to the first, of islands lying half a mile to the west. The second line consists, from north to south, of the islands of Watch, Whiskey, Papoose and Club. The third line, from south to north, includes Wild Goose (also called Arabella) and Hickory, and finally the uninhabited isle called Black Ant. Hickory Island, though small, had long had a place in Canadian history as the mustering-scene, in February 1838, of 300 insurgents against the government of Canada who were assembled on the icy island to seize Kingston the next day by force of arms. Learning there for the first time that more than a thousand soldiers were ready in Kingston to receive them, and that some were even moving toward them on the ice, wisely the rebels decided one by one to go home. The battle of Hickory Island ended before it began.

Speaking of summer homes, we shall begin with the cluster on the northwestern headland of Grindstone and with the the estate called Mid-River Farm. Its manor-house was built in 1903 by the parents of Charles "Chip" Bohlen who grew up to become a power in the Department of State and President Kennedy's appointee as ambassador to France. From the first, discussions at Mid-River Farm were lively but they did not center on the market price for pigs. Interest in international affairs has remained warm in that ample house throughout its history. Fanny and Harry Murray, whose ownership began in 1911, passed it down to their daughter Virginia who had married Robert Low Bacon in 1913. At the time her husband's father, a former Secretary of State, was America's ambassador to France. The groom was to have a long career as a congressman representing New York—a career in which his wife Virginia gave him important support. As a hostess she made the Bacon home in the capital a hub of Washington social life. The whirl continued in the summer on Mid-River Farm. There diplomats and statesmen of many nations were entertained as guests throughout her long life as wife and widow.

There was a second residence on Mid-River Farm, Les Roches, that was inherited with much of the land (the "Murray farm") by Virginia's brother, Dr. Harry Murray, a Boston psychiatrist. The Murray line continues today with Harry's daughter Dr. Josephine Murray, a pediatrician who practices in Boston and summers in a cottage called Nohawkers that lies just around the northwestern point of Grindstone on the western shore.

Further to the south at Cement Point James Hewett Morgan and his wife Martha built a summer home in 1909—a house which Martha, surviving him, continued to own until 1945. Below Cement Point the next noteworthy feature was, in the 1930's a unique barn-like covered dock called the Red Boathouse. It extended out into the water at a point above Buck Bay. There on Wednesday evenings during the summer rousing square dances were held that were the delight of local boatmen and Irish maids and farmers and the teenagers of the summer families. Johnny Johnson called the steps and played the fiddle, using as a shell the prow of a propped-up boat. The nearness of the dancers to the water was dramatic, and occasionally useful. Once a sturdy farm girl, irked by a too-fresh swain, cooled his wicked ardor by picking him up physically and dumping him into the deep cold water.

Next, at Rum Point, in an indentation below Buck Bay, stands the house that was the summer home from 1917 to 1957 of Camilla Morgan White, daughter of Lewis Henry Morgan, and her husband, Dr. James C. White. Michael White, their son, lives there still. Dr. White was a Boston brain surgeon of great note. By the young and the young of heart, Rum Point was and is appreciated especially for its baseball field, a little plain that is priceless in this terrain of jumbled rocks. There on that diamond, for a century, the generations of the colony have mustered on Sunday afternoons and contended with each other in a version of baseball, using dead tennis balls for the game.

South of Rum Point, the last of the houses on the west shore is Kumtuit, built by Mr. and Mrs. Francis MacNeil Bacon (not related to the Bacons of Mid-River Farm). The Francis Bacons were Gotham friends of William Fellowes Morgan. Their descendants occupy Kumtuit to this day.

The Grindstone shore, like Scotland's has its inner and outer Hebrides, and we turn to the first reef of islands, that lie just off the southwestern shore. The northermost, Watch Island, belonged about 1880 to Henry Sheldon Leavitt and in the 1920's was the residence of his daughter Louise Leavitt Thacher. Mr. Thacher was a wool merchant of Boston. In the 1930's the island came into the possession of Thomas C. Thacher Jr. and his wife Vera Morgan Thacher.

To the south lies Whiskey Island, once decorously called Coral Island. In the 1870's a summer home was built there by the pioneers of the community, Emma Leavitt Wolfe and her husband Christopher Wolfe who was a New York architect. After the turn of the century it became the summer home of Hope Thacher Carter and her husband Bernard S. Carter, head of the Morgan bank in Paris. Paul Carnegie of the central island community was the Carters' boatman. Whiskey Island is the scene annually of the mustering of a far-flung Wolfe-Morgan-Leavitt clan, of dumbfounding genealogical complexity, and like the sands of Potter's Beach in number.

The next dot of land, between Whiskey and Club Islands, was once called Hen Island. About 1884 William Fellowes Morgan bought it as a present for his bride-to-be, Emma Leavitt. Emma was pleased with the island, but was not pleased to become the hen of Hen Island. She exercised her bridal prerogative at once to change its name to Papoose. There she spent every summer of her long life until her death in 1958. Her husband was a trustee of Columbia University and of the Episcopal Theological Seminary in Cambridge. Their boatman was Corbett Carnegie.

On the southernmost of these inner islands, Club Island, there were two summer homes. On the western half stood the home of Mrs. Fredric Pruyn, the daughter of William Fellowes Morgan. She was a landscape architect in New York City. Her second marriage was to David M. Goodrich, chairman of the rubber firm.

The other half of Club belonged to a remarkable Broadway actress named May Irwin who built a large stone house there at some time before 1900. Her fame was great and her career long, continuing from age 13 to age 60 in quite varied roles and directorships. For years she brought to Club Island the castes of her coming plays and trained them for their winter roles. When she died in 1938 David Goodrich united the two halves of Club Island, which has passed now to Elizabeth Dodge Haxall and her children.

The outer range of islands begins in the south with Wild Goose or Arabella. It belonged early in the century to D. S. Hicks of Brooklyn and was bought in 1929 by Cleveland E. Dodge and his wife Pauline Morgan Dodge. Cleveland Dodge was a geologist by training and an executive of the Phelps Dodge Corporation. His responsibilities had much to do with the supervision of copper mines. He was also a trustee of Princeton

University and of Teachers' College, Columbia University. He and his wife were national leaders of the Y.M.C.A. and Y.W.C.A. respectively. They were also audacious Democrats living in a sea of Republicans. Wild Goose under their care became a center of very active summer entertaining. It is now the home of Cleveland E. Dodge Jr.

Hickory Island, just to the north, was the home, early in the century, of the broker J. Walter Wood. It was bought at the beginning of World War II by Trude and Raymond Pfeiffer. Dr. Pfeiffer is an eminent eye surgeon, a professor of ophthalmology at Columbia University and a pioneer in the development of X-ray-guided surgery for dealing with industrial accidents to the eye.

Virginia Murray Bacon, c. 1911
The mistress of Mid River Farm

The high incidence in this community of medical men of great skill has probably been noticed. The tendency continues. At Mid-River Farm the great house now belongs to Joan Dodge Rueckert and her husband Dr. Frederic Rueckert, professor of plastic surgery in the medical school of Dartmouth University. Just east of Kumtuit on the southwest corner of the island, Dr. Paul MacLean of Washington's National Institute of Health has long had his summer home. He is famed for his studies of the evolution of the brain.

This close community at the head of the island has survived now for a century with exceptional continuity of personnel and of traditions. Its distinctiveness in the island life is not as sharp now as it once was, because the rest of the island has changed in its direction. Like the quarrymen before them, the island's farmers, too, have gone, and only summer people are left, anywhere in the island, in any number. The whole island shares in one single all-comprehensive economy. But the colony at the head of the island still remains recognizable, by reason of the cultural homogeneity of its founders and the unusual persistence of its traditions and its family lines. Vestiges survive, also, of the glitter of the Edwardian Age in which the community was created. The wealth of residents is comparatively high. Their productivity is noticeable also. One perceives at the head of the island a rare concentration of human skill and accomplishment.

13.
The Heritage Of The Great Quarries

On Grindstone Island beginning in 1880, quarrying red granite was the name of the game. The age ended in 1896 when a strike closed the quarries forever. The major quarries centered around Thurso Bay. The Forsyth Quarry (legally the Thousand Island Granite Corporation), lay at the outer end of Thurso Bay on its west side. The Chicago Quarry (the Chicago Granite Co.) operated at the head of the Bay, on the eastern shore. Its name reflected the destiny of the cobblestones produced there—to pave the streets of Chicago. A third Thurso quarry, far in the back reaches of the McRae farm, had cut into a rock outcropping above the Upper Marsh.

In 1909, many signs of the intense activity of these quarries still remained. Their derricks still stood lonely and motionless in their granite amphitheaters, their cables dangling. Railway tracks ran along their loading docks with pairs of wheels still on them that sportive boys could roll about. The cars that the wheels had carried had long since rotted away. Rusted machinery, still slimy with grease, lay about everywhere—great cog wheels, drive shafts, enormous pulleys, and steam boilers. Many wooden sheds remained, with gaping windows and fallen doors, and in them lay tools just where they had been dropped the day the quarries closed—crowbars, sledgehammers, drills, spikes, wedges, wheelbarrows. One old shed in the Chicago Quarry had been a blacksmith shop and its high hearth, surrounded by tongs and crowbars and the skeleton of an aged bellows, was still filled with a mound of coals. No one had ever felt it worth while to salvage any of these things. It was as if some magic spell had been cast over the region, and everyone had suddenly vanished. For an operation that had lasted only 16 years, the energy that had gone into it was enormous. The quarries had employed about 250 men.

A conspicuous visible sign of the Chicago Quarry was a great dump line of rejected shards that had been laid from the base of the excavation, continuing outward along the entire east side of the Thurso Bay. It was a jetty of great red granite rocks that resembled a seaside breakwater. Its top had been leveled and smoothed for railway tracks that led to a long wooden dock extending to the center of Thurso Bay in the direction of Leek Island. The facing of the dock soon rotted away, but its rock-filled cribs remain visible, deep down below the surface of the river. A deep trough could be seen in the mud of the bottom beside them, cut by the churning propellers of the tugboats which towed the schooners loaded with granite blocks out through the Leek Island Channel to the WideWaters above. There, they could hoist sail for the big cities up on the Great Lakes.

Where the dock had ended out in Thurso Bay there still stood in 1909 two high pilings projecting well above the water, a landmark that lasted for years. They were a menace to boats coming and going through the Bay, especially at night. They finally rotted away at the water line and the submerged stubs then became even more of a menace. These too disappeared in time, leaving the Bay safe for navigation at last.

The long rock pile from the Chicago quarry drew its materials from great excavations into the rock of the hillside to the south, a chasm that extended almost to the limit of the McRae farm at the North Shore Road. High on the cliff there, the ghostly old boarding house stood sentinel. It had housed many of the stonecutters who worked below. Down in the broad pit a derrick still stood in 1909, surrounded already by wild raspberry bushes and burdock and mullen. A blinding redness pervaded the whole scene as sunlight rebounded from red cliffs and red boulders and the red granite chips underfoot.

The long line of refuse that the Chicago Quarry had dumped into the shallow waters at the eastern border of Thurso Bay had of course shut off the owner of the McRae farm from access to the water. After Lew Webster bought the McRae farm, this loss of frontage on the bay became a source of irritation to him and material for a revealing interaction. The jetty was considered to be the property of Horace Kelly, the Clayton man who had succeeded to the ownership of the Chicago Quarry lands. The deeds were vague as to the boundary lines and Lew Webster became convinced that the dump belonged to him. He decided to bring suit in the Jefferson County Court to obtain title to the property. To avoid trouble, Horace Kelly then offered to sell the entire quarry, dump and all, to Lew Webster for $500. Lew Webster refused the offer. With a consummate self-confidence that was characteristic of him, he brought a lawyer from New York City to press his suit — and to his astonishment he lost. It was the first of many humiliations he was to know in consequence of a proud belief in his own infallibility. As we shall see, though he was astute and shrewd, he was too proud to be wise.

The west side of Thurso Bay was fringed by forest in 1909. Much of that forest must have been there all during the time of the quarrying. Deep in the bay on that side stood the Hi Marshall and Turcotte boathouses, with ramshackle walkways into the woods. Midway, a high embankment of rock-shards rose up from the shore, a bluff made up of refuse that had been dumped there as the quarrymen hacked out their paving blocks. Northward from that, near the mouth of the bay stood the high bald granite dome that the Forsyth Quarry cut into, and had partly cut away. Even its remaining half could still be seen for miles up and down the river. This was the largest quarry of the three, operated by an immigrant from Scotland, a wealthy man from Montreal named Robert Forsyth who had been born in Thurso on Scotland's northern coast.

A great gash had been cut into the dome, leaving a wide amphitheater that slanted downward in a series of giant steps to a waterside platform made up of chips of rejected stone from the cutting operation above. Here too in 1909, a great derrick still stood, dangling cables and heavy chains that were fastened to rings set in the rock faces, and even to boulders in the bottom of the bay. At the edge of the loading platform schooners tied up to take on their heavy cargoes. The planking of the docks had all crumbled away but even today remnants can be seen, underwater, of the supporting piles. To dispose of the useless chips and rejected stones of the quarrying the quarrymen kept extending the loading platform northward until it ceased to be a loading platform but the line of a railroad dump, proceeding necessarily straight ahead. The line of the dump followed at first the relatively straight cliff-face on its left, then was compelled to launch into deep water and create a causeway across an indentation in the cliff. The chord of stone captured and enclosed a bit of the river to create a pool [today the prized boat basin of the editor of this book]. I recall an occasion long ago, when it served as a fish pond. Two shadowy monsters of the deep river were imprisoned there. Davy Black and Sid Chase had caught two sturgeon and were keeping them there for some special occasion. Back in the amphitheater of the quarry and near its base, a road came down out of the woods onto the rock-fill, and there a log cabin still stood, with a tall thin smokestack rising out of its roof. Inside lay a collection of greasy machinery and cable drums. Outside stood an upright steam boiler, surrounded by remnants of the coal that once fueled it. In another dilapidated building high up on the rock behind the dome even more massive machinery could be seen, including great cog wheels. The road that rose up into the forest there led ultimately to the Cross-Island Road at the house of Davy Black. On the right of this road, just behind the dome of the quarry, stood my favorite of all the derelict sheds. A gloom created by overarching white pines above it filled the interior of that shed with special mysteries, half-concealed as well as half-revealed by the building's single shaft of light from a broken window. The silence of the scene was broken only by the buzzing of mud wasps in the rafters. I loved all these abandoned buildings and their ghostly machines, tokens of mighty men of old and their mighty enterprises.

Today, every remnant of the old machinery is gone. Not a scrap remains. Before World War II, the Japanese came and picked the entire region clean. Where it ultimately went, we must ask the men who suffered the impact of it all at Pearl Harbor.

Although the quarries were active for only 16 years, they had prodigious effect on the island landscape: the great landfills, the immense scars cut into the hillsides around Thurso. Unlike many of man's works, these will endure to the end of time. No place on Grindstone or the surrounding islands was immune to the quarrymen's hammers. In winter, when the workmen weren't hacking out paving blocks for the big companies, on their own they would cut into rock ledges wherever the grain of the granite gave promise of acceptable cobblestones. The locales of these small operations, none of which fulfilled their promise, were called "notions" and they are everywhere. Only the stone of the three quarries around Thurso had the fine grain that could be cut into long clean blocks. The Forsyth Quarry was the most productive, but all three Thurso quarries, and also a quarry on Picton Island, were profitable. The Picton granite was used in building the American Museum of Natural History in New York. As far as we know, the granite from Thurso was used only for paving blocks. Other building materials have been developed, now, that have replaced the red stone in all of its former uses.

In the 1920's, there were those who could not agree that granite had been out-dated.

The Heritage of the Great Quarries

Horace Kelly came over from Clayton with a partner and did a little cutting in his Chicago Quarry. Their efforts came to nothing. But there was intense excitement when an amiable stranger from Pennsylvania or Maryland suddenly appeared. His name was Hartwell. He brought big news. He was going to resume operation of the Forsyth Quarry. Like Lew Webster, he had all the signs of affluence. One was a Stanley Steamer automobile. He kept it in Clayton. I recall a memorable ride with him to Watertown one day, and my astonishment when after coasting down the hill into Depauville, the car coasted with equal ease up the opposite hill without the vibrating uphill struggles of other cars of the time.

Mr. Hartwell had long consultations with Hi Marshall and Mr. Black. All indications were that big business was in hand. Finally one fine summer afternoon, Hartwell brought over to the island the supreme expert who might, if he gave the final favorable word, finance the new corporation. Together they walked over all the ledges of the Forsyth Quarry and then, standing on the high dome of the quarry in sharp silhouette against the afternoon sun, the three came to a stop and awaited the departing pundit's final word. From a skiff down on the bay, the expert's voice came up loud and clear in the stillness of the late afternoon. I heard him say: "Mr. Hartwell, you are crazy to think you can do anything with this rock." He said no more. The bubble was punctured. Mr. Hartwell vanished in his Stanley Steamer, never to be heard of again. The Forsyth property on Thurso Bay sank back into its serene repose, still owned by Miss Jeanie Forsyth, old Robert's daughter. And the no-trespass signs remained where they were on the trees, bearing the lady's name.

Once a year on a still summer afternoon, Miss Forsyth would appear on Thurso Bay, seated under a parasol in the stern of a skiff, an imperious old woman arrayed in billowy black taffeta and a veiled hat, with Davy Black at the oars. As they drifted along the shores of the shimmering bay, she would point out this and that and in a rich throaty voice tell Davy what she wanted done with the property—for Davy, her cousin, was the custodian of all the Forsyth land. Then without stopping, Davy would row her out of the bay and across the Leek Island Channel to Canada and to distant Granite Island, off Gananoque. There Miss Forsyth spent her summers in a large green wooden mansion with a castellated tower, called for her mother "Dorasdale." Then Davy would row back to Grindstone alone, family obligations done.

14.
Davy Black

Davy Black remains one of the most memorable characters I have known. Of medium height and build, he had a black jutting beard and a shining bald head. He was born in Scotland in a good family, a nephew of the eminent Robert Forsyth. His father was a physician, apparently of some prestige, for the infant Davy had been dandled on Queen Victoria's lap during one of her visits to Scotland. This was regarded as his great claim to distinction. He was highly intelligent, well-educated in Scottish schools, and extremely well-read. His spoken English was beautiful to hear, crisp and precise, spoken in a rich voice with a wonderful Scotch burr. He had been brought to Canada by his uncle, who had immigrated about 1870. Davy for a time traveled as a salesman for the Forsyth Quarry. Then his uncle made him paymaster of the quarry. Davy soon married Kate Kelly, a daughter of Jim Kelly, owner of the Chicago Quarry. The pair settled in the fifth house in the row that stood on the east side of the road that ran down from Hi's store to the cove under McRae Point. Davy was still living in that house when I appeared on the scene in 1909.

Kate Kelly in 1886 became the first post-mistress in Thurso and the Black's house became the island's first post office, the mail arriving there twice a week. From all the stories that one heard, it must be true that Davy had treated his wife abominably. He was drinking heavily by then. In his drunken rages, people said, he was unmerciful. Kate was remembered as a kind pleasant long-suffering woman, hard-working and thrifty. Davy's abuse of her must have been too much, for she was dead long ere I saw Grindstone. I always felt a pity for her as I looked on her weed-grown grave in the Grindstone cemetery. Why Davy drank and abused his wife is a question whose answer we shall never know. Was she a nag? A bore? Was Davy, himself, intolerably bored on an island peopled by stonecutters and roughnecks? Age had mellowed him by the time I came to know him, but even then he was a man impatient with fools and dullards, and his tongue could be sharp. I tasted of his scorn once and never forgot it.

In New York, when I was in my teens, one could buy stickers of fashionable European hotels, together with baggage markers of the big steamship lines. It was a day when foreign travel still lent real distinction, and by plastering one's luggage with these symbols of sophistication one could give the impression that one was part of the elegant life. Like some of the other teenagers in my Brooklyn neighborhood, I had pasted two or three of these stickers on my suitcase, advertising myself as a sophisticated young traveler. One, I recall, was of the Hotel Crillon in Paris, a menage I had never heard of, let alone seen. None of my friends had this one and I was proud of it. This sticker business had become an aspect of one-upmanship. Like much teenage behavior, it was a stupid business. I don't know how I would have responded if anyone who knew the place had asked for any detail about the Hotel Crillon. Luckily, no one ever did. But Davy Black did not let me get away with this pretentious bluff.

One morning as I was about to leave the island for a long trip and was waiting for Hub's mail wagon on the store's porch, with my brightly-stickered suitcase beside me, Davy came along. He gave the thing a glance and then looked again. He took his pipe from his mouth and the withering derision in his voice would have curled asbestos: "And will ye look at the young swell we've got with us now!" He said. "Who do you think you're foolin', lad? Damned if I didna' think you had more sense."

But in 1909, Davy Black was already in his cups, living in squalor in the weathered old house he had always occupied since he came to the island. The islanders considered him a drunken sot, yet in a strange way he always commanded their respect. To everyone he was always "Mr. Black." My father too recognized his innate dignity. This man was no Jay Robinson. My father always stopped to talk with him when they met in the store or on the roadside. Davy was appreciative. In our third or fourth year of camping on Webster Point, Davy appeared suddenly one day. Quietly and confidentially, he told my father of a piece of land at the head of Thurso Bay which, he was quite sure, could be bought from Alfred Dorr. There was a house on this land, which, though it was far back from the plot's waterfront, was in excellent condition. The little unpleasantness with the Websters of which we have spoken had made us wish for a place of our own. Waterfront land even at that time was hard to find and my father was grateful to Davy for the information. The contact was made, the price stated. Sold!

Davy Black

To this day, I feel indebted to Davy Black for my summer house on Grindstone.

In 1912 or 1913 Davy received an inheritance from some mysterious source in Scotland. While nothing specific was ever mentioned, Hi Marshall implied that Davy was to receive for the rest of his days an annual income of about $600—at that time, no mean sum. With this, a miracle occurred. Davy sobered up. He became comparatively neat and presentable and was completely accepted by the community as a solid citizen. To his new respectability, he added a more respectable residence, moving into the white house on the square, just vacated by the Ben Garnseys. Living diagonally across from the store, Davy was now at the center of the village, where the action was. He became a trustee of the Grindstone Church, attending regularly. I can recall his figure seated there in a front pew, his bald head gleaming. There was a considerable fringe of hair around the back of it, lying on his neck. My father insisted that if one painted a face on the back of Davy's head, one wouldn't know whether Davy was coming or going.

David Black

A memorable incident in Davy's performance of his churchly duties occurred one dreadful Sunday morning when the collection plate—a small wicker basket—was being passed along the pew while Davy waited at the end to receive it. As the basket passed from hand to hand toward me, there was some confusion as to who was holding it and suddenly the basket dropped to the floor in a jangle of scattering coins. There was a mad scramble to recover them; heads were bumped, there was fumbling beneath the pews, and of course the service was interrupted as the coins were picked up one by one and replaced in the basket. Meanwhile, the look of intense disgust on Davy's bearded face was memorable. It was far from Christian.

My warm feeling toward Davy began while I was still a little boy. One day I was standing beside him on the porch of Hi's store when suddenly Davy reached into his pocket, took out a shiny new dime, and gave it to me. In those times, to a small boy, a dime was a very considerable sum. I was touched by the generosity of this gruff stranger and as I grew older I came to appreciate Davy more and more, and we became close friends.

Sometimes, we would row together to Gananoque in Davy's skiff, Davy rowing one way, I the other. In Gananoque, there were always errands to do: shoes to be repaired, things to be bought which one couldn't get at Hi Marshall's store such as Canadian bacon, Canadian cereals, and the Canadian bread, which was much better than the wretched stuff made in Clayton. And while I was off on errands of my own, Davy would invariably stop at the International Hotel, on the way down to the docks, for a glass of ale, and a visit with the proprietor, another Scotsman named Willy McCaddy. With peaked plaid cap and all, he was a true bearded relic of the Edwardian era. Then I would come along, and together we would go on to our boat and embark on the long row back to Grindstone.

On these trips, as we rowed through the islands, Davy would relate stories about the places that we were passing. For instance, there was a long breakwater on Granite Island, connecting it with a rocky islet on which stood Miss Forsyth's castle, Dorasdale. "Old man Forsyth" had put in this rock-fill for reasons known only to himself. And to his intense fury, the Canadian government, always ready to levy an impost on everything in sight, immediately laid a heavy tax on Miss Forsyth's new causeway.

And as we passed Leek Island, Davy told me that his uncle had purchased that island from someone in Montreal for $500 and a marble fireplace, and he pointed out "notions" along the shore, where usable granite had been sought but not found, causing the idea of quarrying on Leek Island to be abandoned.

When we approached Thurso Bay and saw Uncle Hub Garnsey's old house in the cove to its west, Davy remembered old Hub and his negotiations with Davy's uncle for the sale of the west side of Thurso Bay with its high granite knob. The year was about 1877. Mr. Robert Forsyth and Davy and an attorney had rowed the three miles across the river in a skiff to meet old Uncle Hub at his farm on Grindstone. The deal had to be consummated in Clayton. So taking on Uncle Hub as a passenger, they continued on around the head of Grindstone to the U.S. shore. It was a nine mile row over open waters that were very rough. Their skiff took on water, and it was leaky, and Mr. Forsyth was impatient over the whole arduous business. In Clayton, Mr. Forsyth asked Uncle Hub to buy a dipper for bailing out the boat and insure a more comfortable journey on the return trip.

They concluded the purchase of Uncle Hub's great promontory on Thurso Bay. By Davy's report the sum paid to Uncle Hub that day was $5,000. Whatever the price, it was a goodly amount in those days. Then all four returned in the boat to Grindstone, landing a greatly enriched Uncle Hub on the shore of the cove below his house. Then the weary trio from Gananoque set out for home. They had gotten some distance out on the river when they saw Uncle Hub running down to the river-bank, shouting and gesticulating wildly. Thinking that something serious had gone amiss, they turned about at once and rowed back toward where Uncle Hub was waiting. Fifty feet from the shore they called out to know what was the matter. "You forgot to give me the fifty-cents I paid for the dipper," Uncle Hub shouted. Wordless, Mr. Forsyth bent down, picked up the dipper from the bottom of the boat and flung it at his feet. Then, he gestured to Davy and they turned about, still without a word, and rowed their boat to Gananoque.

For many years, Davy had a small skye terrier called "Little Sid," a namesake of Sid Chase, we may presume. When Davy went fishing, Little Sid was his unfailing companion, perched on the foredeck of the skiff like a small figurehead, his spindly legs braced tightly against the sudden movements of the boat. As the dog aged, he grew quite stiff and his fishing trips must have become an ordeal. For on their return, just before Davy pulled his boat up into the marsh-grass Little Sid would shake himself in a frenzy of relief and run up into the woods, uttering fierce growls all the way.

Somewhere, Davy acquired a cat called "Ada," probably named for one of the Turcotte daughters. Davy must have felt much solicitude for Ada, for I remember his standing on the little front porch of his house across from Hi's store with pipe held out in hand and calling in a loud brusk voice "Come, kit, kit, kit!" And kit came. With Davy, there was none of that dulcet falsetto "Here, kitty, kitty, kitty" with which most cat-lovers lure their felines homeward. Ada often came down from Davy's house to ours to hunt and to solicit handouts, which my mother always gave her. Sometimes we wondered whose pet Ada was—ours or Davy's. Early one fine September morning we were closing the house and putting on the heavy shutters that covered the doors and windows in winter. Ada as usual was about, hopeful of a handout. At this time, Ada was "heavy with child" and the blessed event could not have been far away. Hub's arrival with his horse and wagon was imminent and with many last minute responsibilities we paid little attention to Ada. The final shutter was clamped over the kitchen door; then Hub arrived, the trunk and bags were put aboard his wagon at once, and we were off to catch the 12:01 train out of Clayton for New York. It was always a sad and absorbing business, this putting away of the good times we had known that summer. And the small boy was thinking of ominous events that might happen during the long winter ahead—deaths or disasters—that could make summers at Grindstone never the same again. Grindstone would soon be as far away in terms of the travel of those days as Europe is now. It was easy to forget Ada.

A day or so later, back in the city, my mother suddenly recalled that we had not noticed Ada during that hurried last hour on the island. With horrid premonition, she dispatched a telegram to Hi Marshall, who had a key to the house, asking him to go there to see if her worst suspicions were true. They were. Ada had slipped into the house, dark as night within with its shutters on. She had gone upstairs, and had her kittens in the middle of my parent's bed. And the little family was all right, not in the least disturbed by their imprisonment.

My prestige with Davy was greatly enhanced in my boyhood by an episode in which I was more favored by luck than by skill. Davy's skiff had vanished one night. A theft was a rare happening on the island and no islander was suspect. It was believed that some miscreant or other had been brought from Gananoque under the cover of the darkness, and had stolen Davy's skiff to take him on to the U.S. mainland. Everyone had an eye out for the skiff for days thereafter, but it was not found on either side of the river.

Then one morning I was in Clayton on errands that I accomplished quickly. I had a considerable time to wait until the noonday departure of the mail boat for Grindstone. Hating the town, I wandered out into the countryside. I soon found myself exploring the borders of the cattail marsh that lined the shores of French Creek on the west side

The Church

of Clayton. I had Davy's boat in mind, but it was an unpromising place and the sun was hot. The redwinged blackbirds scolded, protesting my invasion of their marsh, and I was about to walk back to town. Suddenly, as I parted some tall grasses, I saw a skiff pulled up high, hidden among the reeds. I took a closer look and to my astonishment it was Davy's skiff. That it was his, I could be sure. I had rowed in it with Davy far too many miles not to recognize it.

With all the endless bays and marshes along the river where the skiff could have been hidden, the fact that I had stumbled upon the very spot where the thief had landed was a miracle. In no way could my discovery be attributed to intelligence. But from that time on, I could do no wrong in Davy's eyes.

Over the years Davy and I wrote each other faithfully in winter, when I was absent from the island. In the summer we played endless games of cribbage, sometimes at our house, sometimes on his kitchen table while a clock on the shelf went "spang-spang-spang as it marked the hours." Then he grew deaf and talk became difficult. But he kept his alert mind into his late seventies, and he must have been eighty before his heart began to fail and he became unable to look after himself. That autumn, Jessie Carnegie, who was then living with her son on a farm below the marsh, took him into her house and cared for him. And there he died, just before the outbreak of the Second World War. Again, as was the case with many islanders, he died in mid-winter.

When I returned the following June, he was at rest in the highest part of the Grindstone cemetery, under a polished new granite monument bearing the name "Black." There now, in summer, the birds sing happily and the wild roses climb everywhere. And a rose blooms for him in my memory, in summer and winter too, for he was to me the dearest of friends.

15.
Elizabeth Brown

East of Frank Slate's house stood the home of Will Pettit, captain of the little tanker that delivered gasoline and oil to the various marinas up and down the river. The Sturdevants' house was next; and then, in the last house in the row, lived old mother Brown, not far from the old boarding house whose lodgers, in the days of the operating quarries, had been her clientele. Mrs. Brown was a stocky Scotswoman in her 60's when we first knew her, spotless in her neatness, with a wonderful swirl of snow-white hair. Her strong bony face was livened by deep-set blue eyes that could flash pale fire in fun or anger. Because she had no lower teeth, her lower lip would quiver and pull inward as she talked, making her pointed chin even more sharp and prominent. And that chin was covered with a sparse scattering of stiff grey bristles whose prickling I recall well from times when I kissed her as I came and went from the island, for she became like one of our family. She had come to look upon my mother as a daughter and my mother returned her affection.

Mrs. Brown had a strong burr, stronger than Davy's, and we loved to hear her talk. She called the cows "caes" that grazed on the meadows behind her place, and when she wanted to point out something elsewhere, she would always say "o'er and feruent." When she approached our house along the crooked narrow path leading to our kitchen door, as she did almost every day, she would always announce herself with a call of "Hoots-toots!" and I came to call her, out of her hearing, "Hoots Toots," in the jeering way of unthinking teenagers.

The walk to our place from hers was a strenuous one. It was down a steep hill into our back lot, and then up again over a rock dome to the small plateau on the cliff that bore our house. It was a difficult walk for Mrs. Brown because she had a stiff leg that gave her gait an eccentric rhythm. As she walked the Thurso roads, somehow she made me think of an oncoming paddle-wheel steamboat with its walking beam rising and falling.

Mrs. Brown lived in a long low pleasant house—a sort of ranch-house—with a veranda across the front and dormer windows above. Woven baskets, dripping petunias and ferns, hung from the veranda eaves, and a huge trumpet vine with its morning glory flowers and heart-shaped leaves always enwrapped one corner post of the veranda. At the east end of the house a kitchen extension had been added, with its own door opening into the front yard and its own much-used path leading across the neat lawn to the road.

Mrs. Brown had the usual front parlor, that was shaded by the veranda and thus quite dark. In it there were victorian tables and chairs, and a desk, and a rocking chair upholstered in red velvet. A flowered Brussels carpet covered the floor wall to wall. This room lay totally unused in the summer, suffused with a depressing stillness. It may have become more cozy in winter when the stove at one end was glowing and Davy came to Mrs. Brown's house to play cards and talk. Sometimes he must have written letters for her also, for the fine spencerian hand of her letters to my mother was surely Davy's. Though never mentioned, the fact was that she was illiterate.

According to the islanders, the warm affectionate old lady I knew had been in the quarries' heyday a hard, toughminded, shrewd woman who could meet the roistering young quarrymen on their own terms with no holds barred. When the old boarding house across the road was a hive of young roughnecks spoiling for a good time on Saturday nights, Mrs. Brown had met the challenge; she ran a pub, so to speak, and her public house became notable for its hospitality. It was bountiful but strictly disciplined—and as strictly covert. The cup that cheers was offered freely—at a price of course. There were those who long afterwards referred to her place as a saloon. Whatever it was, it was unlicensed, illegal and mysteriously countenanced by the authorities in Clayton.

Whether anything other than liquor was offered in the rooms upstairs at Mrs. Brown's, no one ever said, but since Mrs. Brown was raising a large family at the time it is extremely unlikely that she was very permissive. Mrs. Brown had engaged in her business, not from choice, but out of stark necessity. While she had a husband, he must have counted for little in her scheme of things. A photograph of that gentleman stood on the fringed velvet table cover in her parlor revealing a weak-looking individual with a wispy moustache and very little of that quality we call character. For the masterful Mrs. Brown, he must have been a minor appendage. He had spent most of the years of his marriage far away from the island on mysterious business the nature of which I never heard, and had gone to an early grave. When my family came to the island Mrs. Brown had already been a widow for many years. And as a widow, she had borne alone the responsibility for raising a large family of children who reached maturity and entered into varied careers on and off the island. A son David became a prosperous businessman in Philadelphia, and another, Ernest, remained on the island to farm on the south shore and raise not only crops but a large family. And then there was Ella, who married Les, one of the island's numerous Carnegies. Les was a respected and intelligent man who for a time carried the mail back and forth from the island after Hub Garnsey had quit. Her sister Jessie, the eldest, married Robert Carnegie and moved to the former Murdoch farm downriver from the marsh. Robert did very well as a boatman for the wealthy Gillespie family of the Grennell Island area.

Old mother Brown had other children, wee bairns who in infancy had been consigned to some other Paradise than Grindstone Island and whose names the island never knew. The old lady deserves all the respect we can give her for having raised, under the most difficult of circumstances, such a decent and wholesome family. And my family became a sort of addition to her own. She loved us all and we returned her affection.

For years, she saw to the plowing of my mother's vegetable garden on our back lot and she herself would plant and weed it before our arrival at the end of June. It was a service I did not appreciate until recent years when I had to do the work myself. But my mother did understand, and rewarded the old lady with affection and many thoughtful gifts she would never have had otherwise. The braided rag rugs and bright quilted coverlets which graced our house were her handiwork. My mother saw to it that many of her rugs and coverlets were bought by our friends at a price that rewarded the old lady handsomely. Mrs. Brown played a key role in our lives in those first twenty years of our time on the island. For me, the echo of her cheerful "Hoots-Toots" still sounds along the path leading to our house on the cliff which she appropriately named "Cliff Cottage." She had many ideas for improving the looks of the place, that involved bordered pathways, the planting of flower beds, and hanging baskets of petunias for the veranda. Her ideas were excellent and undoubtedly would have made Cliff Cottage more attractive, just as they had beautified her own house up on the hill, but she was doomed to perennial frustration. My father and I rebelled at the work involved. My father had no high esthetic appreciation for flowers and I have been afflicted lifelong with incurable sloth.

Mrs. Brown endured our indifference and our relations continued happily over the years. She always understood well how sad we felt at summer's end when the time to leave Grindstone was drawing near. The impending separation from us pained her as well. Then she would give us the old island couplet:

> Oh, it's hard to depart from this lovely green isle
> Where the river St. Lawrence flows by with a smile.

Like so many others, she left the lovely green isle when it was neither green nor lovely, but at a time when even a lover of the island, if old, might be glad to leave it. One spring in the fateful thirties with the second World War approaching, we came to the island and found her no longer there.

16.
Charlotte McIntosh

Directly across the road from Mrs. Brown, in 1909, lived the family of Claude Hutchinson, in a green house of two stories. Though these respectable people soon moved to Clayton, the home is still to me the Hutchinson house. A Mrs. Faust from Syracuse lived there with her two sons for some years and then it was taken over and kept well by Mrs. Jay Robinson, whose descendants have kept it in the family until today. Time is not available to trace the unfolding genealogies and humdrum events in all these quiet households.

There was nothing humdrum about the life in the next house to the east, the house of Charlotte McIntosh, that stood between the Hutchinson home and the desolate old boarding house.

The widow McIntosh was a lean snaggle-toothed old woman (at least to me in my childhood she seemed old). She walked with a long loping stride in gingham skirts that were patched and soiled. Her slate-gray eyes were sunken, her face pale, and her two or three prominent front teeth gave her a rodentine appearance. I understand now that she was desperately poor, and that my estimate of her might have been more generous if I had perceived that fact.

Beside her large unpainted house ran the footpath that was the shortcut from the McRaes' to Hi Marshall's store. The path emerged from the thickets of the Chicago Quarry and ran up over the ledges across Mrs. McIntosh's yard to the North Shore Road. Everybody coming and going from the store passed close to her always-open door, and one could see inside her house. It was bleak and bare. Mrs. McIntosh never seemed to mind the intrusion of visitors as they went by. Often they would stop for a moment's chat with her, for she was always friendly. She spoke in a high treble voice with an astonishingly pure and flowery diction that revealed some heritage of education in her background. She was kind to the island children. The McRae girls told of her giving them small parties under her apple trees, and she was always generous with the apples that covered the ground, seasonally, in her unkempt yard.

Yet for some reason difficult to define, she never aroused in us the warm feelings of friendship with which we looked on other islanders. The idea of social visiting with her did not occur to us. We had heard that she was light-fingered. Hi Marshall always kept a sharp eye on her in his store. The deep pockets of her skirts offered much room for mischief.

My commonest recollection of Mrs. McIntosh is that of meeting her down in the thickets of the old Chicago Quarry, with a bandana around her scrawny neck and wearing a floppy straw hat. There in the amphitheatre of the quarry the wild raspberries grew lush and high in the bright sun that poured into this big pit. With pleased surprise she would always greet me in her high-pitched wavering voice: "Why Stanley, what are you doing down here?" Obviously, like herself, I was picking the sweet berries, trying to fill a quart pail—a tedious task that my mother often gave me, much against my wishes. Our talk was friendly but brief as Mrs. McIntosh went on, intent on finding more productive berry bushes elsewhere. I could hear her trampling the briars far across the quarry until I left, my quart pail finally filled. On less urgent occasions when we met, I always liked to talk with her. She would tell me about other days in other places, long ago. I especially liked to hear her talk about the time when she had lived in faraway Cold Spring on the Hudson River where her husband, Donald, long since dead, had once worked in the trap rock quarries.

When we arrived on the island each June, Mrs. McIntosh always knew of our arrival by some mysterious clairvoyant sense, and appeared at our kitchen door within the very first hour. She would be bearing a pail of choice wild strawberries which my mother was delighted to buy from her, and from that time onward, during the summer, there would be many visits involving berries of one sort or another.

Mrs. McIntosh never entered the house. The berry purchases were always a matter of business—inevitably accompanied, of course, by a pleasant exchange of conversation at the kitchen door. On the first visit, the talk would be more lengthy with the happenings of the long winter to discuss. It was during one of these early visits that my father and I were removing the long wooden shutters that had capped our doors and windows during the winter, and were stacking them against a tree in the grove behind the house. They were to be stored, later, in the crawl space where the house jutted out over a rock ledge. These shutters were heavy and clumsy and hard to handle and I detested them heartily. As we worked with the shutters, at the door Mrs. McIntosh and my mother continued in their protracted first talk of the season. When my mother finally went inside to get her purse, Mrs. McIntosh watched our spring ritual without manifesting the least flicker of interest. When my mother paid her, Mrs. McIntosh with her innate sense of decorum refrained from an abrupt departure, lingering to chat for a few moments more. Then she departed, her floppy straw hat and red bandana disappearing around the rocky dome.

A day or two later, on a Sunday afternoon, we left the house empty while we went to visit the Dick McRae family to learn how they had survived the vicissitudes of the preceding winter. Although there was a trickle of customers in their tiny store, they did no farm chores on the Sabbath other than milking, and there was plenty of time for visiting on the broad McRae veranda. The pleasant visit was prolonged in order to wait for the milk, which we carried home every evening in a covered pail. When we finally got home, one of the house shutters was missing that had been resting against the tree.

There wasn't much question in my father's mind as to who had taken it. Over the years, Mrs. McIntosh had acquired a formidable reputation on the island for coveting wood. Once on a dark night she had been seen in silhouette carrying a privy on her back along the road near her house in Thurso. If there was doubt about the actuality of that feat, there was none whatever about an event that had happened in the quarries years before. The evidence had been quite public, and shattering, both literally and figuratively. It had become a first-class island legend, still related with gusto some twenty years later as if it had happened yesterday.

It had been the custom of the quarrymen, on the evening before ending any day's work, to cut and stack a pile of kindling for use the next morning in starting the steam engines they used for power to sharpen drills, wind cables, and other jobs involved in stonecutting. This foresight on the part of the quarrymen was frustrated when they began to discover their stack of wood mysteriously diminished during the night. While it was a good terrain for elves and gnomes to perform their tricks the tough Scotch-Irish quarrymen discounted that possibility and they decided on measures that would deal with a more substantial culprit. One night, they prepared a pile of kindling wood in which they had drilled small holes and packed them tight with blasting powder. They stacked the wood as usual in an innocent pile beside the boiler and went home. Again, a goodly part of the pile disappeared during the night. The quarrymen waited. The suspense must have been intense. A few days later, to no one's surprise, there was a loud explosion in Mrs. McIntosh's kitchen. It must have been heard all over Thurso. Though the good lady herself was unhurt, the top of her stove had been blown off. No one asked her about the fuel she had been using or about where she got it, but from that time onward, every morning the quarrymen found their kindling pile quite untouched.

Now, it was difficult to imagine how this scrawny old woman could have made off with a heavy house-shutter. But years of practice must have made her adept. With a tact that was rare for him and seldom evidenced in his relations with me, my father made no accusation. A few days after the shutter's disappearance, Mrs. McIntosh, completely unabashed, arrived at our kitchen door with another pail of berries, greeting my mother with her usual flowery amenities and her snaggle-toothed smile. Hearing her high plaintive voice, my father casually came out to join in the small talk for a moment. His manner was pleasant and disarming as he glanced casually at the remaining shutters, still piled against the tree. His expression became suddenly perplexed.

"Do you know, one of the strangest things happened here the other day. One of those shutters disappeared. I can't understand it. They are heavy and hard to carry. I haven't the slightest idea what anyone would want with one of them," he said. Mrs. McIntosh's deep set grey eyes remained as dull and lifeless as ever. She nodded in agreement that the shutter's disappearance was indeed strange.

My father went on. "Of course, it doesn't bother me in the least. Everything here is covered by insurance. "But..." he added ominously, "I am afraid the insurance company will investigate this thing pretty thoroughly. It's a matter of principle, you know. They'll want to make an example of whoever took it. They can't afford to let such things slide." Again, Mrs. McIntosh nodded agreement and the subject was dropped. Soon, Mrs. McIntosh made her usual cheerful departure up the rocky path homeward.

Charlotte McIntosh

One morning a day or two later we looked out to find that the missing shutter had reappeared. It was resting innocently with its fellows against the tree. It had arrived mysteriously and silently, during the night. And nothing more was ever said about it —at least to Mrs. McIntosh.

In advanced old age Mrs. McIntosh finally went to Clayton to live with her daughter Maggie Calhoun. In the nineteen thirties, which like the plague brought termination to the lives of many island people, Mrs. McIntosh died.

Today when I hear a stick break or a tree fall in the dead of night in the woods that now fill the pit of the Chicago Quarry, I fancy that the ghost of Mrs. McIntosh is prowling there, with the ghost of her old hound True Boy, continuing her lifelong hunt for wood.

17.
Emmet and Nellie Dodge

The story of the Forsyth Quarry would be incomplete without a sketch of those who wrote its final chapter. Emmet and Nellie did not belong to the line of the quarrymen. They were its terminators. They gained control of the land of the Forsyth Quarry and turned it over to another use.

Nellie Dodge grew up as Nellie Cummings, on one of the island's more prosperous farms. Superficially speaking, people always spoke of her as Will Cummings' daughter, yet they knew, and Will Cummings always acknowledged, that she had been adopted. Who her actual parents were, the Cummings' never explained. Island gossip filled the gap, hinting that Nellie was Will Cummings' daughter by some woman other than his wife Addy, and pointing out that Nellie had not even one of the physical characteristics of Addy. It could have been said as truly, that Nellie in no way resembled Will Cummings either. It was only late in her life that Nellie silenced all such talk by finding, deep in Canada, her biological parents and her own natural identity. Nellie was the legally-acknowledged Cummings daughter, however, and their sole heir, and when Emmet Dodge married her and took over the Cummings farm, he set himself in line to become the controller, eventually, of the farm and a number of properties, and the Forsyth Quarry would eventually be included.

Nellie Dodge was a pleasant and easygoing woman, with a mind so simple that it sometimes seemed to be empty, but she was warm at heart, and always sympathetic. In facial contour she reminded me of Judy of Punch-and-Judy renown. She had Judy's long hooked nose, and the sharp upturned chin that promised to meet it. But her face was much broader than Judy's, and she had an agreeable smile, and a nature totally alien to that of the showman's puppet.

The Dodges raised three daughters, none of whom settled on the island when grown up. A son named Willie died tragically when still young, by accidental drowning. Jim and John were identical twins—clownish lads, full of mischief, known particularly for a quaint stunt of running across the fields of the Cummings farm with heads turned sidewise like manipulated rag dolls. Both spent World War II in the navy. Then Jim returned and married and settled on a farm below the marsh. John worked for a time in Kansas, then returned to Thurso in ill health to live in a little house on the former Turcotte site until he died in the 1960's.

Emmet Dodge's family came originally from Dexter and had, apparently, some appreciation of education. A brother of Emmet was a bacteriologist in Albany. Emmet himself had already served for some time, before my arrival on the island, as schoolmaster at the island's upper school, and must have had some advanced education. Whether he had a keen mind as well as an education was a debatable question on the island. In his own view he belonged definitely to the island's educated elite and was destined to be the mediator between the island community and the highly educated summer people. To those people he often was, indeed, a source of valuable advice and help in negotiations. He loved to challenge people to solve his conundrums. I recall his favorite: "Brothers and sisters have I none, but that man's father is my father's son. Who is he?" But many called him, in their plain vernacular, a "smart-Alec," given to showing off his learning but possessed of very little.

Emmet Dodge

Emmet had close-set eyes and ears that were very large—a combination that in my apprehension gave him a simian appearance. In 1909 when I first saw him he was the customs officer of the island, and much too strict in enforcing the regulations for the islanders' liking. He was truly skillful with figures. His mastery often stopped, however, with the mathematical aspect of a problem. He could calculate in seconds, without paper or pencil, the number of board feet of lumber needed for the completion of a construction job. But with hammer actually in hand he could not or would not make any two of those boards meet with true precision. Many liked to point out and laugh at Emmet's "dutchmen"—specimens of his faulty joints and hasty ill-cut pieces. Mrs. Packard's cottage was a famous display of his handiwork, with its sagging roof and sticking windows. The consensus was that Emmet was a slack farmer, a poor businessman, and an atrocious carpenter.

The low estimate of Emmet's acumen in business had a substantial base in accounts of how he disposed of the Forsyth lands. These had been one of the acquisitions of his father-in-law. When Jeanie Forsyth died, Will Cummings had bought the entire twenty-five acres from the executors of her estate. Emmet and Nellie moved immediately into the last and finest house in the line of quarrymen's accommodations, the neat demesne of the deceased Sid Chase. In the inevitable course of nature Will and Addy Cummings died. Nellie in law and Emmet in fact became the controllers and disposers of the glorious western shore of Thurso Bay. Emmet now proceeded to sell that lovely shore, so dear to my heart, without any consideration of how it could be used best, or even of how it could be divided for sale to his own best advantage. First, for a thousand dollars he allowed the very heart of the shoreline—a one-acre grove at the halfway point—to be plucked out for objectionable use by the Clayton Guides Association, a group of five professional fishing guides who used it as a spot to which they could bring their clients — sometimes large and noisy groups — for shore dinners. The sounds of merriment that they generated carried even as far as the next bay and to the retirement home, there, of Bertha McRae, who dubbed their grounds the Grindstone Biergarten. The unity of the shore was destroyed forever, and also its peace.

Then, six months later and just before he died, Emmet sold the remains of the Forsyth plot—they say for a song—to a group of summer people from Connecticut who formed the Thurso Bay Association. Soon the land was laid out in sites for five cottages, and in no long time there were summer homes on most of them. Emmet's children protested vigorously and brought suit to have the sale annulled, but in his mathematics Emmet had made no slip. They lost.

That was the end of the Forsyth saga, and of the wildness of the bay that was so precious to the Websters and to me. We cursed Emmet heartily. But the shore of Thurso Bay had only gone the way of all the shoreline of the island. Farmers who could no longer wring a living from their acres were accepting the offers of persons who hoped for pleasure rather than income from the land, and could pay.

Bertha McRae

18.
Fire on the Island: Mort Marshall's House

"Fire! Fire!" were the most terrifying words in all island experience, ringing through the village on a black night. Where buildings—all of wood—were totally flammable, and all heat came from wood stoves and all light from kerosene lamps, fires were frequent, and almost always utterly destructive. The nearest fire-fighting equipment —a fire boat on the mainland shore—was nine miles distant and at least half an hour away. All that it could bring was consolation. While still a child I was to see the islanders in action in this most critical of circumstances.

Mort Marshall, our nearest neighbor to the west, was usually working out of Clayton as a conductor of fishing parties. But he was not in sturdy health in either mind or body and even in the summertime he was often found at home, sitting on his veranda and nursing his infirmities. When sent by my mother on errands to the store I often took a shortcut through the apple orchard that separated our houses and came out under his eaves. There I liked to stop and talk with Mort.

Mort Marshall was a ponderous man with very short legs and a bulky body shaped rather like a bottle. His talk was hearty and affable but not very winsome to islanders, many of whom had experienced a streak of meanness in him. Though he was not reputed to be a pleasant man, he enjoyed these chats, and so did I.

One time, when as usual he was moaning about his health, I remember his complaining about having no appetite for any food he could think of. Together we talked over a long list of goodies. He shook his head sadly at the mention of each of them. Suddenly I had a thought. "How about graham crackers with milk?" I suggested. He slapped his thigh. "That's exactly what I want," he exclaimed. "I'll get some right away." And the next day he reported that my recommendation had gone to the very spot.

Mort did not live long after our conversation about delicacies. When he died, as usual it was in winter. I missed visiting with the old codger. Mort Marshall had not died however, without providing the village with more excitement than it had known for a long time.

One still night about one a.m., my father and I were awakened by a great shout ringing in the street: "Come! Come! Mort Marshall's house is all afire". In Thurso, a cry of fire was hair-raising. It usually meant the total loss of the stricken home.

Quickly pulling on our trousers and shirts, my father and I rushed up through the apple orchard. As we neared Mort's house, we could see ahead a gaping hole in its slanting roof and tongues of fire rising out of an ugly red glow in the attic below. The chances for saving the house seemed nil. As we neared, in the baleful glare, we could see black figures rushing through the shadows. A bucket brigade of men, women, and boys was already bringing water from Hi Marshall's cistern across the road. The downstairs and the stairwell of the house were free of fire. The bucket brigade could go up into the attic. A steady line of buckets were being carried up to throw on the fire. Meanwhile, the stairwell became more and more awash with spilled water and there were thumps and curses as one or another person would slip, and slide down the stairs with a bucket full of water following. It is a wonder that no one was seriously injured but there must have been many bruises. To the bruises, feelings of outrage were soon added. For on the lawn in front of the house and to one side of the line of bucket-passers sat a large figure, wrapped in a blanket and apparently insensible to the uproar about him. It was Mort Marshall, supposedly in a faint, and certainly not lifting one finger to save his house from the fire. Someone came with a bottle of spirits of ammonia and held it beneath his nose. With an angry sputter, the old man sat up suddenly and pushed the bottle away. Then he sank back into his convenient coma again. He didn't rouse even when someone came near looking for Hub Garnsey's spectacles, which had gotten lost in the excitement. People searched about in the wet grass in vain. They were nowhere to be found. Suddenly someone espied them on top of Hub's head.

By some miracle, the fire was put out. Mort's reputation on the island was not enhanced by his role in extinguishing it. A wide belief was that he would take no part in fighting the fire because he had set the fire himself in order to collect insurance money.

Fire on the Island: Mort Marshall"s House

After Mort Marshall died, Hi Marshall bought his place and renovated it. He fixed up the small outbuildings, and in summer used it as a guest house for Eliza's mother, old Mrs. Delaney, and for her sisters Allie and Bertha and other casual visitors. They were a jolly lot. As the fireflies sparkled over the lawn the air would be full of merriment and laughter. It was always fun to join them on warm summer evenings.

19.
Hub Garnsey and his Family

Just south of Hi Marshall's store on the Cross-Island Road, we have noticed the large white house of the Hubbard Garnseys. Once the first house one saw in approaching the village, soon it was to vanish utterly, in circumstances that will be described.

Hub Garnsey, for as long as anyone could recall in 1909, had been the island's Charon, ferrying its people, its mail, its cattle, its cheese, its hay, its school children and its freight across the wide river between Grindstone and Clayton every weekday, winter and summer, over the years. The United States Post Office slogan of getting the mail through in spite of sleet and snow and ice and fog and rain described Hub's role. A winter river full of jagged ice floes and fierce sudden storms that would have given pause to an Arctic wanderer, Hub faced without fanfare and without talk.

Hub was an oddly taciturn man. I never came to know him intimately, and I doubt that many others knew him better. He was a big block of a man, square of shoulders and square of face, with a scrubby mustache and sunken cheeks and pale eyes framed by gold spectacles. I never saw him without his old felt hat. Very strong, he handled heavy crates and oil drums with ease. For one in the public eye, Hub's talk was absolutely minimal, confined to grunted commands and brief discussions of the business at hand. Hub's family, too, lived a life apart from the rest of the islanders.

Although Hub had innumerable relations on the island, there never seemed to be a warm family feeling among them. When Hub would deliver freight at the McRaes' for their little store, Mrs. McRae, who was his cousin, would give him a curt greeting and go on about her work. There were no smiles, no questions such as "How is Martha?" or "Is little Ruby feeling better?"—none of the cousinly cordiality that I knew among my own "kissin' kin." Once the freight was unloaded, Hub would just cluck to his horse and drive away.

This familial indifference seemed to be widespread among the island people. There was little exchange of visits, there were few of the small family pleasantries. I recall no visiting between the Dick McRaes and the Tom McRaes, although Dick and Tom were brothers. And it was the same with other island families that I knew. Perhaps in summer, the only time I knew them, the island families were too busy. Perhaps on an island where half the population were one's cousins, relatives weren't remarkable enough to fuss over.

Martha was Hub Garnsey's wife. Born in Canada in 1871, she died when she was only 56 and she lies now beside Hub under the Garnsey monument in the cemetery. She was called "Marthy." I remembered Marthy well. In fact, one couldn't forget this strange woman—swarthy, heavy-set, with an intimidating scowl and a slow measured stride which seemed full of menace. In my memory she is always wearing a sort of mother Hubbard dress, long and shapeless. In my first year or two on the island, when I saw Marthy coming toward me on the village road I was frightened of her. She seemed to be the personification of the Cro-Magnon woman one saw in popular cartoons. Yet when I finally got to know Marthy, I found her to be the gentlest and kindest of women, and that she had a ready laugh.

I shall always remember her laughter one time when I was playing tag in their yard with the two oldest Garnsey daughters, Alice and Dorothy. All three of us were about 13 or 14 years old at the time. While I never went into their house, I often stopped to play with the Garnsey girls when sent by my mother to Hi Marshall's store.

The Garnseys had a large black dog they called "Old Pete" who was of a serious turn of mind, and on a certain occasion he disdained to enter into the spirit of the game. At one point in our revels, the girls darted screaming down an outside cellar stairway. I followed in hot pursuit. Old Pete misread my intentions. Suddenly I felt a sharp nip in the rear. It was Old Pete. The nip was sharp enough to draw blood. The girls emerged quickly from the cellarway and when they saw me, hands behind me, dealing with my wounds, they burst into gales of laughter. And ever after, even when they became grandmothers, the girls would remind me of the occasion. "Remember the time ole Pete bit you in the seat of the pants?" And then they would dissolve as always

Hub Garnsey and his Family

in fits of uncontrolled merriment at the thought.

By a previous wife, of name unknown, Hub had two grown sons, Bob and Fred, who had their own large families, Bob's on the south shore of Grindstone, Fred's in Clayton. Bob would eventually succeed his father as carrier of the mail. We have already spoken of David, who was about 10 when I came to the island. Eventually he married Hildred Dano and raised several very normal children. Mental difficulties plagued him all his life, however. He died in 1979 in Adams, New York, where he and Hildred had retired. Hub's three eldest daughters, Alice, Dorothy and Katy, were jolly tomboys, exuberant and full of fun. His two youngest daughters, Ruby and Bertha, were more restrained. Ruby was a florid child with unusual eyes quite properly described as "gooseberry." She married a Matthews and died in 1926 at the age of 18. Bertha was a fair doll-like little creature with very blue eyes and blond hair who lived to raise four daughters. All the Garnsey girls were saucy and straightforward. I remember Dorothy in hot controversy with one of her sisters. "Shut up!" she shouted; and then she added the last word in Grindstone vocabulary of insult. "You miserable old Sears-Roebuck-catalogue house!"

Dorothy and Alice married the brothers Corb and Paul Carnegie, sons of old Jim Carnegie, and raised respectable families on the Carnegie farms below the marsh. The two girls and their husbands survived to about 1980.

The third girl, the warm-hearted and vivacious Katy, was my favorite. On growing up she soon left the island to marry and live in New York City. Like so many of the island girls who left the island, Katy's life thereafter became remote and beyond all island knowledge. One was never quite sure whether they were married or not, divorced or widowed, or what they did in these far places.

We have mentioned the weedy lawn of the Hub Garnsey house. The interior of the house, too, was not famed for fastidious maintenance. The burgeoning life of the house was not limited to bipeds. Creatures were plentiful there that had six legs, or even more. There were some sniffy people who carefully identified Marthy's casseroles at church suppers, and took only the dab that courtesy required. This perception of the sanitary situation all came out when, one night about 1911, the rambling house just south of Hi Marshall's store burned. In the gossiping line-up of milk-wagons at the cheese factory the next morning the news was proclaimed by someone all too cheerily: "Hey, did you hear what happened last night? A terrible tragedy! Thousands of lives were lost." There was a dramatic pause. "Hub Garnsey's house burned down." The laugh that followed along the line of wagons was callous but it was knowledgeable. Hub and his family quickly took possession of old Phrone Slate's empty white house, just east of the Marshall store. That was the house in whose yard Old Pete made his foray upon me from the rear. Hub lived there until Marthy's death and then retired to spend the rest of his life in a house below the marsh. Phrone's house then stood empty until it was torn down in the early 70's.

Hub Garnsey suffered from hernia for years. The ailment brought him his brief moment of public prominence. One day just before the first World War, at noon time when he had just brought the mail to the island from Clayton, the hernia Hub had borne for years "came down," as island diagnosis described the situation. Probably an unusually heavy load of freight that day had brought it on. The usual expedients of manipulation failed, and by mid-afternoon Hub was in acute pain. By chance, I happened to arrive at the McRaes', to find Hub stretched out prone upon their gasoline dock, surrounded by a small crowd of islanders. He was groaning mightily. The intention had been to take him to Gananoque. Then someone had thought of Dr. Benedict who lived with his wife and daughter on a houseboat, the "Halcyon," anchored in Leek Island's southern bay, a half mile away across the Leek Island Channel.

Dr. Benedict was a small man with a prissy little moustache, a gynecologist down in suburban New Jersey. He was a friend of the Kipp family, who owned Leek Island. Like many little men, he had a towering and formidable wife and a buxom teenage daughter. Sometimes, when I rowed my skiff near the "Halcyon," mother and daughter would be sitting on deck in languorous ease, looking very bored. Aloof, they never waved or called a greeting. Nor did they ever come over to Grindstone for mail or to participate in the church socials as the Kipps sometimes did.

Aloof or not, Doctor Benedict was approached by boat, and by great good fortune the mission found the good doctor aboard his house boat, and he was willing. Although reducing a hernia was not exactly in line with gynecology, he consented to attend Hub and arrived quickly, clad in knickerbockers and the white duck summer hat he always wore. He found Hub writhing in pain among the reptilian coils of the gasoline hoses on the McRae dock, his skin as white as a toad's belly and plastered with a repulsive shiny mess of hopleaves with which someone had made a poultice.

All the while reassuring Hub with a "Just a moment, dear, everything will be all right," and a "Don't fret, ma dear, its going nicely," one wondered if Hub's groans were in protest against the doctor's strange terms of endearment or due to the pain of his protruding gut. "Ma dear" or not, Dr. Benedict remembered enough of his residence training to reduce Hub's hernia. The fastidious man returned to his "Halcyon" and Hub returned to his chores and I am sure carried that hernia unrepaired for the rest of his days. Not long after Marthy's death in 1927, and the breakup of his family, Hub moved to his retirement farm under Black's Hill, below the marsh, and soon quit carrying the mail. He did not live long.

Unlike old Uncle Hub of dipper renown, there was no cupidity in our Hub. My family's relationship with him always centered on business. Over the years, he carried us back and forth to Clayton, hauling our trunks and everything else we needed and his charges were always fair. To a small boy for whom time ahead seemed endless, Hub and the mail seemed as permanent a part of the island as its granite ledges. Almost up to the time of his death in 1932, he carried the Grindstone island mail and to this day, despite the long succession of carriers who followed him, Hub is still for me synonymous with the mail.

20.
Life on the Island Farms

Seen long ago from the train as one approached Clayton in early morning hours, Grindstone's field-patched slopes seemed as serene and still as on the day after creation. But a closer view, like the scene in a microscope, revealed a different picture, teeming with life and activity. By sunrise the island barns were echoing with the stamping of cows being milked in the stalls. Horses were being brought in from the pastures, and the wooded roads were already resounding with the snicker of horses and the grating on gravel of iron-rimmed wheels as milk wagons made their way to the middle of the island. There the cheese factory was already trailing a plume of soft coal smoke in preparation for the day's work. On their way home, the wagons would be loaded with whey for the pigs, always hungry in their whey-sodden pens.

Later, the empty milk cans would be placed out in the yard on platforms to be baked in sterilizing sunlight. The cleanliness of milk cans always got prime attention from all careful farmers. Dirty cans, when the milk stood overnight, always resulted in "gassy" milk, and gassy milk was the bane of the cheese-makers' life. At the factory many full cans were rejected and those families that often suffered this penalty were deemed to be dirty, and the dishes they brought to the church suppers were quietly avoided. The symphony of sounds about the farmhouses always included the clucking and crowing of chickens that pecked in the grass and among the burdocks and clumps of ragweed behind the house. Cats with eager faces and a dog, usually a shepherd, scrounged hopefully around the kitchen door. Not infrequently, a faint aroma of skunk hung in the air, a memento of a visit by a night raider. Sometimes a shamefaced dog would be exiled for a day or two for having been a little too dutiful as a protector of the homestead.

Thus far, farm life on the island was not very different from that on other farms across

America. But there were differences. We islanders had no electricity, no telephones. And our milk went to the cheese factory not to cities. The major difference however lay in the people. Grindstone Islanders were a unique breed. Aside from a very few who worked for the wealthy summer people at the head of Grindstone, they were an independent lot.

Alexander Richard McRae whom we have already met was pure Scotch Irish. His family had arrived in the 1830's and had cleared the land they settled on. Dick had been born in the old house that he was living in in 1909.

He must have had some schooling, for he was literate. As a young man, Dick had worked in the quarries and for an eventful year he had sailed the Great Lakes. By 1909 he had settled down to farming, selling gasoline, and raising his two daughters, Bertha and Mabel. He had become one of the most prosperous men on the island, and one of its most respected citizens.

I write of the farm life out of long experience as Dick McRae's virtual "hired hand" though I never received any hire. For some reason, I had an inner need to do hard work for Dick—a compulsion I have never known since. I may have even been regarded by Mrs. McRae as down right dim-witted for doing it. I don't think I was ever thanked for the work I did, other than by acceptance as an intimate of the family. I suspect that I always very much wanted Dick's approval. It confirmed my manhood in some way.

I helped Dick with his haying in July. I helped him with harvesting in August. And every afternoon at four o'clock or so, I went "out back" after the cows and brought them home for milking. In retrospect, going for those cows was stupid, for on other farms I have known, the cows always returned to their barns of their own accord, glad to do so in order to be relieved of their milk.

Dick's herd were a contrary lot. Fetching them of a hot summer afternoon was a disagreeable job. The air was swarming with vicious deerflies, and Dick's cows would invariably be at the farthest end of the farm. Deep in the thickets of Long Point which jutted far out into the marsh, they were hard to find and reluctant to be driven home. One could yell "Come, boss!" until he was blue in the face and there wouldn't be a sound. Then in the innermost reaches of the woods, a branch would crack and there would be the cows, calmly chewing their cuds, their eyes wide with surprise.

I was never fond of Dick's cows, but I loved his horses. All the while Dick was farming, he had but three horses, Ginnie, Nellie, and Jack who was Ginnie's son. Ginnie died soon after I arrived on the island but Nellie, a pretty red mare, survived for years. Jack was the love of all of us who knew him. As a foal he had been a pet, eager and responsive to attention, and he always remained an amiable horse. And Dick, a man never noted for demonstrations, always greeted Jack with obvious affection.

Haying is hard work, especially the way Dick did it, but it had its pleasant aspects. Necessarily, the weather was always fine when one hayed, and the fields were blanketed with the heavenly scent of sweet clover. Out on the hot meadows, cool oatmeal water laced with vinegar was unbelievably refreshing for the men who worked at cocking the hay and then at pitching the cocks onto the wagon as it slowly made its way across the stubble to the barn. Driving the horses of the hay wagon was a coveted job. That I was never allowed the privilege remains one of the sharpest disappointments of my young life.

In the barn, the new-mown hay was fragrant, and it was fun to wade waist deep through it in the hayloft while the alarmed barn swallows fluttered above in the dim light under the peak. Always there was a swallow's nest or two perched on a high beam, filled with naked nestlings who were all open mouth. These nests were never touched and the little birds were always allowed to mature and fly their nests in peace.

Then there was the smell of sweaty horses, stamping impatiently as they waited in their harness in the bay between the lofts, and the not-unpleasant smell of horse urine, which would persist for years in barns. And always there was the moan of the wind blowing through the cracks in the siding.

Pitching hay off the wagon high into the haylofts was the most disagreeable of all farm labor that I have known. It was a hot, heavy, dusty job in which one's sweaty clothes got full of chaff and dust that caused itching and irritation until one could get a swim later in the cool river. I still cannot understand why Dick never installed in his barn a horse-powered hayfork which from a high track could pick up half a load of hay from the wagon and drop it into one of the lofts that lay on each side of the barn's center bay. Tom, Dick's penurious brother back in the middle of the island, had a hayfork, probably of necessity, for Tom had the largest barn on the island. One night, some years later, Tom's barn was struck by lightening and burned to the ground. It was a sharp lesson that thrift and frugality, which Tom practiced, are not always rewarded in this contrary universe.

Another piece of equipment that Dick refused to buy, much to my exasperation, was a hayloader—a contraption dragged behind the hay wagon—which raked up the hay as it went along and conveyed it on racheted belts upward, tossing it into the wagon, where a man with a pitchfork distributed it across the wagon bed. This machine would have saved us the tedious work of cocking the hay and later pitching it up into the hay wagon as the wagon crossed the field.

Harvest time was much more fun than haying time. Then the grainfields would be sliced away, strip by strip, by a chattering binder with shuttling mower blades. They were heavy machines that would cut, gather together and tie and drop the grain in golden sheaves, with which the field would be studded. In time a professional thresher would bring his machine to the farm, and the sheaves would be thrown into that noisy monster. The threshing machine consisted of a huge horizontal gasoline engine on wheels from which a long wavering belt ran to a complex van, full of machinery, into which the bundles were tossed. From the front end, a steady wind-driven stream of straw would emerge through a blower while the threshed grain poured out of a vent into bags on one side.

The engine had a characteristic ugly bark—a sharp "Bock Bock-Bock, Bock-Bock-Bock-Bock"—that was heard far over the distant hills on the summer air and let one know that the threshing season had arrived. It usually lasted about two weeks. While haying would call for a hired man or two, harvest time called for ten or twelve to handle the many aspects of the threshing process. It was a tacit understanding among the farmers that they would help one another with the threshing. And, in some ways, threshing became a festive occasion. The women would prepare steaming meats and potatoes and pies and set up long tables in the kitchen or, sometimes, on trestles out of doors. There the men would sit down for a fine dinner and a brief half hour of talk and rest before going back to work. It was a scene repeated everywhere across the nation wherever grain was being harvested in the days before the combine. John Stuart

Life on the Island Farms

Curry's famous painting of Kansas harvesters at dinner could have been made on Grindstone Island.

The haying and harvesting always had their small tragedies. Baby rabbits were overtaken by the sharp knives of the binders and horribly mutilated. Cats would be lured by the darting field mice suddenly routed by the advancing machines, and would be overtaken themselves and dismembered by the vicious knives. A cat with a missing leg, a the victim of the hay mower or binder, was not an uncommon sight on the island farms.

There were other aspects of farm life that were traumatic. I was never around in the springtime to see pet calves led off to slaughter. But I did see tokens of the slaying of the old cows. Skulls, ominously fractured by a sledge hammer, lay about on the pastures. And I did see the killing of a hog or two on the first chilly night of September when the carcass would be safe from being flyblown. Most children, if not downright cruel, are known to be quite heartless and I was no exception. Today, I would go far to avoid being present at such killing. But then, butchering time held for me a morbid fascination. The grim rite began with the setting up, in the yard beneath the stout branch of a tree, of a big barrel to hold boiling water. Hooks, ropes and a pulley dangled ominously from the branch. A neighbor or two arrived to assist in the killing. The men talked in low voices as though a conspiracy was in process, which indeed was the case. It was a particularly ominous business when one thought of the goodnatured unsuspecting hog, grunting complacently nearby in its pen, oblivious to the final action toward which these horrid preparations led.

The hour was always at dusk, a time of day when all should have been at peace in the world—a time certainly incongruous with the sinister acts that now followed. With the others standing by, one of the men would enter the pen and deftly slip a rope around the unsuspecting animal's hind legs. Then the other men would take hold and drag him, squealing in protest, outside onto the grass. There they would pin him down and a long sharp knife would flash as one of the men with quick expertise would thrust it deep into the animal's throat. The poor beast's squealing rose to a frenzy. Then, the knife withdrawn, the men released him, and in sudden relief the hog would get to his feet again and for a long moment he would stand there in the shadows, grunting softly. The men would watch in silence while the dark blood poured out of the poor animal's neck.

And then suddenly he would become aware that something was terribly wrong, and begin to squeal again. This time, his outcry became almost human as he weakened and sank to his knees. Then suddenly, grunting gently, he would fall over on his side and after a few reflexive kicks become still.

His limp body would be hauled up quickly and thrust head first into the barrel, now filled with scalding water. The carcass was repeatedly dragged over its sharp edge and scraped until it was clean of bristles. In the lantern light, the body would look disconcertingly human. With the hooks, lines, and pulleys, it would then be hung head-down from the branch of the tree and eviscerated. It was left there for the rest of the night. The next morning, it would be taken to Clayton, looking like a thousand other carcasses one saw in the butcher shops and certainly not like the friendly hog who had grunted a grateful response when scratched in his pen a few days before. In this fashion one more hog had been given what Ernest Hemingway was to call "the sweet gift of death."

All kinds of animals played a significant role in our life on the island. The McRaes, always fond of pets, had a succession of cats named Spiffy, and a water spaniel named Laddie, and later a sharp-toothed spitz named Teddy, of a disposition quite congenial with that of Nettie his mistress. With Hub Garnsey's Old Pete and Mrs. McIntosh's True Boy, these animals comprised the entire pet population of Grindstone through the 30's as far as I was concerned. And there were cows and horses that broke through our fences. Raccoons would invade the gardens, and skunks would be encountered on our paths at night. And of course in our wanderings across the pastures, there were always the bulls to be considered. Usually they ignored us and went on about their business. But on one occasion, one did not. The result was my one and only <u>corrida</u> on the island. No self-respecting matador would have given a peseta for the spectacle. But it was bull fight enough for me.

It took place in the barnyard in front of the old McRae barn which stood behind a clay bank on the edge of the cove. The barn was a picturesque old building, weathered grey, with a long sloping roof. Beneath was a central door through which the cows would file twice a day from the barnyard to take their place in stanchions and be milked. That the barn was picturesque was apparent when a young esthete from one of the wealthy families off the head of Grindstone came down one morning in a small boat, anchored it in the bay before the barn and spent the entire day committing the barn to canvas. No one paid him the slightest attention.

The path from our camp on the Point crossed the connecting isthmus and followed along the top of the bank just mentioned and entered the hoof-printed yard in front of the barn. It was there that I found myself, early on an eventful morning, planning to ride with Dick to the cheese factory. Not only did I like being with Dick but the three-mile ride through the fragrant woods behind Nellie or Jack was always an adventure.

I waited while Dick and Mrs. McRae finished the milking inside the barn. One by one, their duty done, the cows emerged to wander down the lane that led back to the pastures. Suddenly I noticed that a large black-and-white bull was appearing around a corner of the barn. He was a visiting bull—one who had found the temptation of a new harem on the far side of his fence irresistible and had broken through to disport among Dick's herd.

At first I paid him no attention. Then I noticed he was coming toward me, following the front wall of the barn, and that he was regarding me with a lowering look that was not to my liking. He was between me and the central door of the barn that was my only avenue of retreat. I decided to outflank him around the end of the barn and I walked slowly in that direction, hoping that he would lose interest. Soon I saw that, far from losing interest, he was playing a game. He too walked slowly toward the end of the barn, paralleling me and eyeing me with steady menace. Then he took a step toward me. I turned and walked in the opposite direction. So did he. Then I stopped and turned and reversed my direction again. So did he. And with each turn, he took a step closer and I took a step further toward the edge of the bank. He had no idea of letting me get around him. And as we walked back and forth, he stalked closer and closer. It was a bull fight in slow motion but no less ominous for all that. The bull was out to get me.

The game went on—back and forth—until I was halfway down the river bank. The slow deliberate pace of it was sinister and I was frightened. Just as I was about to take refuge in the river, suddenly Dick appeared in the doorway of the barn. He saw at once what was happening and gave a stentorian shout that echoed from the high ledges on Leek Island a mile away. In sudden ignominy, the bull spun about and retreated while I found safety at last in the barn. The *corrida* was over—or almost, for there was a brief sequel.

I was waiting in the doorway while the McRaes concluded their milking when the bull, who had left the yard, returned. Slowly he walked up to the doorway and stood lowering at me, obviously for a showdown. His hatred of me was not quenched, and by now I reciprocated it fully. There was a stout club leaning against the wall inside the door and I seized it. Standing in the door frame I raised it, ready to strike at the first chance. With tentative steps, the bull approached until he was within a foot or two of the doorway. The sill was high, so that the bull stood a little below me—in perfect position to receive the blow I had in mind. And now I saw my chance. I knew when that club hit him in the head it could kill him. I didn't care. And I knew that Dick wouldn't either. I swung that club, hard—and of all things, the doorway was too low for the swing. It hit the top timber of the barn door's frame with a resounding bang that could have celebrated the victory of another Manolete! Though the bull was unharmed he was terrified by the thunderous noise and spun about and ran off as though the knackers were just behind him. He never bothered me again. Later I heard that he had been badly teased by boys. For this reason he may have had an urge to do a little teasing himself.

21.
Aboard the "Whistler"

Dick did not depend much on Hub for bringing his freight from Clayton. He usually fetched it himself in "the Whistler." The little "Whistler" had belonged to Will Sturdevant. After Will abandoned it on the day of his elopement with the Calhoun girl, Dick had purchased the boat. It was always great fun to go with Dick on these trips and when he went alone, as sometimes happened, my disappointment was acute.

Starting the old Barber engine was tricky. First, each of the four cylinders had to be primed by squirting gasoline into a little cup with a petcock which would then be opened. Next the heavy flywheel at one end of the engine would be turned over slowly to suck the gasoline into the cylinders. This procedure was called "priming." Then the petcocks were closed and the flywheel was turned again—this time vigorously. Sometimes the engine would start at once, sometimes it didn't. When it didn't, adjustments followed that were as mysterious as the Eleusinian rites. When the engine was finally running, Dick would open the petcocks one at a time and each would explode sharply for a few seconds until he turned it off again. This operation presumably cleared each cylinder of excess fuel. It could have cleared them of evil spirits, so far as I knew.

None of the boats went faster than ten miles an hour. Dick's Whistler always took the best part of an hour to go the nine miles "around the Head" to Clayton. If the wind was as usual out of the west, the waves could be big and our course exciting, as we rolled off the western Grindstone shore with little but clear water between us and Kingston, twenty miles away.

If the weather was very bad and the "Whistler" heavy with freight Dick would return home the longer way around the foot of Grindstone—a trip that I enjoyed especially because it took us through narrow channels among the lovely islands that lay off the island's eastern shore. I doubt if Dick took that aesthetic view of the matter, however. He had to endure an additional drain on his time.

It was a great privilege for me when Dick allowed me to steer the boat by manipulating its forward steering wheel. In addition to that wheel, there was a steering lever at one side amidship where Dick sat beside the engine. Sometimes when I had run too close to a shoal, I would be startled by a sudden twist on the wheel as Dick pulled the lever to correct my course. But Dick was ever good-humored when we were alone together, always humming a tuneless murmur, just audible over the noise of the engine, and if I did something which pleased him, he would shout "Good old Tanny. Tanny's my boy!" And when we got home he would give me a penny for my steering. He was not so munificent as Davy Black had been with his gift of a dime, but a penny would buy me a Tootsie Roll, a confection of which I was very fond.

Sometimes Dick would discover that the freight he had expected to find in Clayton would not arrive until the coming in of the one-o'clock train. Then we would go up the street together for a noonday meal at the Rattrays, Mrs. McRae's parents. They lived in a rambling white house (long since razed) on a street which curved along the upper bay. The country-style meal of boiled meat, gravy, boiled potatoes and a canned vegetable was a novelty for me, and I enjoyed eating not in a tent but in a cool dining room on a real table cloth with table talk on unfamiliar topics.

Captain Jim Rattray was a lanky old man who owned a little steamboat, the "Niagara," of which I recall little except its odd clipper prow and a cavernous hold full of polished brass pipes and the smell of steam. It was probably in this boat that he had started a ferry service to Gananoque and enroute carried the first mail to Grindstone.

Captain Rattray also owned a pretty little sloop called the "Roamer" in which he paid social visits on our side of Grindstone, always anchoring it in the cove before the McRae farmhouse. There were at that time very few sailboats on the river. I liked to fancy myself sailing to far away tropic isles and "the Roamer" provided a focus for my dreams.

Mrs. Rattray, Nettie's mother, had been a Garnsey—perhaps a sister, or at least a cousin, of old Uncle Hub of dipper renown—which of course made her a Grindstone Islander. She was a heavyset well-spoken woman with a plaintive voice, like her husband given to venting many complaints in the course of conversation. It wasn't difficult to see where Nettie McRae had gotten her chronic dissatisfaction with life.

She had inherited a dose of "frowning chromosomes." The Rattrays were always warm and kind to me however, and I loved the times when Dick took me to their house for dinner.

When Dick went to town, he invariably dressed in a blue serge coat, grey trousers and a dark boatsman's cap with a black visor and his black shoes were always shined. Yet he remained the farmer he was, dressed in Sunday clothes.

Dick McRae

22.
The End of the Webster Saga

Although Lew Webster was not a Grindstone Islander, he was the owner of the most beautiful property on Grindstone's north side, and he had an important role in the island's history during the first forty years of the century.

One could say that he was engaging, genial, ingratiating and likable, and all these words would describe him truly and still fail to describe the great charm he exerted on everyone he met. He had a bigness about him that made you feel that here was a man of importance. He had a marvelous sense of humor, full of whimsy and wit. In conversation, he would convey at once that the person to whom he was talking was the only object of his interest—that nothing else mattered.

I found a curious sensitivity in him one time when a little girl from a distant state had visited the family and, on leaving, said, "Tomorrow I'm going to my faraway home in the west." Later, Lew Webster commented on her use of the poignant phrase "my faraway home in the west." It uttered the nostalgia of the westward-moving American people and Lew found it touching

He was flattering to women—even to women whom I knew he disliked. Later, he would be merciless in his ridicule of them, always in such a genial clever way that one was bound to laugh. In short, he was a superb actor. My mother always marveled at his duplicity.

As a small boy I worshipped Lew, always trying to elicit his pleasant amused chuckle. And I so wanted to emulate his looks that I thrust my lower lip out in what I fancied to be a resemblance to his lip, which was a little heavy. My effort created an effect that, far from accurate or humorous, won me the name of "groucho" from my hero. For all his superficial geniality, he had a counterbalancing streak of ruthlessness below the surface. I was to discover that coldness one day when with him and my father I was walking across the sandspit from the Point toward the McRae barn. I was teasing him to get the attention from him that I craved, and I got it in a way I didn't expect. No doubt I was being annoying to the point of complete exasperation, for suddenly he gave me a hard shove downward that forced my face deep into the sand. To this hour I remember vividly the horrid grit that filled my mouth when I got to my feet again. Uncle Lew, smiling and talking, walked on oblivious. But as a rule, he was tolerant and fun to be with.

Lew Webster was ostentatious. With a wave of his cigar, he would point out the great things he was going to do to improve his property. He was to be known, clearly, as the Lord of the Manor. The camp on the Point did indeed become elaborate, with platforms, sleeping tents, a dining tent, a kitchen tent, and guest tents. There was running water, and a large storehouse to house the camping gear in winter. Mrs. Webster, proud and politely patronizing, was always elegant with her stylish and expensive clothes. Even the Webster's small son, Bill, was an immaculate Little Boy Blue while I was a grimy Huck Finn. To complete the atmosphere of luxury, Mrs. Webster brought to the island from Brooklyn her Swedish maid, Lena, replete with her blue uniform and white apron with its bows and criss-crossed straps. The McRaes were impressed to the point of downright groveling. They responded to the Websters' every beck and call. Whenever Lew wished, Dick would take him back and forth to the Clayton train carrying his expensive leather bags.

Even from the beginning however, I noticed that Dick was a little suspicious of Lew Webster in the way that country folk can be suspicious of city slickers. At his gasoline dock Dick had had experience with imposing summer people who failed to pay their bills. He called them "ten-dollar millionaires" and he was a little worried that his landlord might be one of these. Dick felt intuitively that there was something not quite forthright about Lew Webster and, as we shall see, he was right.

Meanwhile, no cherub trailing clouds of glory could have been more indulged by Mrs. McRae and her two girls than little Bill Webster. They went into raptures over his cute ways. His father's own child, he could be winning and immensely likable with a gay laugh and sparkling elfin eyes for those adults whom he wanted to impress. With

The End of the Webster Saga

others, he could be a calculating little monster. He always knew exactly when and where to play his lovable act. And when it didn't work, as happened sometimes, he would display a vicious temper that was not to diminish over the years. On these occasions, I still can hear his mother's angry expostulation: "Lew-ell-yn!". She had a quick temper of her own. Of course, I disliked him heartily. In the presence of him and his adorers I felt myself to be, in contrast, unattractive, unlikeable, and a lout. I felt that my status, for the McRaes, was that of a poor relation of the Websters, to be tolerated and little more, and that my family were hangers-on, living ignobly under the sufferance of their princely landlord. Thus for me, the atmosphere on Webster Point at this time was unpleasant. I was very happy when Davy Black made it possible for us to buy a place of our own high on the bluff on Thurso Bay and I recall exulting: "This is our own house and our own land and no one can put us off it!"

The events that were to follow could be evidence that Divine Justice is a reality after all. Inauspicious developments now occurred in all the inevitable progression of a Greek tragedy. Trouble began in 1915 with, of all things, a matter of house-paint. The McRae farmhouse needed painting and Lew Webster suddenly had the notion that Dick should not only have the responsibility for painting it but should purchase the paint as well. In a letter, Lew issued that flat demand. Dick rebelled. I suspect Mrs. McRae wrote the reply. Its style was tart, I'm sure—tart enough to anger Lew Webster for he immediately replied, ". . .next year, the farm will not be for rent." And so, the McRaes were abruptly ejected from their little paradise with its flourishing gasoline dock and its store, and from the house in which Dick had been born and where he had raised a family and prospered. It was a heavy blow. It was also humiliating, after all the years of service and servility that the McRaes had shown the Websters. "And that's all the thanks we ever got for kissing Lew Webster's ass," Mrs. McRae said bitterly. When angry, she forgot her ladylike airs and reverted to island vernacular.

The McRaes predicament was grim. Even at that time, land was difficult to get along the river, and especially land that would be suitable for a public dock and a little store for profitable sale of cigarettes . By a stroke of immense good luck, however, Dick was able to find a farm on the little bay just west of the Forsyth quarry and Thurso Bay, at the headland that we now call McRae Point. It was the Uncle Hub Garnsey farm— the farm of Mrs. McRae's great uncle. The large rambling farmhouse was occupied temporarily by the Turcottes when we first came to the island. We had skulked past it with muffled oars when warned by Mrs. McRae about that "terrible" family.

Here at McRae Point Dick could reestablish his gasoline dock and tanks, and Mrs. McRae could continue to have her little store. The farm was prime land with a well-built barn and broad clear meadows sloping up to the cemetery without obstruction. The beautiful peninsula had McRae's Cove on its eastern side, and westward lay the Wide Waters. It was a fine farm that had everything the McRaes needed to carry on.

For me at least, the new place never had the charm that the old farm had had. The old Garnsey farmhouse was set far back from the river, and from its front veranda one could catch only a narrow view northward and a long sweep downstream with nothing to engage the eye. There were no dancing waves splashing almost on the doorstep, no sundowns to see in the framework of the splendid pines on Leek Island. And the docks which Dick built were exposed toward the northeast and when the wind blew a gale from that direction, his shores got a heavy pounding. There was something a little bleak about the new McRae establishment. However, over several years, the McRae's surrounded their new house with social graces that gave it a beauty of its own.

Mabel brought her children to the island in summers and Bertha's schoolteacher friends would visit for a week or two and the large old house was filled and warmed. It became a jolly place on summer afternoons and in the long northern twilight hours on the veranda. The Canadians, coming over to the dock for gas, would wander up the long lawn to the store and stop for pleasant visits. At Nettie's strong request Dick replaced his old "Whistler" with a fast new mahogany "Whistler II" for frequent jaunts to Clayton and in Clayton their Model A Ford was always waiting for trips to Watertown. Thus the good life eventually was resumed. Mrs. McRae mellowed. Perhaps she felt, as I had, that at last they had a place of their own and no one could throw them out. Now she had more to talk about than ever, and gradually the old place was forgotten.

The new place had one feature that the old place did not have—a bathroom. It was a pity that Mrs. McRae could not put it on display. She was very proud of it. Not many on the island had bathrooms—not even the elegant Websters. It must have been a thorn in her side that Dick still preferred, quite publicly, to use the backhouse outside. It was easier than climbing the stairs.

The End of the Webster Saga

Dick and Nettie lived on into the 1950's at McRae point, yielding steadily to the years. Painful arthritis finally made Dick a cripple. One summer when I came to the island, I found Nettie thin and scrawny, her large head set on a painfully emaciated body that had once been plump. It was the ravage of a bad heart. One summer, in her 70's, she died, and I walked with her body in procession to the Grindstone cemetery.

The island winters grew too much for Dick. He went to live with Mabel in the house he had bought in Clayton, and which he now gave to her. Miserable with pain and dispirited by increasing blindness, he attempted suicide, vainly, by slashing his wrists. Shortly a natural death ended his life. Thus ended a story that I felt to be a part of my own family history as well.

After Lew Webster's rude eviction of the McRaes from their old home, a curse seemed to fall him. The course of events that was to overtake the resplendent Websters was harsh.

Shrewd as he was, for some reason Lew Webster never repeated the killing he had first made on Wall Street. For a time he did well enough to maintain the old pose of opulence on those summers when he still came to the river. He abandoned camping on the Point and occupied the farmhouse vacated by the McRaes. He continued to commute to New York and to hire Dick to take him back and forth to the trains. Dick's resentment did not prevent his acceptance of a ten-dollar fee for making the trip.

But Lew's grandiose plans for developing the farm were not discussed now, nor the house he would build atop the cliff at the head of the Point, nor of the boathouse that would stand in the bay beneath it.

The final Webster debacle was sudden and dramatic. It came one winter night. Mrs. Webster telephoned my mother in desperation. The astonishing news was that Lew was in the Tombs—the grim jail in downtown Manhattan. The charge against him was embezzlement.

He was soon released on bail and then the story was revealed. At the end of the war years, Lew Webster somehow became the New York agent for a new Russian trading organization named Amtorg. The organization showed great promise. In exchange for

Lew Webster as Insurance Man, from one of his flyers.

a $5,000 bond, to be held in escrow, an American company could become a member of Amtorg and have exclusive trading rights. One such bond was put up by Mr. Wickwire, head of a large business. The bomb fell when Mr. Wickwire one day accused Lew Webster of misappropriating the Wickwire bond money for his own purposes. Strong enough evidence was presented to have Lew Webster immediately

144

jailed. At astronomical expense, Lew Webster hired one of New York's top criminal lawyers, Robert Elder, and eventually the case was settled, I don't know exactly how.

My affection for Uncle Lew gave me strong doubts at the time about the validity of the Wickwire charges. I felt all had been a hideous mistake. But years later I learned that Lew had also misappropriated money that a nephew had given him as an insurance premium. I concluded sadly that Uncle Lew was indeed capable of violation of trust.

Lew Webster was now a pariah on Wall Street. He sought refuge in the insurance business in which he found slim pickings. Slowly, his fortunes wore way. The depression years finished him. He borrowed money on his fine house in Flatbush, taking out a government mortgage under a system set up for victims of the depression. With typical assurance he was certain that the benevolent Roosevelt administration would never foreclose. To his astonishment, it did. The Websters were now compelled to move into a shabby two-family house in a second-rate neighborhood in Flatbush and there they spent their last days in oblivion.

In these later years, the Websters often rented the deteriorating farmhouse in summer to friends. The lovely meadows became overgrown with scrub. The arable fields disappeared and the long views were gone. Not maintained, the barn roof decayed and the barn itself then collapsed, leaving scarcely a trace that it had ever existed.

In the early '40's, Lew Webster and his wife sought refuge in the old farmhouse for their summers. Refuge is the exact word, for process servers were often at their door in Brooklyn and only by departures on midnight trains did they escape such unwelcome visitors.

The house was by now in sad disrepair. Uncle Lew's efforts to patch the exposed laths with cardboard and to make a garden were pathetic, for by now he was not only very poor but he was in his seventies with a failing heart.

Yet he remained genial and warm and clearly fond of me, while Gertrude Webster became mellowed and much more tolerant. Their son Bill was now scarcely a factor in their life— distanced from his parents because he had married a girl whom Mrs. Webster detested. At great sacrifice, they had sent young Bill to the exclusive Lincoln

School in Manhattan, and then to Union College where he got a degree in electrical engineering. As a naval officer living in Washington during World War II he prospered, but as far as I know he saw little of his parents in their last days.

On summer evenings when I was on the island in this period, I loved to row over to "the Webster place" as it was now called and spend the evening playing rummy with Uncle Lew and Aunt Gert, as I always called them. And he and I would play checkers together. Uncle Lew was reputed on occasion to have tied professionals. Almost always, I lost. I would explain to him that some of the world's best checker players were the inmates of lunatic asylums, and Uncle Lew would laugh heartily. He never lost his wonderful Irish sense of humor. And he would lean down and stroke his big yellow cat Butch, of whom he was inordinately fond. As I pulled away from the Webster dock and left their farmhouse warm with glow of kerosene lamps, I wished these times could last forever. Such happy times did not last very long, for in the mid-forties, at the close of World War II, Uncle Lew finally died in Brooklyn when I was far away. Aunt Gert moved into a forlorn tenement above stores near a Brooklyn subway station. I was able to visit her briefly once or twice and found her cheerful, but the humiliations and the loneliness of these last years had taken a heavy toll. In 1946, she too died, of a perforated ulcer. Ironically, as if to even out a score, their estranged son died of the same affliction, childless, some 40 years later.

Lew Webster in his lifetime committed some wrongs, no doubt, against certain people. But in the end I must declare, on reflection, that in no way did he ever do any real wrong to me. On the contrary he gave me much affection—affection as sincere as the adoration that as a child I gave to him. If at the Great Assize hostile witnesses raise a clamor against him, I will not join it.

23.
The Cheese Factory

One of the island's major institutions, the cheese factory was central in more ways then one. Built in the year of the closing of the great quarries it was the principle source of income for island families for more than fifty years. The economic story that began with Dick's cows browsing in the thickets will be continued now to tell of the marketing of the final product. The cheese factory was not only the island's economic center, however. It was one of its primary social centers as well. Thirty-three farmers brought their milk every morning to the cheese center when it was founded and the number remained stable for half a century. Necessarily almost every farm on the island was represented there in each morning's queue of wagons. It was one of the primary spots where news and views as well as dairy products were exchanged. Located almost exactly in the center of the island geographically, the cheese factory imposed an equally heavy burden of haulage on its suppliers. All of their milking sheds and homes were far away near the shores, in every direction.

The early ride to the cheese factory with Dick was a daily ritual in which I loved to participate on a fresh summer morning. The drive by clover-scented hayfields, the slow climb between rock outcroppings on the Baseline Road, and the run over the rolling lands to the factory never failed to be fascinating. It was always good to be with Dick, ever showing his good spirits by humming his tuneless drone. And there was the pleasant smell of the horse—either Nellie or Ginny or, later, Jack—whom we all loved and petted. The wagon wheels made a grating sound as they rolled over the gravel road, while the songs of larks and song sparrows—the sweetest of music to city ears—filled the air on every side.

At the factory, the farmers lined up on the road that circled the building, waiting their turn for their heavy milk cans to be weighed. The cheesemaker stood on a high platform manipulating the crane that hoisted the cans and adjusting the scale balances.

Sometimes he would reject the milk as too "gassy" and send it home with a grumbling farmer. Gassy milk was the result of unclean cans or failure to cool the milk properly. Several farm families suffered frequent rejections of their milk, and with these rejections came a questionable reputation for general cleanliness, and distrust of their dishes at church suppers.

After the milk cans were weighed the farmers drove on with their empty cans to the rear of the factory. There was a sunken vat there filled with a byproduct of the cheese making process—foul-smelling whey. Swarmed over by buzzing flies and filled with repulsive debris, this whey certainly was not the whey that Little Miss Muffet relished. To the farmers' pigs back in their pens, the yellow slop was both delightful and nourishing, however, so the farmers dipped up pailfuls and filled their empty milk cans with the stuff. Then they drove on past the boiler room and its coal pile out to the Base Line Road and home.

With thirty-three farmers lined up at the factory on a summer morning, there was inevitably much gossip and small talk. The quality of the hay crop, the price of hay, the market for cattle, the prospects for getting in grain before rain, and what Charley Cerow was paying for hogs. The price of lumber at Daggert's or at Brooks' lumber yards where they bought materials for silos, barns and granaries was often discussed. It was at the cheese factory on these summer mornings that I got acquainted with the island farmers as they really were, quite free of their stiff deportment on Sunday mornings at church, the principal other place where I saw them. I never ventured to participate myself in the talk of these imposing adults but I sat silently beside Dick and took it all in.

And on those mornings, the factory was the distribution-point for the news of what had happened the previous day on the island—often of cattle killed by lightning, and of barns burned far away. Because radio and television were unknown on the island at the time, national news of politics, train wrecks, and high crimes arrived by word of mouth. Probably the most striking news, which was to shake the entire region, came one morning in 1912 when I was 10 years old. I was at the factory with Dick and when he heard it, he exclaimed, "That's the end of it. The Bay is finished and so is Clayton." And Dick was right. The elegant Frontenac Hotel, the social hub of the Thousand Islands, had burned to the ground the night before. People who had seen the glow of

The Cheese Factory

the fire thought sunrise had come. Symbolically, what people had thought a sunrise proved to be a sunset—the sunset of a graceful era that would never return. Indeed it was the end of the Thousand Islands as a grand resort in the class of Newport and Bar Harbor. Actually the age of elegance was moribund anyway as the 20th century rolled on. But the Frontenac fire ended it sooner in the Thousand Islands.

Sometimes I went to the cheese factory on my own, walking the long road there and back, to chat and watch the cheesemaker make cheese. The cheesemakers differed from year to year, coming from far-off places down state. They seemed always glad to have company, for most of them were living alone in upstairs quarters in the factory building, remote from the general populace. No one ever seemed to know much about them. All that the islanders were interested in was whether they made good cheese. Always the first news we got when we arrived on the island in June was a report on the quality of the art of the new cheesemaker, for he was a critical factor in the Islands's economy.

The factory had two immense vats for the handling of milk. I do not recall the second's having ever been put into actual service. The vats were lined with metal. Hot water pipes were encased in their sides, which heated the milk to about blood-temperature. The cheesemaker would add rennet and colorants to the warm milk and then, walking slowly around the vat with a wooden rake, would slosh the milk back and forth for two or three hours. I would usually arrive at the factory about eleven o'clock when the monotonous task of raking was over. By that time the curd had been precipitated out by the rennet and the whey was being drained away. On the bottom of the tank lay a heavy mass of golden curds. With a great knife the cheesemaker was now cutting deep gashes to drain the remaining whey into a channel that ran the length of the vat. The result would be a row of "loaves" of curd on each side of the vat. For an hour or two thereafter the cheesemakers would keep turning these loaves over and over until they became quite dry and easy to handle.

One by one the loaves of curd would be put in open-ended round boxes separated by cheesecloth, and taken into an adjoining room which was cool and dark. Here, end to end, they were placed in a long horizontal press where a turnscrew would compress the curds under great pressure. The next morning the boxes, now filled with bland cheese, would be sealed and stacked. Then they were stored for several weeks until they were "cured." On "cheese drawing day" they would be taken to Clayton and shipped from there to Lowville, the cheese center of New York State.

One of the pleasures of my visits to the cheese factory was an opportunity to feast on curds, always a gustatory delight. The cheesemakers were always glad to give you as many handfuls of the rubbery green cheese as desired, and, further, to wrap up a tidy lump in cheesecloth to take home—a largesse, never begrudged, that everybody took for granted.

It was certainly unusual to find a woman in this strenuous business of making cheese but for several successive years Grindstone Island had Mrs. Claflin as its cheese maker, and she proved to be one of the best the island ever had. I always enjoyed going out to the factory and visiting with this strong, wiry woman in her sixties.

I always found her warm, and hospitable despite her reputation among the farmers as being extremely tough and uncompromising with regard to the quality of milk accepted on her weighing platform. We sometimes talked about Mrs. Claflin's name, for there was in New York City a wealthy and notable Claflin family and Mrs. Claflin was a distant relative. I heard much about her life in Little Falls, New York, where oddly enough, the rennet used in our cheese-making was produced in a factory that I had often noticed in going through Little Falls by train. Thereafter when I passed by the high stacks of that Chris Hansen Junket Company I always thought of Mrs. Claflin, wondering what had become of her after she left the island.

Before electricity was brought to the island in 1955 the Grindstone cheese factory had already closed its books. Without refrigeration and other controls that electricity provides, the cheese factory could not meet the demands of stricter and stricter sanitary regulations. Even after electricity arrived, a factory serving so few contributing farms could not hope ever to recoup the cost of the very expensive equipment that the newer laws required. Great plants were rising in Lowville to create a national center of cheese manufacture but our island farmers were excluded from that market by the high cost of shipping their milk ashore and to that place.

The making of the famous Grindstone Island cheese came to an end. All that is left is a legend, like the legend of heather ale. A few connoisseurs remain alive who dare

The Cheese Factory

boast from experience of its unmatched excellence. But today the quality of its cheesy aroma has to be asserted and accepted increasingly on faith.

taken from experience of researches and excellence. But today it is a crude practice, soon it is to be asserted and irregular increasingly on life.

24.
The Post Office

Even more important than the cheese factory as a center for the exchange of news and views was the post office. We have followed the course of the mail from Clayton to the unloading platform at Hi Marshall's store, and the dragging of the heavy canvas bags into the partitioned sanctum that was the post office. The most inclusive assembly on the island was the crowd waiting for the mail to be sorted. It filled all sitting and standing space. Almost every family on the populous north shore, at least, was represented. At the cheese factory, men assembled; here, women and children, too, were present. Summer people and islanders of every kind of livelihood met there on an equal footing, and members of the local church and of other churches and of none. Canadians from Leek Island and from Gananoque, surprisingly, were often there, and especially farmers from the lonely Grindstone shore below the marsh, who were dependent on Thurso for many of their needs. All these people came early and stayed late and met and chatted and became acquainted with each other and made themselves a community.

After the departure of the mail wagon everyone waited for what seemed an interminable time while a great rustling of papers and thumping of packages went on behind the post office partition. There Hi and Flossie were sorting the mail. For a small village the volume of mail was great. Not the least factor in its bulk was the great number of parcel post packages from Sears Roebuck and Montgomery Ward, those great suppliers of farm and family needs in remote places. There were always packages for residents of Gananoque and Leek Island, who ordered American mail-order treasures for delivery here and in their small boats took them illegally across the border. Finally, the sorting finished, the window would open. One by one, the people in the store would step up, receive their mail and soon vanish outside in the bright sunshine. By two o'clock, the store lapsed back into the somnolence of the summer afternoon. Later, stragglers

153

would appear—perhaps one of the Turcottes, who had been working unrelentingly in their vegetable gardens. Sometimes small parties of Canadians lingered long over the merchandise, trying on endless shoes without the least sign of impatience on the part of Flossie or the ever-obliging Hi Marshall.

In these gatherings at the post office we met persons whom we could not meet or know through any other contact. One of these was Billy Gauthier, called Go-chee by all who knew him, a Canadian who carried a large brass-studded pouch for the mail of the Kipp family of Leek Island. The Kipps, of West Orange, New Jersey, summered in a luxurious lodge at the head of Leek Island, overlooking the Wide Waters. They never appeared personally at the post office, yet they were immensely popular on Grindstone Island as donors of the ice cream and cake consumed at the island's ice cream festivals, in which their popular daughters took part merrily. Such distinguished summer people were never at the center of my interests, however. My heart was with the island and the islanders.

Among personalities from Canadian islands who were often seen at the post office were the Sharples family of Netley Island, important in the eyes of Grindstone farmers because they were the manufacturers, in Philadelphia, of the cream separators used on most of their farms. Sometimes they brought guests, to enjoy with them the fascinating rusticity of such a sequestered place. The Sharples were friendly people and their daughters were gay and full of fun. The family was most often represented at the post office, however, by their boatman, Hiram Russell, who lived opposite their island on the U.S. shore. Tall, round-shouldered, clean shaven and neat, Hi Russell was a smooth-talking Lothario, ever attentive to the island women who might be present in any crowd. The girls of Jay Robinson's family were often there, from their home on the border of the upper marsh, and Will Johnson, from far down the river, with whom I had often worked in Dick McRae's harvest fields. These Grindstone families that lived "below the marsh"—i.e., eastward from Thurso—were a distinct sub-community, as dependent upon Thurso as the people of the North Shore Road but much less often seen in the village. Shortly we shall look at the wild coastal country that was their home.

These gatherings at the post office began not later than 1880, when Kate Kelly Black, the wife of Davy Black, was appointed director of Grindstone Island's first post office.

The Post Office

Before that time mail was being brought over from Clayton by ferryboats bound for Gananoque. The ferry boat "Yennek" under captain Kenney was one of these. How the mail reached the island farms I do not know. Nettie McRae's father, Jim Rattray, was the carrier in 1875 and was succeeded in that function by Merrit Garnsey and John Slate—men whom I never knew. In 1909 the carrier was Hub Garnsey, who has been introduced to the reader. He continued to bring the mail to the Grindstone post office almost until his death in 1932. It was Leslie Carnegie of Clayton, the husband of Mrs. Brown's daughter Ella, who won the government contract in that year, and moved to the island and into the tall green house that was being vacated, north of the square, by Harry and Maggie Gordon. Les Carnegie was a capable intelligent man, a redhead who brooked no nonsense. He had once turned down the offer of a job as first mate on the beautiful excursion boat "Alexander Hamilton" that plied our Hudson River waters from New York City to Albany. In my young eyes that position was analogous to sitting at the right hand of the Deity, but Les stayed loyal to the St. Lawrence and was content for several years to carry the mail summer and winter to our island.

Because of the hazards of winter in particular, the Grindstone mail carriers had to be, and were, a special breed, resolute and daring. The firm ice of midwinter was rather safely traversable with special vehicles, but the soft and broken and patchy ice of late autumn and early spring tried mens' strength and courage. Then the main channels of the river are broken into jagged patches and jumbled ice floes, alternating with ribbons of open water occurring helter-skelter. Even in the coldest weather there are open patches along the shores where winds and changes in water level often tear the ice away from the land. Then neither wheels nor runners nor boat bottoms can take man or mail all the way across the river. The mail carriers must resort to strange vessels called "ice punts"—shallow square-ended boats with handles at both ends and with double runners as their keels. They can be pushed over the ice where the ice is solid, and where it is not, the ice punt becomes a boat, paddled with difficulty among the ice-chunks. Where a firm ice shelf rises again, a punt has to be dragged up onto the shelf with much danger and great labor. In recent decades airplane engines have been mounted on these punts to push them along. They have eliminated much of the physical strain from the task of the carrier, but none of the peril. The risks of travel on these ice punts is never inflicted on the high school students of the island. They commute to Clayton during the unfrozen months, but when the river freezes they are lodged in Clayton for the winter.

Les Carnegie's successor in this hazardous occupation was "Let" Conant, the husband of Les' daughter Florence. The Conants lived in mother Brown's former house. Let was a handsome young man, in his late twenties at the time, who carried the mail in summer in an old truck and a large cabin boat called the "U-otta-go." "Let" combined faithfulness to his job with whole-hearted devotion to the bottle. Especially on Saturday nights, he made old Mrs. Brown's onetime pub ring again with guitar music and wild partying. When Let Conant reliquished the job and moved to Clayton, the commission returned to the Garnsey family, where it has rested since. Bob Garnsey, first of the restored dynasty, had a farm on the south shore near the town dock. He was the son of Hub Garnsey by his long-deceased first wife. Tall, broad shouldered, with a heavy ambling stride, Bob Garnsey was quick and explosive in his speech. All business, he never encouraged intimacy. He added to his work with the mail a good deal of activity as an entrepreneur, buying and selling many plots of land on the south shore. After World War II he bought the many buildings of Robert Koenig's onetime camp and moved them to plots on the shore to create highly saleable summer cottages. In the 1960's the postal franchise fell into the strong hands of Francis Garnsey. Francis and his boat the "Debby Lynn" were the last mail carriers of my experience.

25.
The Shore "Below the Marsh"

A glance at a map of Grindstone Island reveals two parallel gashes driven deeply into its northern shore. They appear to be transverse cracks that may have opened at the time of the long fission in the rock that created the river itself. Each cuts more than a mile into the island, dividing it into three distinct realms of human habitation. In the geography of the islanders these indentations are called the Upper Marsh and the Lower Marsh. In published maps the Lower (downriver) Marsh is sometimes called Delaney's Bay. The Lower Marsh separates off from the more westerly parts of the island an almost unpeopled northeastern peninsula. Between the marshes, however, there is rich land that once supported many farms. Thus the Upper Marsh was the north shore's real demographic divider, setting apart a major group known as "the people below the marsh." From the point of view of mainlanders these were the people from beyond the beyond, the wildest of the wild islanders. And indeed they had special difficulties in keeping contact with even the centers of the rustic island.

A description of the Upper Marsh will serve for the lower as well, for they are alike as representatives of a single type of landscape. Mud has no place in the usual scenery of the St. Lawrence, where crystal waters, typically, run over well-washed rock. In that respect, the marshes are different. They are pockets of rich mud, rooting-places for masses of flowers and reeds and bushes not seen elsewhere on the island.

The mouth of the Upper Marsh opens just to the east of Webster Point, in a channel that runs along the east shore of Dick McRae's onetime farm. A long vestibule of water runs southward with great dignity for half a mile, flanked by eye-high cattails on both sides and growing gradually narrower. Then fronds of waterlilies begin to appear. They become so compacted that the channel seems about to close. At the same time a wall of rock rises out of the water ahead—jumbled ledges with heavy forest cover.

It is Long Point, and at first it appears to be the utter end of the Upper Marsh. If one pushes on, however, one finds that it is only a gate standing slightly ajar: at left a ribbon of water circumvents this great spur of rock. Paddling through it, one's view widens out, and beyond Long Point one enters the marvelously different water-world of the marsh proper. One is confronted by a southern sea of reeds and myriad kinds of water plants, and by a maze of inviting water-lanes, several of which can be explored either by canoe or in shallow-draft boats propelled by poles. One gleaming lane turns sharply westward and skirts the rocky southern side of the Long Point peninsula. Green cedars grow thickly on the high ledges and yellow finches flit about, seeking the blue-green berries. In the shallow water at the foot of the slope in those days beavers were always building their brushy homes. On the shore the conical stumps of trees could be seen that the beavers had gnawed and felled. Out in the reeds at left redwinged blackbirds teetered and twittered. Suddenly there would be the scream of a kingfisher as it dove abruptly into a pool from an overhanging tree. Up ahead, as one proceeded, alarmed mud turtles were constantly dropping into the water from jutting rocks and seeking safety by sidling into concealing clumps of underwater weeds. In the thick brown waters along the bottom mysterious mighty swirlings would appear again and again as heavy-bodied creatures—fish or reptiles, who knows?—adjusted to the dangerous intruders. Off in the green thicket of bordering marsh grasses one would hear strange clucks of invisible nesting birds. If one pushed the nose of one's craft into the cattails one might look down into a nest full of open mouths, or send a clutch of baby ducks scurrying away. One heard the constant refrain of song sparrows calling out their lusty invitation, "Poll-Poll-Poll put the kettle on we'll all take tea!"

High on the peninsula again, among great trees, the rock face opens and one could discern then—as one can even now—a pile of cobblestones, and a dilapidated toolshed. It was the work site of Thurso's third quarry. Through the door of the shed a jumble of drills, crowbars, wheelbarrows and sledge hammers could be seen, just where the striking granite-cutters had dropped them. Moving on, one saw looming up ahead, the faces of high monoliths of cut stone. But the channel ends, and one must return to the water-gate where one entered this green ocean.

From that entrance, an alternative channel meanders southward to the neighborhood of the Baseline Road. On it the vistas narrow again and again until forward movement seems impossible; but a hearty stroke of paddle or pole creates a breakthrough and one

The Shore "Below the Marsh"

goes on, and on. Finally, deep in the island, mudbanks rise up out of the water and the heads of cattle appear above the grasses. One has reached terra firma and pastures of the farm of Billy Graham or perhaps of Tom McRae.

Even then, in times of high water, one's exploration does not have to end. By a sharp turn to the right one could push one's canoe almost to the little iron bridge we have noticed before as a former landmark on the Cross-Island Road. That bridge was part of the long detour that any farmer living below the marsh was forced to take if determined to go to the village of Thurso by land. Most preferred to face the difficulties of the water way, protected as it was from wind and waves in most reaches by the fringe of largely Canadian islands that lay off Grindstone's northern shore.

No shoreline road serves the farms along the river in the land below the marsh. By viewing the countryside from the water we see the homesteads from the highway on which they fronted in the conception of their builders. As we proceed eastward by boat from the mouth of the Upper Marsh one's vision clears the tops of the reed-fields at last and plays over a lush country of rolling meadows that rise gradually upward for a full mile to Black's Hill, the highest point on the island. The rocky bluffs that comprise the shore of the island elsewhere are absent in this section. The meadowlands descend to clay banks that drop easily to the water. Cattle stand in the shallow water on hot summer afternoons, wading out to knee depth in the refreshing river. The houses of the farmsteads, most of them gone now, stood well back from the shore on this wind-swept land.

The people of these farms entered into my acquaintance slowly. Practically speaking, their homes were not accessible to Thurso boys whose roaming was by foot. Connection could be made by land only via the Baseline Road and mile-long dirt tracks running northward to the homesteads. But teen-age mastery of small boats finally gave me direct access, by water, to the wondrous territory that lay below the marsh.

We have mentioned Jay Robinson's farm, which lay along the eastern shore of the Upper Marsh. The next farm eastward was still owned in 1909 by a Murdock family who soon thereafter left the island. Then it became the home of Mrs. Brown's daughter, Jessie Carnegie, who took in Davy Black and cared for him there in his last days. Then came Van Slate's shipyard, an unusual establishment. Several decrepit boats were always hauled up there on ways extended out into the water, waiting for the attention of Van, whose real name was Sylvester and who was also called "Old Stearage" for reasons still obscure to me. I remember Van as an old man with a straggling moustache, puttering endlessly on his dock. He was seldom seen in Thurso. Van and his wife Elizabeth lived above the dock in a plain white box of a house reminding me of the homes of rural Maine. Aquiline-nosed Elizabeth Slate was a strong-minded and shrewd old lady. I enjoyed visiting her, and would often beach my skiff and climb to her door and find her peacefully smoking a pipe. We would chat for hours over the soft sound of flies buzzing against the window panes, an old clock intervening from time to time with a spang spang spang while our talk went pleasantly on.

Van Slate was not a farmer. Consequently the land once attached to his plot had been given over to others whose dwellings made up a little settlement about the shipyard. Well back from the shore against a rock face stood a green house on a narrow strip of land, the homestead to which Hub Garnsey retired from the carrying of the mail. Just east of the shipyard Walt Cummings had a cottage, one of the earliest of all summer residences on the island. In a grove of trees nearby stood the house to which old Phrone Slate retreated when she left Thurso Village. Again, south of the shipyard, lay Jim Carnegie's farm, the childhood home of his sons Paul and Les and Corb. Just downhill from their house lay the island's earliest cemetery where burials began to be made in 1830, and nearby also a Slate family burial plot.

Next eastward lay the farm of John Black, who lived with his wife Etta in a charming two-story white house that stood in a grove of trees on a bank by the a riverside. Its white porticoes provided a splendid view upriver to the west. It was a manor that could have held its own with the mansions downstate along the Hudson, had it been preserved, but perception of its worth was lacking on the island, and it moldered away and collapsed like most of the homes I have been mentioning. On a beach below the house stood the Black's pump-house, painted red with a white-framed window in its center. Seen on the river from a distance the pump-house building looked exactly like a target—a highly-identifiable landmark for all navigators. Behind the Black's house, on a knoll, lay the Black family cemetery within an iron fence that enclosed a tall monument. There, in time, John and Etta too would be buried.

The Shore "Below the Marsh"

John Black was one of the island's most prosperous farmers. He was a heavy man with a pleasant face, reticent, and a person of some culture. His wife Etta, was a Hutchinson by birth and a sister of Deed, the wife of Tom McRae. She was a roly-poly woman of pink complexion and pleasant unobtrusive manners. The pair had a son Wella, a young man whose thick purplish lips and puffy eyes gave him a grotesque appearance that one forgot at once when one met him and knew his affectionate nature. Wella and his son Lawrence farmed in Maryland till Wella's father died; then they returned to the island and kept the Black farm running until the 1960's. At that time Mrs. Howard-Smith, a wealthy widow, bought the Black farm, and shortly her son Douglas Howard-Smith bought the Carnegie and Robinson farms as well, and thus consolidated into one great ranch the entire slope running from the Upper Marsh eastward to Black's Hill, the highest point on the Black farm and on the island.

I never came to know John or Etta Black intimately. They came too seldom to the village for that. But the Black farm became very important to me, because of Black's Hill. Many a time I trudged up from the shore to lose myself in enjoyment of the view from its summit. The best prospect was from the north side of the hill's wooded crown. There one looked down on the array of Grindstone's offshore islands, like strung emeralds. On only one or two of them did the outline of any summer cottage obtrude itself in those days, and the coves and channels among the islands gleamed blue, not with the white and red of massed fiberglass hulls at anchor. Beyond the Canadian shore one could see miles of rocky woodlands and very far away a precipitous blue hill, almost a mountain, on the edge of Charleston Lake. Black's Hill seen from the south was a delight-giving vision—the first token of the island that one saw in the spring when coming to the river by train. Black's Hill meant the island. When in September departing trains were carrying the summer's children away from Clayton and the river, Black's Hill again was the logo of the island—the last bit of the island that could be seen as their train chugged southward toward the cities and their waiting schools. One small boy, with nose pressed against the window of the railway car, ordinarily took those last glimpses of Black's Hill with filmed eyes that could scarcely see.

Downriver from the Black farm the shore turns rugged. Clay banks give way to granite cliffs and to small coves alternating with wooded headlands. The farm of Corbett and Dorothy Carnegie lay eastward from the Blacks, their house situated at the point where a rude cross-island road from the lower town landing touched the northern shore. Corb

161

was a steady reliable person who worked all his life as boatman for people "up at the head." Dorothy was Hub Garnsey's merry daughter with whom I played tag—and lost—at the Garnsey house near Hi Marshall's store. Corb and Dorothy had a handsome son, Lloyd. Amiable and modest, he was one of the most promising youths on the island in the 1930's.

The farm of Hi Russell was next in the downriver direction, running southward on the east side of the just-mentioned road from the lower landing. A summer cottage of the Rossmasslers already occupied an enclave in the Russell shoreline, the Russell house itself lying eastward still and set back on a high ledge amid maple trees. The little house of Will and Ella Johnson came next, standing in a grassy glade at the base of a bold peninsula that points downriver like a rocky finger. Taciturn Will lived by odd jobs and by working occasionally as boatman for the Sharples family on nearby Netley Island. Will's lean gaunt head gave him some of the appearance of the Jolly Roger at the masthead of pirate ships. His wife was an unobtrusive dark-haired little woman. They were a childless couple who left little impression, biological or other, on the island. The isolated Ben Calhoun place, well down the river, was in the 1930's the easternmost of the farmhouses on the shore between the marshes. It was located in a deep cove, with its verandas overlooking its dock.

Only two summer cottages yet existed in these several miles of delightful nooks and shelters. The entire eastern half of the island was unexploited—even unfrequented—and very lonely.

The story of the just-mentioned Russells is worthy of a pause here. Hiram and Florence Russell lived on this remote shore, but Hi was much seen at island gatherings, always the too-smooth ladies' man, attentive, flattering and seductive. Just how far Hi actually went in his seeming quest of liaisons is not clear. I never heard of his involvement in any specific scandals. But the facts about his actions hardly mattered: his public manners oozed seductive intent. The air of infidelity about him was perceived by the islanders and surely by Florence herself. She had their sympathy.

Florence Russell was a good-looking woman with honey-colored hair and high cheekbones. In Toulouse Lautrec's painting of the dinner party at the Moulin Rouge the woman at the head of the table is a coarsened image of Florence. Trimly athletic,

The Shore "Below the Marsh"

she used to appear at the store in Thurso after rowing her skiff alone through the islets from her distant downriver home. I perceived her as one who in a more sophisticated milieu would have been the center of a coterie of artistic people. The fate of this flower, however, was to blush unseen and waste its sweetness on the air of a desert isle and on her husband's callousness. She faced the philandering public behavior of her husband with tossed-hair defiance of the indignity involved, and by staying aloof from all island women.

I liked Florence Russell—enough to call on her on one of my rowing expeditions among the islands. Tying up at the Russell's dock I climbed the bluff and knocked on the door of their pleasant green house. Florence was surprised by my visit but responded cordially. Caroline Black, her aged mother, was living with her—an elegant old lady in billowing black taffeta and a corona of odd-colored hair which, I heard later, she dyed with coffee. My call was a pleasant one but for some reason I did not repeat it.

As the years passed Florence, like so many islanders, came to know great suffering that was very physical. In the 1930's she died of cancer. I shall never forget going with Bertha McRae to see her in her last days in a nursing home in Gananoque. As we approached we could hear, even in the street, her unforgettable whimpers of pain drifting down from an open window. A few minutes later we were shocked when we saw her pathetic emaciated body stretched out on her bed. A week later she was dead. Even to this day when I pass the site of her now-vanished house I think of the deeper cancer that she endured with such courage. Which kind of cancer hurts more, I can only guess. Florence knows.

The Russells had a son Clarence—dark, clean-cut—who married and moved to Clayton and lived an honorable and respected life there, dying in the late 60's. It is only fair to say of Hi Russell, who worked for the Rossmasslers occasionally, that someone thought well of him. Sometime after Florence's death, he went with the Rossmasslers to New Jersey, at their invitation, to live with them in his retirement. East of the house of Ben Calhoun the line of the north shore undergoes the deep interruption of the Lower Marsh, which runs so far to the south that only a narrow isthmus preserves the unity of the island at all. The Lower Marsh is a wilderness of water lilies and reeds that is even larger than the Upper Marsh in the center of the island.

It begins as a north-south avenue of great dignity, a water promenade with high impenetrable walls of green reeds on either side. Then it narrows and becomes a morass of water plants so like the inner reaches of the Upper Marsh that it calls for no separate description. Midway down the marsh there is a narrows, and there one sees near the western shore the only human construction on the borders of this swamp. The building of the Lower School stands there still. Always a closed building in my experience, it has been completely closed since World War II began the depopulation of the island. The Baseline Road nears its eastern end here, passing south of the school and on eastward over a causeway and bridge to the eastern shore of the Lower Marsh. There the public road comes to an end. Only private tracks continue into the dense undergrowth of Grindstone's eastern peninsula, a different island world. In a moment we shall look into those trails, but we have a few tales yet to tell about the north shore, tales of several ghastly misfortunes.

26.
Death on the River

At the end of a golden afternoon in summer, the view downriver from the northern massif of the Forsyth quarry is one of the most serene that the world anywhere affords. The calm blue expanse of the Canadian Ship Channel lies straight ahead, and at the right the gleaming white lighthouse on the Punts is the central jewel in the lovely Lake Fleet string of Grindstone's offshore islands. The St. Lawrence does indeed run by with a smile. The ship channel runs alongside this chain and at a certain gap passes through it. It makes no moiling as it does so that is visible, nor is there any flaw anywhere in the benign calm that extends downriver as far as the eye can see.

Before one becomes utterly lost in the peace of that scene one does well to notice, on charts, the names of some of the islands in view: Deathdealer, Bloodletter and Dumfounder—names surely given by traversers of this reach of the river who found it to be less maternal than it seems. And in fact the historical lore of the river records two shocking events that occurred in the waters just off this lovely lighthouse. Both disasters involved aspiring islands beneath the surface, that never rose up with their fellows to attain full visibility. They remained below as reefs. Our stories tell of how these reefs wrought deadly mischief in two quite different ways.

Some of these underwater pinnacles were high enough to threaten keels and to worry the creators of the Canadian Ship Channel. Early in 1913 the Canadian government undertook to remove a menace and straighten the channel by blasting away an underwater rock formation near the Punt lighthouse. In the spring of that year a drill boat came up from Montreal and anchored over the offending rocks. Its sides bristled with stanchions that held long drill bits. With these drills the crews began to bore deep holes in the granite below them. Daily, when these holes had been filled with dynamite, the drill ship would be moved far away and the charges would be detonated, breaking portions of the reef into removable fragments. Twenty-two drillers, divided into night and day shifts, worked at this removal night and day throughout the spring months. But it was slow work that continued into the summer. Islanders and summer people occasionally rowed by to note the progress of the project but little of the operation could be seen, hidden as it was beneath the surface of the water. Some of the workmen lived quietly in their nearby houseboat, some came and went from Gananoque, but none came to our post office or stores. We ceased to be mindful of them and their enterprise. Now and then we heard the muffled boom of a submerged blast, and that was all.

On Wednesday July 9th, 1913 the drilling proceeded as always. The noise of the chattering drills was monotonous and unremarkable. Thirteen drill holes were bored during the day, and as dusk approached the day crew finished their work by tamping into them 130 pounds of dynamite. As they were rigging the charges for the detonation that would end their day, a darkening of the sky occurred that was not clearly distinguishable from the darkness of the approaching evening, and then a typical summer thunderstorm, with noisy wind, moved over the river and the islands. Grindstone island people retreated into their houses and sat down to supper and were not much disturbed as jagged bolts of lightning lit the sky and shook the earth again and again. No single flash, no special clap seemed greater than the others. In time the storm moved on down the river in a familiar pattern. Silence returned, save for peaceful dripping from the eaves. Farmers who would have to rise at cockcrow went to bed with the chickens as usual and slept soundly, totally unaware until morning of what the night had wrought.

While the drillers of the day were finishing their work with the dynamite, and were preparing to cast off and remove the drill boat from the scene, the electrical charge in the black clouds above was attracted to a protruding drill rod still seated in the rocks. A bolt descended and the whole store of explosives went off. The steam boiler of their ship also burst. Every man was lifted into the air and hurled far, and not one escaped serious injury. Backs were broken, legs and arms were broken, and, worst of all, the crashing and flashing of the storm kept the occurrence from being noticed on the island or on the mainland. The few survivors who were able to move had no means of going for help. Only the arrival of the night shift revealed the devastation of equipment and of men. The first rescue boat that set out from its dock in the Gananoque River struck a pier in its hasty exit and was delayed in its arrival on the scene. On Grindstone Island we slept sweetly through it all.

Death on the River

Our account of the second disaster takes us forward a full twenty years. The time is the early thirties. The reach of the river remains the same. Again it is a matter of the channel through the islands, and of the reefs between the islands that often rise up toward the surface there, unseen. Not in this case, either, were these rocks to tear a vessel asunder as in familiar tales of marine disaster elsewhere. It was a question of the effect of these sunken rocks upon the speed of the currents when they were forced to make their way through the impeded passages between the islands. Forced through the narrow gaps they pick up speed, and swirl with special turbulence around and over the sunken rocks. These roilings create great differences, in winter, between one spot and another in the speed of freezing and in the thickness of ice—differences totally invisible to anyone who views the ice in its usual light covering of snow. This is a winter's tale, not of ships but of cars, and of a couple bound for Canada in an Essex automobile.

They had come from Syracuse, and in that age of moral rectitude their venture was clandestine. For they were not man and wife. Driving over the ice, they were bound for Canada and for freedom, escaping the fury of their respective spouses.

They had rounded the foot of Grindstone Island safely and were driving up through its offshore islands, intending to venture out upon the broad reach of ice below Leek Island and reach Gananoque, whose winter lights glittered bright on the Canadian mainland. Here, where the river was broadest, the downstream current was generally slack, and that was deemed to insure solid ice "that would bear a car."

They passed Deathdealer and approached the last islands of the group. One was high and bristling with pines, with a bald granite knob. As one came down the Leek Island Channel from the west, it could be seen ahead for miles. Next to it is a smaller island known appropropriately now as Ghost Island. Together they comprise the group called "The Punts." Both islands are surrounded by hidden rock shoals, and the current there becomes rapid.

The Syracuse travelers, unfamiliar with the vagaries of ice and currents, were soon on thin ice. The ice cracked, the car broke through. In an instant it sank and disappeared, carrying its passengers, trapped inside, into the depths.

For several days, the hole in the ice was not seen by anyone. Then the tracks and the snow-free spot in the ice were noticed and understood. The islanders gathered and grappled for the car, Frank Slate taking the lead among them. Somehow, they recovered the woman's body. But the driver's side of the car was inaccessible. They could not extricate the body of the man. The winter weather became severe and finally they decided to defer all further effort until spring. Then the man's body was at last recovered.

It was Frank Slate, finally, who was able to raise the car, using the gear of the Slate shipyard. He brought the car to the island. It was never claimed by any heir. Since the folk law of Grindstone Island has never recognized New York's authority to register or license island cars, Frank got involved in no formalities. He took full possession of the car. For years, it was a familiar sight as Frank drove it on the island roads. But the car always carried a grim reminder of its history. On the leather of the driver's seat a large white blotch remained, marking the spot on the upholstery where, to the end of winter, the body of the philanderer had rested. No cleanser was found that ever could remove it. A pale scarlet letter, it continued to remind restive island men of the dubious fruits of adultery.

For much lesser offenses—mere unwariness, for instance—many a time the St. Lawrence took other lives, some in a careless tumble from a boat. Thus it was with Duke Moneau, and Willie the eldest son of Emmet Dodge; and Alden Pettit, grandson of the Turcottes, and with a son of Orlando Potter. Charley Soulier, who had moved with his family into old Mrs. Brown's house after her death, set out one winter day to walk to Gananoque but got no further than the troubled waters and rotten ice under the cliffs of Kalaria. His body was found in spring, wrapped around the intake pipe of the water system of a summer cottage. And there were a few others who were the rivers' victims. However, in all this account of death on the river, I have no tales to tell of homicide, on water or on land—or even of robbery, in the whole century open to my knowledge. No sheriff or sheriff's deputy has ever resided on the island. Effective surveillance by officers of the law is not the explanation of this remarkable fact. This community of about three hundred people lived throughout remembered time in a state of apparent anarchy but without violence. In their tradition they found no justification for bloodletting.

27.
Canoe Point

Facing eastward at the bridge across the Lower Marsh, one enters a roadless peninsula, attached to the main body of the island by a mere thread of land. It is Grindstone Island's third world, a tail of the island that is very different and very broad, and yet nameless. For lack of better language the whole is sometimes spoken of loosely as Canoe Point, after the very popular state park now located on its northern tip. Here below the Lower Marsh the wildness of Grindstone Island reaches its apogee, the supposed wildness of the islanders giving way now to true wildness of terrain. Before the coming of the summer cottage, and even now, the plough has hardly mattered here. I have heard of only two efforts to wrest a living from the soil, and those efforts did not last long.

Near the beginning of the track that continued beyond the bridge lived Josiah and Ida McAvoy and their large family, in a low ranch house with ample verandas. Of the McAvoys I knew principally the children. A daughter named Ruth was a beautiful girl—in my father's pronouncement the most beautiful he had ever seen. There was a son Si, a harum-scarum young fellow. He had the distinction of bringing to Grindstone its first automobile—a touring car in which we often saw him on summer evenings at our crossroads store in Thurso. Si died very young of pneumonia or a like disease. Not long after, the McAvoys left the farm.

Further north and nearer the end of the peninsula lay the Delaney farm. Still operating in 1909 when I first came to the region, it ceased to be farmed in the following year. We have met Eliza Delaney Marshall, a daughter of that Delaney family, at the store in Thurso, and have noticed her merry guests, her relatives from the foot of the island. Old Mrs. Delaney was a sprightly little woman, wizened and shrunken but with bright eyes. Her lips were drawn tight over a few remaining rodent teeth that gave her the look of a cheery little squirrel. A widowed daughter, Bertha Martin, plump, assured and capable, managed a successful shoe store in Watertown while her sister Allie, a subdued spinster, seemed entirely content to take care of Bertha's children—Barbara, Junior and Bill. Eliza did not resemble these sisters of hers in any way, nor did Eliza's daughter Mary resemble any of her Delaney kinfolk. Tall thin and tense, she graduated from St. Lawrence University and then married Stanley Phelan and left the island to live entirely in Chicago till her very recent death. The Delaneys were a Roman Catholic family but they made little manifestation of their faith save refraining from attendance at any other church. Neither Hi nor Eliza took any part in the worship of the Grindstone church, but Eliza mingled cordially in such church events as slide shows and ice cream socials and contributed generously to potluck suppers.

When the Delaneys stopped farming, saplings of course began their work. The farm buildings began to sag. Before the second world war Clarkson University used the area for some years as a training ground for its students in surveying. Then the land was totally abandoned. The buildings fell to the ground and all signs disappeared that a farm had ever been there.

Such abandonment was not to be the fate, however, of the area north and east of the onetime Delaney farm. There, on an extensive shoreline acreage at the northeastern extremity of Grindstone Island, stood a glacial drumlin, a high conical hill covered with windswept grass. A spot of great beauty, it provided splendid views of the Lake Fleet and Navy groups of Canadian islands to the north. As late as the 1880's the St. Regis tribe of Indians, once the recognized owners of Grindstone Island, were still using this point as an occasional camping ground. In 1892 the State of New York acquired the point for public use. For a long time it was called merely "the state land," since it did not yet enjoy the status of a state park.

In 1910 Chet Reese of Clayton, Gertrude Webster's brother, was supervisor of the Town of Clayton. It was a position that included some responsibility for the oversight of Grindstone Island. He conceived a project that was most unusual for its time: that of planting "the state land" in oak trees. And it was done: he planted the entire drumlin in trees. Now, after eighty years, they magnify the hill's apparent height and clothe it in the dense foliage of great interlocking oaks. "Uncle Chet's" vision was foresighted, and the rising forest is a delight now to the campers and boatmen who crowd the shore of the Canoe Point State Park. How can one uttter any word today that casts a shadow on this achievement, in a time when the nobility of planting trees ranks with honoring God and country? Yet sometimes I do murmur, none the less, that I rather wish Canoe Point were still a windswept open hill with summer breezes surging through golden grass, and that I could climb it and see the broad river and its islands once again.

I cannot take much further this survey of island homesteads as they occurred in close geographical sequences. The Baseline Road might seem to claim attention, but in fact almost no farms faced on it, from the Lower School to Flynn Bay on the western shore. There at last a full-scale farm was encountered. The original surveyors of the island created the Baseline Road as only the back alley, so to speak, of the island farms. The cheese factory was the one center of human concourse on all the desolate miles of the Baseline Road. A mile or so east of the cheese factory on the north side lay the foreshortened little Billy Graham farm, connected with the world necessarily by the Baseline Road because the Upper Marsh blocked it from access to the river. The isolation of the Grahams was extreme. I was never aware of the existence of their lonely house save when, rarely on a summer evening, a speck of light from one of its windows could be seen from our camp on Webster Point. We knew nothing about Billy Graham other than the fact that he had two daughters, who came to church. One, Belva, who married Alec Lember, saved the Graham place from the usual ruin by living in it in her retirement until about 1990 as a very aged widow.

Unlike the heart of the island, the south shore was peopled early and fully. A description of the eminent residents in the setting of their homes wouid be interesting, but impossible for me to write, because I almost never travelled the difficult cross-island roads to visit them. It was only as churchgoers, that I knew them and, will be able later on, to speak of them. I have already mentioned persons who were often seen at the upper town landing, and I shall tell of other acquaintances who worked at two camps located on the south shore.

28.
Mary Crouch

In the twenties and thirties on Grindstone Island, there were two boys' camps. They were as different as night and day. At the eastern extreme of Aunt Jane's Bay lay Camp Frontenac, run since 1909 by one Robert Koenig. He was a tall blond man with hair *en brosse* and a marked Prussian look about him that brooked no nonsense. He recruited his campers from his school in New York City. Herr Koenig ruled his young campers with an iron hand. They were mainly Jewish boys and it was a nice irony that these families entrusted their children to a Prussian-style martinet. The camp's counselors would take the boys on occasional hikes around the island and bring them to Hi Marshall's store where they would make quick forays upon the candy and cookie counters and then depart. Neither counsellors nor campers were a genial lot, so I learned little about them. As I recall, the Koenig camp survived the First World War and continued into the thirties when the director retired and left. The land was then bought by Hub Garnsey's eldest son, Bob, who made a good thing of moving its abandoned buildings to various sites along the river to create valuable summer cottages.

Quite different was the smaller Tip Camp, located on the South Shore westwards from the town dock at a spot where young Ray and Lolita Pfeiffer now have their summer home. Tip Camp was established in the early twenties by Walter Crouch—a man as unlike Herr Koenig as one could possibly imagine. He was a heavyset man with a large round florid face, who always wore a large straw hat. He was a warm man—even a little too demonstrative in his geniality. He was a teacher at the Friends Central School in a western suburb of Philadelphia and he and his boys were all Quakers. They were bright, likable, gregarious lads, more athletic than the boys at Camp Frontenac and more open to friendships with people of the island. Mr. Crouch was always very kind to me. He died in the late thirties and the camp was closed, but his old campers for many years thereafter kept returning for sentimental visits to the camp site and the island.

After the closing of the camp, Walter Crouch's wife Mary lived on in their large house on the edge of the river, after renovating it for more comfortable living. She was a plain woman whose facial lines made me think of a parrot. Like Herr Koenig, she was a no-nonsense sort of person and there was little of the sentimental in her character. Business was in her blood, and she prided herself on her efficiency and orderliness, which had helped her husband make the camp a success. The people who worked for her had to submit to her methodical ways. It was said that, as employer, she had given Lizzie Rouse a hard time, and I do not doubt it.

If Mrs. Crouch had within her some small spark of sentimentality, I believe she reserved it for me in those last years, before World War II threw the island world into chaos. After Walter's death, I would often walk across the island using little-known trails that brought me out at the Crouch Place. She was always effusively glad to see me. We would play croquet together as the shadows grew long and then she would insist that I stay for supper and for some savory dessert she knew I liked. To see her one fine day with my favorite north wind blowing I sailed around the island instead of walking, and landed at the Crouch dock. Though surprised at my unusual arrival "by sea," she gave me her usual warm welcome. The wind was still fair and the river was blue and sparkling under a cerulean sky. Its call was irresistible. I suggested to Mrs. Crouch that she join me in a sail down river. We would tack against the wind as far as pleased us, and then the northwind, behind us, would quickly blow us home.

Mrs. Crouch showed a schoolgirlish eagerness for the idea. "Oh, that would be wonderful!" she exclaimed. "Wait till I get a hat."

For a woman of her age, she was remarkably slim and agile. She ran down to the dock and settled herself in the boat and we were off. The sailing was glorious. We tacked two miles or so down river before we decided to return to Tip Camp—and then the northwind we had counted on to blow us home began to fall off! Soon we were wallowing along slowly against the current. After a half-hour, Tip Camp seemed no nearer. The wind had become a whisper.

Suddenly, Mrs. Crouch, who sat behind me, spoke. "How soon do you think we'll get home?" she asked.

Mary Crouch

"Oh, in half or three-quarters of an hour," I replied.

The course we were sailing ran parallel to the island's south side. After a moment or two, she spoke again "Do you think we could get to the shore over there?" she asked. "I think it would take us as long to get over there as it would to get home," I replied.

There was silence for a few moments. Then suddenly Mrs. Crouch burst forth and there was urgency in her voice. "Oh Stanley, do you have a sponge?"

At last I awoke to the situation, and knew exactly what she needed. Any half-witted moron would have known by that time. "Oh, I've got much better than that", I told her. "I've got a bailing pail". "Oh wonderful!" she exclaimed fervently.

I reached for the pail and handed it back to her. Then I went forward about some business with the sails From that time, I felt that I was a member of the family! I corresponded regularly with her over the years until, in the mid-50's, she died.

29.
The World Wars and the Rum War

The first world war had no great impact upon me, or on the island. The few men who went to war were much older than I. I barely knew them. And the islanders were not greatly impressed, apparently, with the tales current in 1917 of Kaiser Wilhelm's wicked Huns bayoneting infants and frying scarce fats from human corpses. But on the north shore of Grindstone Island that war did bring some spectacular developments. The Kipp family opened their rustic retreat on Leek Island to the Canadian armed forces as a convalescent hospital for wounded soldiers. Soon limping men in uniforms were swarming over the island with their white-coated nurses. Surprisingly, they were a jolly lot. They loved to row across the Leek Island Channel in skiffs. We saw much of them on the McRae farm on Grindstone, and at the Saturday night ice cream festivals at the church. The McRae girls were the first to welcome them and the other island girls joined in the merrymaking. There were the inevitable crushes. Bertha's fancy was caught by a high-spirited Irish boy named Joe Flynn who was very engaging in his white sailor's uniform and his black curly hair and charming grin. Fifty years later she still cherished fond recollections of his sunny ways. He was soon gone, however, like the others, and we never heard of him again.

Fishing was of course an especially suitable diversion for convalescent men. Three or four skiffs were soon poking about Leek Island's shores, and then venturing out into the currents of the channel. Now a round-bottomed St. Lawrence skiff is an excellent boat for rough waters, but it does not tolerate the liberties that landlubbers in careless ignorance persistently take. Inevitably the inexperienced convalescent men and their equally inexperienced nurses took such risks, and one fair summer day two skiffs capsized in the Leek Island Channel. Two soldiers and two nurses were drowned. Now the sad ritual was enacted that always follows such events, Dick McRae and Hi Marshall playing the principal roles as always in the grim business of searching for the bodies. The sight of slow-moving boats in formation, dragging their lines in a systematic search after a drowning, is not something that one ever forgets.

At the end of the war the Leek Island Hospital of course closed. Soon after, the Kipps' great mansion burned and was replaced by a modest central lodge and a cluster of surrounding cottages. These facilities were used for some years by the Kipps and their many guests. Then the Canadian government took over the island to create a national park. The buildings that were not destroyed, decayed. Today the lovely island has reverted to a wilderness.

World War I was followed in this border region by the decade-long war between U.S. federal agents and the rumrunners. This was a guerilla war, in as much as it was of the essence that the operations be covert. I do not claim to know how deeply Grindstone Island people may have been involved in it. But the forbidden liquor was only three miles away on the Canadian shore, and those miles were a maze of islands and of dangerous water passages known only to the initiated. The labyrinth certainly made Grindstone well-positioned for illegal liquor traffic. With snickers and knowing smiles, people make sly innuendos even today about the island's role in rum running during that noble experiment, Prohibition. But I doubt that many islanders were involved. It was too sophisticated a business. The real rumrunners were agents of the big city syndicates, who could afford fast boats, bribes, scouts, radios and all the other paraphernalia of an organized operation. Those outsiders undoubtedly made use of Grindstone in their fast night runs across the river from one mainland rendezvous to another, but if the islanders knew about them, they said nothing. A case of Scotch brought over from Gananoque in innocent wrappings sometimes ended up in Clayton, I'm sure, via Grindstone, but not as a part of a commercial enterprise. It was done as a favor for a friend or business acquaintance. And occasional bottles were easily carried in a string-bag or suitcase. Never did I know any government agent to examine anything that came into Clayton on the Grindstone mailboat. For Grindstone, there was a presumption of innocence.

However, I am fairly sure that one or two islanders were involved in liquor trafficking. One of these was Duke Moneau. As I remember him, he had a wild clownish way about him that made him different from the other islanders. Rakishly dressed in boots and a hunting cap he guided fishing parties on the river, and was famed as "The Muskie

The World Wars and the Rum War

King" in that capacity. At other times, he worked at odd jobs wherever he could find them. In short he was a "river rat." Duke had married Aleitha, Ben Calhoun's daughter, and lived down at the foot of Grindstone in a lonely place.

Later, Duke and Aleitha moved to Mrs. McIntosh's old house in Thurso. I don't think I ever said five words to Duke in all my life, for his orbit was far removed from mine. His comings and goings were always mysterious and for that reason, I always surmised that Duke made good use of his fast boat to carry more than fishermen. He had the reputation for partaking with much gusto, himself, of the cup that cheers. He partook of that cup once too often, for one night he did not come home, and his body and his boat were found among the weeds in very shallow water. The conclusion was that he had fallen out of his boat too intoxicated to raise himself up. Aleitha's mourning period was brief. Very soon she married Harry Slate.

The first World War had inflicted no great harm and brought no great changes in the island. The second World War was longer and its impact upon the island and upon me was greater. It was not that the second war took greater toll of island life, but that the persons who served in the second war were men of my generation, men whom I knew. Their names are all remembered on a plaque in the island church. Only one lad did not return. That was Lloyd Carnegie, the son of Dorothy and Corb Carnegie. The family lived on the north shore near Black's Point. Their tall son Lloyd had an engaging way with him that won everyone's liking instantly. His laugh was full of innocence and he was ever pleasant. I remember him as the most attractive boy I had ever known on the island. Little wonder that Dorothy was devastated when in 1945 a telegram came saying that his plane had been shot down in the Pacific and all aboard had been lost. It was a blow from which Dorothy never recovered. She was bitter up to the time of her death thirty-eight years later. The war had taken the most promising of all the island's youth. Was the weapon that brought Lloyd down made from the iron, perhaps, which the Japanese had salvaged from the deserted Grindstone quarries?

In taking the life of even one of the island's youth the impact of the war was acute, but the island's great wartime loss of population did not occur on the battlefield. The war that drew a few islanders into military service drew many more into the industrial cities to serve in offices and factories. Successful in the country's centers, and savoring the pleasures and opportunities of urban life, they had little reason to return to scratch a living again from the rocky soils of a disadvantaged island. Few did so. Tilling stopped on farm after farm as the old people of island families retired. The Marshall store ceased to thrive and soon closed. Gasoline was not sold any longer at the McRae dock. Bertha McRae would—only in the summer time—keep a tiny general store, the last on the island. The cheese factory would soon cease operations. The course of postal service is another story of decline which we shall tell later. The end of World War II marked the beginning of the end of an era.

30.
Bertha and Mabel McRae

No two people could have been more unlike than the two McRae sisters. So different from the calm and placid Mabel, Bertha was forceful, mercurial, and unpredictable. She had little concern with domesticity. Her interests followed a more intellectual bent.

Much more ambitious than the home-loving Mabel for whom such intellectual interests were unthinkable, Bertha persuaded her father to put her through normal school at Cortland, New York. On graduation she began to teach in the one room country schools in the north country, first in a small school on Wellesley Island, then in the Lower School on Grindstone, and later in the Upper School at the Crossroads. After a year or two she accepted a position in the public schools of Tuckahoe in Westchester County, and there she remained for the remainder of her teaching career, teaching classes of backward children.

Bertha's hair was brown, her eyes blue, and her mouth could in a flash change from a delighted grin to a scornful sneer. She was taller and more aggressive than her sister. Ordinarily she was slow-spoken, hesitating for the right word, and speaking finally with a slight lisp. She seemed sometimes almost to have a speech defect like her father, who, as we noted, had a very marked one. Like so many of the north country people, she accentuated her R's and her speech was always precisely articulated. Again like her father, on outings she could be exuberant and full of fun.

Yet she could be tart and voluble. I realized that her reputation in this regard was more widespread than I had thought when I heard a man in Clayton giving directions to some workmen who were going to the Island: ".. and you go down the road to the house by the river where there is a little store run by a woman who talks too much. Ask anyone. They'll tell you where it is."

Bertha had a strong feeling for what she thought right, and when she felt justice had been disregarded, she could lash out with intense anger. Sometimes her reactions were hasty, with unhappy consequences. I experienced her outrage on one occasion long after she had retired to the old farmhouse on Grindstone. On Bertha's recommendation I had rented a garage for the summer from an old woman in Clayton. And now in mid-season, when garages were hard to get, the old lady had announced that she was going on welfare. The move involved a condition that she have no outside income such as my rental payment of six dollars a month. I suggested to the old lady that she tell the welfare people that she had a rental contract with me for the summer and that she did not wish to break it. Would they permit her to honor her commitment? They would either accept or refuse her request. It was as simple as that.

The old woman vehemently refused to make that petition. She could not take a chance on losing her precious welfare. I tried to tell her that she was taking no chance if she explained matters. But the old woman became defiant and I departed to seek another garage. I thought that was the end of the matter. But when I returned to the island late that afternoon, I called in at Bertha's on some errand or other. To my astonishment, I was met with vituperation. "You should be ashamed of yourself, trying to cheat that old lady out of her welfare. She has no other way of supporting herself. She needs that money and it is a contemptible trick to try to cheat her out of it." I tried to explain the situation to Bertha, in vain. Then I left her quickly and went home, a little angry myself.

She soon forgot the matter and our relationship continued as it always had, with pleasant talks of the books we had read, of the activities of mutual friends, and of island affairs and old times, for Bertha was always interested in the history of the region.

Relentless memory recalls another occasion, some 70 years ago, in which Bertha had given me a taste of her angry temper. It was completely unexpected and completely unjustified. The island girls had been swimming off the McRae dock, of a hot August afternoon, and Bertha had gone upstairs to change. Her bedroom overlooked the path from the dock to the house and I had just come up that path and was standing on the lawn in front of the veranda, talking with someone. Suddenly Bertha appeared, came up to me, face red with rage and slapped me smartly across my face. "There!" she said angrily. "That will teach you not to go peeking into upstairs bedrooms." And she flounced off. I don't think I have been more astonished in my life. It is possible that inadvertently, I may have glanced upward as I walked up that path but I had been completely innocent of peering into anyone's bedroom. At the thought of this 20-year old girl's accusation, I still find myself a little resentful.

I am sure that Bertha was always conscious of sex, unlike her serene sister Mabel, who had but one love affair in her life and that with the man she married. Bertha was always involved with one man or another over the years. All of them dropped out of her life, one by one. Her quick temper probably had something to do with her spinsterhood.

Her first young man was Paul Houghton with whose family she boarded during her first teaching in the school on Wellesley Island. Her friendship with the Houghton family lasted for years, but Paul was to marry someone else. Bertha always spoke warmly of him and apparently cherished no resentment over their lost love-affair.

Next in order was a young Clayton man, Potter Kelly. That relationship was intense, protracted over several years, and recorded in many photos I have seen in albums in the McRae's parlor. In most of these Bertha was reclining, fishing rod in hand, in the stern of a St. Lawrence skiff with Potter at the oars. This affair eventually broke up. Potter went to Syracuse to marry and become an engineer in charge of Syracuse's water supply. He returned to the island to summer in a house he built on waterfront land west of the McRae farm. One rainy morning in the late 40's I rode with him, now a widower, across the island. I found him a churlish old man and knew why Bertha was not interested in seeing him again, despite the fact that he was now a near neighbor.

Her next romance, in the mid-thirties, was intense and the most enduring of all. I think that Bertha never outgrew her attraction for this man. He was Bert McFadden, a swarthy slender man with jet black hair and a saturnine thin-lipped face. He had fine ascetic features and a vaguely sullen air that, oddly, made him extremely good looking. Bert came from across the island, of gracious parents and a genteel family. I knew the McFaddens through their active participation in the island church, and liked them. Bertha, on holiday from her teaching in Tuckahoe, would spend Sundays on the river with Bert whenever Bert was not working as boatman for the Bakewell family from New York City who had a summer home on the south shore.
Occasionally there were clandestine meetings between Bert and Bertha that stirred up

snickering talk; and once at a time when my mother had been asked to watch over the McRae house during Dick and Nettie's absence, Bert lied to my mother about where he had been with Bertha. I don't think my mother ever forgave Bert for the deceit. In the light of today's morals, Bert's conduct would be a joke, but at the time, it seemed offensive.

Bert McFadden's relationship with his employer, Alan Bakewell, was unusual. I had met Alan one time on the night-train from New York. He was blonde and handsome and I had found him unusually warm and personable. I was usually intimidated and reticent with the wealthy summer people but Alan was different. I liked him much more than I liked Bert, who regarded me, I think, as a nuisance. The two men were inseparable. Some years later, in the late 40's or early fifties, I heard that Alan had divorced his wife and was spending more and more time on the river. He and Bert were now taking long fishing trips in a cabin cruiser that the Bakewells owned. Rumor had it that it was well stocked with liquor. One autumn morning in the 1950's, the police found the Bakewell cruiser tied up at the Town Dock in Clayton in front of the Old Town Hall, and then they found two bodies in the river. One was Alan Bakewell's, the other, Bert McFadden's. The theory was that they had been drinking, that one had fallen overboard and that the other had tried to rescue him, and both had drowned. I think that Bertha never got over the tragedy.

Not long after, Bertha retired from teaching. She took possession of the old farmhouse at McRae Point that Dick had willed to her along with the farm. In the summer she lived there alone thereafter, taking an apartment in Clayton in the winter. Mabel's family kept her company during long holidays on the island. For some years the two sisters and their families made happy use of the McRae place, which remained the same save that the gasoline tanks were gone, and the little store was abandoned.

Bertha had one last courtship with a bachelor farmer who lived at Green's Corners on the road to Watertown. Carl Gailey was a lean gangling amiable man, highly intelligent in his rustic way. Bertha saw much of him in the '60's. I recall driving to Watertown one day with Bertha and as we passed the Gailey farmhouse, clearly visible to the east of the highway, Bertha exclaimed, "Just think! One of these days I may be living there." She was happy at the thought. But experience had taught me, with regard to Bertha and marriage, that a rough road would have to be traveled first. . She and Carl saw each other for several years—dinners together in Watertown, visits on the island—and

Bertha and Mabel McRae

then very gradually, I heard no more of Carl.

In the 1970's, Bertha was stricken with Parkinson's disease. Slow in onset, it worsened insidiously until in the middle of the decade she was compelled to seek refuge in nursing homes, first in Watertown and finally in Cape Vincent. I visited her as often as I could and she was always pathetically glad to see me. Weak and feeble as this horrible disease left her, she always made a brave effort to introduce me to fellow patients: "This is Dr. Norcom," she would say proudly. "I have known him ever since he was a little boy." She would add with a little smile, "When he first came to Grindstone Island, I was twice as old as he was. We have had many good times together." It was true. Indeed, we had had small differences of which you have read here, but they were minor. I was very fond of Bertha and honored her over the long years. Our families had grown very close. We were like kinfolk. Even Mrs. McRae in her last years had mellowed and I had come to like her. In fact, I felt much closer to the McRaes than I did to some of my own blood-relatives. Bertha became the last with whom I could share many old memories such as those recorded here. With her death much that had made life on the island meaningful to me was gone.

Mabel, the younger of the two sisters, was a plain kindhearted child whose interests were, and always would be, exclusively domestic. As a little girl, "Madie" would build doll-houses in a lilac thicket down on the riverbank in front of the old farmhouse and persuade me to join her in moving her dolls about and creating new rooms for her little family. As she grew older she was quite content to stay at home and help her mother in the little McRae store. Finally, she came of age and married Earl Cummings of the Cummings family across the Island. They lived in Clayton and there Mabel continued to keep a house that was immaculate and replete with modern conveniences unknown on Grindstone. She gave birth to four children. Mabel's husband was an engineer on one of the great ore boats that plied the Great Lakes and thus he was usually away from home from March to November. Alone for three fourths of the year, Mabel had the task of raising her little family with only an occasional letter from Earl, mailed in Conneaut or Chicago or Duluth, to help her carry on. I always felt her life was sad although I sometimes wonder if her total devotion to domesticity may not have mercifully saved her from introspection. But nothing saved her from the sorrow, in 1929, of losing her little girl Shirley at age three. And her son Johnny, 30 years later, was killed in an ambulance accident when he was on an errand of mercy. The death of this amiable boy was overwhelming and its pain was lasting. Both Mabel and Bertha had always been active in the Grindstone church, and Mabel transferred her devotion to the Clayton Methodist Church and drew much comfort from it. When Earl died 11 years later, in 1970, Mabel carried on with the strong support of her two children, Ruth and Richard.

Over the years Mabel seemed to shrivel. In the spring of 1980, when I arrived late one afternoon in Clayton, I was surprised by how little she was when she met me at the door. I took her to dinner at a pleasant restaurant on Cape Vincent; and we talked over old times on Grindstone. I think for her it was a rare treat, as it was for me. I always enjoyed visiting with this kindly warmhearted woman, now, like myself, grown old.

Mabel McRae

It was the last time I was to dine with Mabel. Again a year later, I arrived in Clayton on a late spring afternoon, and I was looking forward to taking Mabel again to dinner and to renewal of our talk of old times. When I went to the door on her little side-porch that I always used, it was locked, and no one responded to my knock. Then a neighbor told me that Mabel had been taken to a nursing home in Cape Vincent, hopelessly disoriented. She died there a year later, in 1982. Tolstoi once said "We all lead tragic lives and are destined for miserable ends." Whether Mabel's life was tragic or not I cannot say, but surely her end was miserable, as was that of so many of the islanders. With Mable gone, I no longer had any more intimate friends in Clayton. I became a stranger to the little town and have remained one since.

31.
The Church

Directly across the road from Hi Marshall's store stood the Grindstone Methodist Church, having a tall white spire in those days, pointing to heaven. It was as truly the center of the spiritual life of the island as the store was the center of its commerce. The church too was unrivaled. There were islanders who had no doings with that church, but not through attendance at any other. Dick and Nettie McRae had a grievance against the Lord, as we have mentioned, over Dick's loss of an eye in His service. For Charlotte McIntosh and for Hub Garnsey and his family, staying away from church was part of their general shunning of the island social life. For the Delaneys and the Marshalls and a few others, Catholics in heritage if not in practice, a residue of Roman Catholic feeling no doubt kept them separate in religious matters. All other islanders acknowledged a tie to the Grindstone Methodist Church. Some people were known as conventional church-goers, others as ardent. Other than this subtle line, religious division was never manifest. Acceptance of the title "Methodist" did not betoken any special sectarian zealotry, but rather a gratitude to the regional conference of that denomination for assistance in finding clergy. Preachers, like cheesemakers, often needed special urging to accept assignment to a small institution on a remote island. The islanders as a whole have prized their church as a part of their identity, and empty pews on a Sunday morning have never been a problem.

The Grindstone church was typical of little country churches of northern New York: a wooden church of white clapboard with a steeple in which a bell was hung—but in this case never rung because it had been hopelessly cracked. Beyond a small vestibule lay the sanctuary, and beyond it, a Sunday school room. On a low platform in the front of the sanctuary, separated by an altar rail, there was a pulpit, and, off to one side, an oaken reed organ. In the floor of the central aisle leading up to the pulpit a large bronze hot-air register was set, indicating that there was a basement space below and a stove for heating the church in winter. This was the stove that had cost Dick McRae his eye, and the church one of its pillars. The heating arrangement indicated that it was not for summer people that the church had originally been built. Another indication was the narrow gothic windows with only the smallest of sliding panels at the bottom for ventilation. They were gravely inadequate for sultry summer days; the air inside could be stifling. The comfort situation was not improved by the hard straight-backed wooden pews that were ranked on each side of the central aisle. The islanders, however, accepted these sufferings without protest.

A prominent but invisible aspect of the interior of the church was a distinctive musty smell. Without identifying it I rather liked it, because I associated it with the happy summer days that I loved so well. Perceptive summer residents in later days were not so complaisant. They recognized the smell of bats, and they took effective measures to remove them from the church belfry. As far as the remaining islanders were concerned, and certainly as far as I was concerned, the bats could have lived on there indefinitely. The odor was a part of Grindstone Island and I wanted to lose no part of it.

On weekdays the church was always open and empty, and as a teenager sent to get the noonday mail I would often enter the church for diversion, not for prayers, and practice the old familiar hymns, pumping away for dear life on the little organ. No one paid me the slightest attention, though my diapasons were surely quite audible on the roads outside. When I paused in my playing the church would be lost in a wonderful silence broken only by the buzz of flies and hornets against the windows and the soft whisper of the south wind as it blew across one of the small window openings. And in June and July one could hear the faraway songs of the meadow larks on George McCarthy's hayfield to the south.

In the years of my first memory of the church it was Flossie Sturdevant with her high thin shoulders and pensive face who was the organist. She presided over this keyboard and accompanied the choir of island girls whose uncertain soprano voices sounded thin and wavering in the air of the crowded church. Recruiting young people for the choir was always difficult: adults were too modest and the boys were too shy to participate. Years later, as islanders diminished in the church and summer people increased in number, the choir and its music throve and became more sophisticated.

The Church

After Flossie left the island, it was my mother who played the church organ until about 1950. Then the freckled face of Nellie Dodge was seen for a long time above the organ, concentrating with great effort on the hymnal before her and nodding the tempo for the choir. After Nellie there must have been others whose names escape my memory. Some of the ministers' wives made great contributions to the church's musical life.

When I came on the scene in 1909 the spiritual needs of the island were the concern of Elder Robinson, who for five years more would occupy the pulpit. On his sermons and other advanced skills, this small boy is not able to report. He did have a patriarchal white beard, and his wife—school-marmish and gold-spectacled—conducted her part of the church's affairs with a benign asperity that was a little intimidating to one of my age. I never felt easy with the Robinsons and about them I have no intimacies to share.

In 1909 the church was already twenty years old, its first pastor and indeed its creator having been an energetic and enthusiastic man named Alexander Shorts, still famed in island stories as a flamboyant character. In the 1880's he coursed up and down the river in a little steam launch founding and building churches. The Grindstone church is his principal monument and there he remained as pastor until his death in 1896. At least one more church was built by him, to my knowledge: a yellow wooden chapel that stood in a glade far down river on the Canadian side just below the present international bridge. Neither it nor the Grindstone church is a Chartres cathedral, and the chapel had the more serious disadvantage of having been built in a deserted place that remained deserted. That forlorn little church already stood abandoned in my earliest memories of it, and each time I passed, it sagged a little more until it finally collapsed and disappeared. But Deacon Shorts tended his Grindstone flock personally and it prospered. To me, a latecomer, he was a figure of hearsay. It was said that he had an impressive beard, and that he lived in a little home in the gully below the boarding house, and that he kept a beautiful lawn with a lovely vista through trimmed greenery that ran down to Thurso Bay. By 1909 nothing could be seen there save a few foundation stones, swallowed in trees and scrub. His plot is still called "the old Shorts lot," but it is only the church and its cemetery, really, that preserves some shadowy memory of Deacon Alexander Shorts.

Well into the 1930's the pastoral shepherding of the island was a full-time occupation.

Church services were held throughout the year, the pastor living in all seasons in the parsonage just to the west of the church. The parsonage was indeed, in those days, a place to provide divine inspiration to those who lived there, because of its lovely view of peaceful meadow and gleaming river, extending almost to infinity.

There are many gaps in my knowledge of the residents of that parsonage. Even though selected by the District Superintendent in consultation with the Deity, they were a mixed lot. The first of these whom I remember with any discernment was a clergyman who served the island in 1915, the Reverend W. S. B. Walsh.

The white-haired heavyset and ruddy Reverend Walsh was one of the most distinguished and yet enigmatic characters the island had ever known. His name, together with the fact that he was unmarried, somehow made him the very figure of a member of the Roman Catholic clergy. There were those who swore that this cleanshaven man had to be an unfrocked urban priest. The black suit, the tie, the white shirt, the vest and heavy gold watch chain he always wore did not dispel the intuition. It was supported also by his speech, beautifully delivered with the faintest trace of an Irish brogue, and by his singing exhortations to follow the gospel according to St. Paul or whatever other saint suited the day. Scholarly and thoroughly professional, one felt that he should be presiding over the rituals of a wealthy metropolitan congregation, or that his true place would be in a procession of distinguished prelates in robes of red and gold.

About his background, the islanders knew nothing and nothing was ever revealed to them. He arrived out of a void and was to vanish into a void after a year of service. Regarding him one could only be sure that he was a man of immense erudition who had been familiar with people of consequence. Although he gave no sign, one felt that his assignment to the island had been a fall from grace. Somewhere, something had gone wrong. The more knowledgeable people on the island were inclined to feel compassion for this lonely and distinguished man. I sensed my father's respect for him because, when the Rev. Walsh suggested that for a small fee he would tutor me in quadratic equations in preparation for school that autumn, my father agreed. Why quadratic equations had been the chosen subject is a mystery to me. But the Reverend Walsh prevailed and I faithfully solved quadratic equations on our front veranda on summer afternoons for a month or two. I haven't looked at a quadratic equation since. My relations with the Reverend Walsh were strictly impersonal, not in the least like

The Church

those I had with the equally erudite Davy Black with whom I would have preferred to play cribbage on those warm summer days. I had come to love Davy Black, but respect was all that I felt for this priestly person with his chill clerical formality.

The Reverend Walsh stayed on throughout the year, alone in the parsonage. He had little to do with the islanders socially. When the winter snows came, the solitude in which he lived must have become extremely trying. He left the following spring. We learned then that he had been addicted to the cup that cheers. And I recalled that, in poring over my quadratic equations with a watchful eye, he carried with him on his breath a trace of the odor of liquor.

After the departure of the W. S. J. Walsh, the spiritual needs of the island were given into the care of a man of quite different nature, the Reverand William A. Whiston. He arrived in January, 1915, and was to remain until September, 1919, staying all through the years of World War I. The Reverend Whiston and his wife not only looked British but they were indeed British — reserved, genteel beyond belief, and always somewhat condescending in their polite tolerance of the crudities of the island life. They disclosed a feeling that they were in an environment that was quite alien to all that they had known, and they felt, I am sure, that they were displaced aristocracy— missionaries in an uncivilized land.

With his sandy mustache and gold spectacles and his formal dress and a white straw hat, in summer he was the very model of clerical decorum. Like old Mrs. Brown, he had a stiff leg (only his was stiffer) and he would swing it out in a great arc as he walked the paths of Thurso with his stick. There was much conjecture on the island that his game leg was a wooden one. No one ever knew. And his manner of preaching was as stiff as his leg. Standing in formal morning dress and delivering a sermon in Oxford tones, he was an utter exotic in the Grindstone Island pulpit. But the islanders accepted him gratefully and without question. The good man must have been in his fifties, yet he had a quavering old man's voice which he never raised even at dramatic moments in his sermon. Rather he attempted to move his congregation with an affecting break in his gentle voice and even a sniffle or two when he was describing some of the more harrowing details in Biblical history. One always longed for him to clear his throat and get on with the sermon for the crowded church was hot and stuffy on summer mornings and I was bored. I had devoured Russell Conwell's big volume of stories of the New

Testament for children with Gustav Dore's marvellous illustrations. As a small boy, I had been deeply stirred by the tribulations of everyone involved in the Gethsemane tragedy. But at fourteen I had become quite detached about the whole business and I looked upon Mr. Whiston's approach as hopelessly sentimental.

Mrs. Whiston was a slender woman with bright gold spectacles gleaming under a straw garden hat. In summer she always looked as if she had just left an English garden party. In her speech she remained, like her husband, uncompromisingly faithful to the intonations of the land of her birth. Mrs. Whiston conceived herself to be an artistic person, and not without reason. On one occasion when I was ill she thoughtfully brought to me the Whiston family stereoscope and an enormous collection of beautiful worldwide views that the Whistons had somehow gathered. These stereoscopic pictures entertained me for hours on end and the memory of them still fills me with a feeling of warm gratitude to this strange English couple who always seemed to take pleasure in visiting us on our veranda.

The Whistons had a son Leo who had had a call to propagate the faith also and was doing so down state in a manner that was quite different from his father I am sure. He was an exuberant likable young man and on his visits to the island he and I became friends. It was at his suggestion one time that we embarked on an overnight canoe trip down river toward Alexandria Bay, about 15 miles distant. Like modern *couriers dubois,* we paddled through the Navy and Fleetwing Groups of islands, and then on into the International Rift past Deacon Short's little deserted church, standing still and peaceful in the lonely woods. Then we crossed the Lake of the Isles, rounded the foot of Wellesley Island and proceeded down river. Our first evening out found us settled in a pup tent on an island near Boldt Castle, a mile or two from Alexandria Bay. In those days we seemed very far from home.

While we were eating our supper (probably of pork and beans), we could hear someone, across a narrow channel, trying to start a motorboat at the Boldt Castle dock. When we had finished our meal, we could still hear ineffectual explosions and sputterings over at the dock, so we got into our canoe and paddled over. We found the island's caretaker, a pleasant young man, understandably exasperated at the perversity of gasoline motors, and very eager to go home to dinner in Alexandria Bay. So in our canoe we paddled him over. He was forever grateful. For years thereafter, whenever

The Church

I took guests sightseeing on the tour boats that always stopped at Boldt Castle, the young caretaker, growing steadily older, always recognized me with a warm smile. The other passengers would be charged a 50¢ fee to explore the castle, while I and my guests were waved through free.

The Whistons in September, 1919, finally left the island to take a pastorate downstate at Westmoreland, near Utica. There they may have lived more happily, for Grindstone Island was missionary country and the Whistons were not missionaries.

The Whistons were succeeded in 1921 by a testy old man who was their complete opposite — the Reverend David Wright. He was a tall, thin and ungainly man with an adenoidal face and a small moustache. He could have been Ichabod Crane grown old. Mr. Wright's God was a vengeful deity. In contrast to Mr. Whiston, this minister would rant his sermons in a high nasal voice and threaten hellfire and eternal damnation for the island's sinners. All in the congregation sat without batting an eye, the whole time sure that his words were intended for their neighbors.

This minister was not only anti-intellectual, but also anti-work. His wife was stout and crippled and confined by arthritis to a wheelchair Yet to the indignation of many of the islanders, he allowed her to do most of the tasks about the parsonage and in the garden, too. A sweet old woman, she was as gentle and kind as her husband was bigoted and querulous. Incredibly adroit in doing the tasks of keeping a house and a garden, she was a marvel — particularly when it is remembered that her chores were especially difficult without the help of electricity or telephones, which had not yet reached the island. Nor would they for 32 more years. Everyone who knew her admired her, even as they derided the selfish old man who did so little to help.

The Wrights vanished into the countryside somewhere near Dexter on the mainland in 1923 and I never saw them again. They left behind in Clayton a daughter, Maude, an agreeable intelligent girl who was to marry Laurence Garnsey and suffer much because of Laurence's mental instability following duty in the navy.

There followed after the Wrights a strange hiatus in the island's pastoral succession. There was series of "fill-ins"—men from about the country, sent to the island by the District Superintendent. I have no recollection of the ecclesiastical events of those years, but somehow, sin was held at bay on the island. Then, in 1925, a middle-aged widow with a chirrupy voice mounted the pulpit to present the gospel with none of Mr. Wright's threats of hellfire and brimstone and eternal perdition. Florence Printer wasn't as fascinating to watch as Mr. Wright and I was bored, but my mother liked her, as did the islanders. Mrs. Printer carried on the Lord's work for five long years. By the end of her term the island pastorate had become a part-time occupation, and in winter Mrs. Printer retreated to her home in Copenhagen.

Her successors again were not memorable. Then suddenly in 1935, with the arrival of the Gabriels, we can say that all heaven broke loose. The Gabriels were, figuratively speaking, to turn the church inside out.

The Reverend B. R. Gabriel was a small swarthy man with soulful eyes and a dark mustache. Years before, he had come to the United States from Armenia and "Armenian" was written all over him, even in his accent. He looked as if he would be completely at home in a Near East bazaar, showing oriental rugs to prospective buyers. And that was exactly what he was currently doing in winter, not in an exotic bazaar abroad but in an exclusive little shop in St. Petersburg, Florida where he and his wife sold genuine oriental treasures.

Saving souls was for Mr. Gabriel a summer vocation. All of his predecessors on Grindstone had given to the church their entire professional lives. Mr. Gabriel's dedication of his time was partial, but his concentration on the struggle between God and Mammon was so intense as to outweigh the efforts of those before him who had given full time to the matter. "B. R.," as his wife called him, was a truly selfless man. One could easily say that he was more Christlike than all those who had preceded him and we could be bold enough to add, than all who have followed him. He was kind, he was generous, he was honorable, and he was highly intelligent. And, furthermore, he was lovable—a trait not always evident in island preachers we have seen.

His wife was a stout woman with a great swirl of fair hair and a gold pince-nez which dangled from a black ribbon. She was always spangled with jewelry—with golden rings encrusted with colorful stones, with festoons of Indian silver and opals about her neck and across her broad bosom. Golden bracelets heavy with jade and amethysts adorned her arms. All of these were drawn from the stock of merchandise that she

The Church

displayed and sold in the St. Petersburg store. Like her husband, she was knowledgeable and shrewd and kind. Mrs. Gabriel seemed to be always hovering over something which interested her intensely, from flower arranging to planning innovations for the church, particularly to the activities of the Ladies' Aid Society which she was inclined to dominate. When crossed, she could become petulant and even vindictive, as we shall note.

Despite a foible or two, the Gabriels were remarkable for their kindly Christian spirit. Long before they came to us they had shown their compassion in a situation where it counted—in adopting as their son a little boy named Azad, whose parents had been killed by the Turks in their infamous massacre of Armenians. The Gabriels would send him to college, and later he would study for the ministry and preach in various parishes in the North Country. In the meantime he was spending his summer holidays with his foster parents and I came to know him well. He was a round-faced boy of brown complexion, with dense black hair and large brown eyes. He was full of fun and laughter, yet with me he seemed always to prefer philosophical discussions. I remember only my taking to him my bewilderment about the prevalence of so much suffering in a world over which an all-powerful benevolent deity was said to preside. He proceeded to enlighten me on the view on that matter that had been taken by the Manichaeans of the ancient Middle East.

The Gabriels worked more change in the Grindstone church than it had seen since Deacon Shorts stepped off his little steamboat to found it. In a mysterious way known only to the Gabriels and God, they found replacements in some down-country church for the pews that Deacon Shorts had built by hand. He had made them straight-backed and stiffly upright and had stained them mahogany. Uncushioned, they had been built to a design devised by Lucifer himself to test the devotion of the faithful. The new pews had inclined backs and were so curved that the entire congregation would face the pulpit in a more agreeable arrangement. A few, of course, refused to join in the general satisfaction at this change, saying that an early American charm had gone with the old pews, and the church was now like any church on the mainland, losing all distinction.

The Gabriels introduced stained glass into the sanctuary. In the tall narrow exterior windows they inserted small memorial panes commemorating members who had passed on, such as Elizabeth Brown and David Black. And behind the alter they cut a circular opening through the interior wall and placed there—their own donation—a rendering in color of the well-known Hoffman painting of Christ in prayer in Gethsemane, his robes flowing out behind him among the rocks.

Another blessed contribution of the Gabriels was a negative one—the razing of the long carriage shed back of the church and the disposal of its contents. For as long as I could remember the shed had sheltered, covered with bird droppings, an elegant horse-drawn hearse. Its windows were of plate glass. They were festooned with tasselled purple curtains and one could see, within, a low dais covered with purple velvet. At each outside corner of the hearse a large silver coach-lamp was ensconced. I had never seen this hearse in actual use, but island funerals occurred most often in the winters when I was far away. The hearse vanished now, I know not where. Then the timbers of the old carriage shed were turned to the service of the living rather than the dead. The islanders built of them, at last, a long-needed parish house. It was complete with kitchen and stove and cupboards and counters—a place to serve church suppers and a place where the Ladies' Aid Society could quilt and do other work pleasing to the Almighty, all of which had had to go on before in the cramped quarters of the parsonage. Emmet Dodge was the chief planner and builder in this worthy work. Consequently the new parish house was an architectural wonder. In a few years the roof had to be rebuilt after collapsing under the weight of winter snow. But in general the building has served well.

Mrs. Gabriel organized small theatricals in the Sunday School. The pupils would stand before the altar clad in white sheets and fairy wings suggesting celestial purity and in quavering voices barely audible beyond the first row they would recite verses telling of Jesus' love and other matters of theological interest. It would go on in tender spirit until the childish treble would hesitate and falter at some critical moment in the drama. Then Mrs. Gabriel's strong mezzo would suddenly break in and complete the story of the crucifixion or whatever other Biblical ordeal was afoot. It was all wonderful fun and the doting parents loved it.

Seizing upon summer visitors to sing, lecture, or give dramatic monologues was another aspect of the alertness of this tireless couple. The church had never been so lively in all its history. These events had a religious slant, of course—lantern slides of the Holy Land, a talk by a missionary from Thailand or by a physician who cared for

The Church

lepers on St. Croix. One man gave a talk on his travels in Alaska and at one point told of an exploit of his that resulted in disaster. He had undertaken it on the Sabbath and for him the lesson was obvious: never do it on a Sunday! And in our family from that time on, whenever any project was proposed for that day, my father would solemnly warn, "Never do it on a Sunday!" and then proceed at once to do it, with a grin. My father occasionally poked fun at some of these amateur entertainments that had comic aspects that the entertainers did not intend, but he respected the Gabriels' efforts to bring good Christian conviviality to the island.

Over the years, a large part of the islands' social life lay in the Ladies' Aid Society whose members met regularly in winter and summer, occupying themselves with quilting, organizing church suppers and the like. They were an enterprising lot. The regulars included Grace Slate, Nellie Dodge, Carrie Garnsey, Mae Packard, Hattie Potter, Mrs. Jay Robinson, Jessie and Ella Carnegie, Mrs. Sturdevant, Elizabeth Brown and my mother. From below the marsh came Ella Johnson and Mrs. John Black, and from across the island, Davy Atherton's wife Jeanne. Nettie McRae, Clara Turcotte and Charlotte McIntosh, along with "Marthy" Garnsey and Addy Cummings and some others remained aloof from the society. The Ladies' Aid in its last years had one unofficial member in Hi Russell, the flirt, whom we have already noted. At all of the society's festivals he became the ladies' handyman. Accepting his flowery attentions with merry laughter, the members refused to take him seriously and put him to work at such tasks as setting up the tables in the parish house for the church suppers or hanging lanterns in the lawn for the Saturday night ice cream socials.

The ice-cream socials of the Ladies' Aid Society were an important weekly institution in the life of the island. They were held every Saturday night in summer, on the lawn in front of the church. The ice cream was made in Clayton—always vanilla, rich and naturally golden. It arrived in large cardboard cylinders from which the ladies scooped up liberal portions and filled cones that were grabbed eagerly by outstretched grubby hands in exchange for a nickle.. The Ladies' Aid considered it a good night if they cleared $15.00. The money went for the church's purposes, which included upkeep and special projects, in which the benighted heathen were always included.

The scene at the socials was lively. Children dashed about, running in and out of shadows, playing tag and screaming and all the while clutching their cones and stumbling over dogs that had followed wagons from their distant farms and now lay panting in the grass hoping for a fallen dollop of the delicacy of the evening.

Off on the lawn at the south side of the church, the men lingered in the dark to talk of the cheese factory and of the prices of hay and cattle. Here and there in the blackness a cigarette would suddenly grow bright for a second. Far to the south the faint glow could be seen of a light in the window of George McCarthy's house. Hi Marshall's store, across the road, lay dark. Behind the church one heard the stamping and nickering of horses waiting with their wagons. In later years there was silence there, where battered automobiles now stood in the horses' place. For island women the ice cream socials were a heaven-sent opportunity for visiting in the midst of the busiest season of the year. The sound of feminine laughter was an aural background that prevailed everywhere. All the while Hi Russell, like a loitering satyr, drifted in and out of the lamplight, offering his flowery tributes to the ladies.

One worker who was always present at the activities of the Ladies Aid was the amiable and buxom Mrs. Packard, whom we have already met. Under Mrs. Gabriel's leadership she became a stalwart, doing more than her part in preparing suppers, stitching quilts, embroidering towels, making potholders and the like for summer sale. Both ladies were collectors, it is to be noted, and fanciers of fine handwork. Now the preparing of covered dishes for suppers was one of the commonest of Ladies' Aid activities. It was on one of these occasions that Mrs. Gabriel and Mrs. Packard crossed swords—or, better perhaps, "crossed knives."

Mrs. Packard had brought for the feast her share of goodies—perhaps scalloped potatoes, or, more likely, macaroni and cheese, cheese being in strong supply on the island. And at the end of the evening Mrs. Packard had taken home an empty casserole dish. Mrs. Gabriel declared it was hers, and not only that, but her own very special imported casserole dish, a classic that she treasured more than life itself. Mrs. Packard refused to return the prized vessel. Mrs. Gabriel turned purple—insisted that Mrs. Packard's act was only one step removed from outright thievery. The precious dish became an *objet d' art*. The two ladies refrained from actual blows but harsh words were exchanged which could not be recalled. People took sides. The Ladies' Aid Society became a house divided until the rift was seen to be intolerable and the ladies pulled themselves together. The islanders laughed the clash away and went on with island business. But Mrs. Gabriel thereafter could not endure the presence of Mrs. Packard, and that old lady just as resolutely refused to attend any more of the Ladies Aid's gatherings.

It was in the Gabriels' time that the Ladies' Aid carried to success the most ambitious of all their projects: providing the church with a well. It was very badly needed. All water for cleanups at the church suppers and ice cream socials had had to be carried in buckets from the parsonage cistern. Almost all houses in the village then depended upon cisterns or on rain barrels for domestic water. The only well in the area, much resorted to from afar, and with great labor was at the Upper Schoolhouse, as we have seen. A well was an expensive luxury. A well-driller had to be brought over from the mainland, and once arrived he had to drill through layers of hard red granite. And so when the ladies set out to raise the money, they did so with great courage. At least a thousand dollars were needed. They were raised, and the well was drilled. Water was found, and it was sweet and potable. It was made available to all comers. People came from miles around, thereafter, to fill pails or large cans with the precious fluid for their household use.

Pastor Gabriel likes the new well

In time an electric pump and small pumphouse was added and a line was run to the parsonage. And thus it happened that the old outhouse that formerly stood behind the parsonage was replaced by a sparkling white indoor bathroom. And of course, a septic tank and leach field were also installed—in heavy clay soil that was very ill-suited for such use. In 1973 a new family of summer residents studied the water problem of their cottage and took a step that no one before had ever dreamed of: they took samples of water from the river and from the parsonage well to a laboratory for testing. The report, returned, caused utmost consternation: the river water was potable, the well's, contaminated. It was a shocking reward that the Ladies' Aid's members received for their labors! A hunt was launched for the source of the offending *bacillus coli*. Not even the reverend occupants of the parsonage were exempted from suspicion. Eventually the use of chlorine and some attention to the slope of the lawn about the well brought an end to the crisis—but, alas, not before all the stout-willed ladies who gave the church its well had gone elsewhere for their reward, via the church cemetery just up the road.

The members of the Grindstone church were from the first a varied lot: stonecutters, farmers, villagers. The villagers continued always to be faithful church attenders, with the few exceptions already mentioned. The farmers were always a majority. They were a surprisingly intelligent and genteel group. Of those who lived near the village we could mention as leaders the Cummings, the Dodges, the Matthews and the Garnseys, and the Murdocks and Blacks from below the marsh. But many of the pillars of the church came faithfully from the far south side of the island—the Rushos and Danos and others too numerous to mention. I remember sharply how the family of Jim Kittle arrived at the church on a Sunday morning. They could have stepped straight out of a John Stuart Curry painting—stern old Jim Kittle with his Biblical black beard and black felt hat, and his pale wife, plain and incredibly neat with black hair drawn smooth over each temple. They always arrived at the church in a trim buggy drawn by a black horse that they tied in the carriage shed. The fact that they drove the island roads in a covered passenger vehicle gave them the distinction that a Cadillac would give today. A touch of class could be expected of the Kittles, however, since Mrs. Kittle was the daughter of Ben Grossman, owner of extensive lands on Grindstone and on Picton Island also, including the site of Picton's great quarry.

The family of Ambrose Dano, the Kittle's neighbors, were prosperous farmers. "Am" was a hearty intelligent man. My father loved to engage him in long conversations, and I delighted especially in his tales of how, in 1903, he barely escaped with his life when attacked and thrown into the air on the horns of an infuriated bull. One of Am's daughters, Mildred, married Aaron Cummings and moved to the large Cummings farm at the southwestern corner of the island. Another, Myrtle, married a Dr. Mix and spent her middle life in Phoenix, but returned as a widow to build the first of the colony of

The Church

houses that destroyed the wilderness west of the upper town landing. Am died in 1938 but his pleasant wife Ardelia for another twenty years carried on the work of the Dano farm and the Dano tradition of active participation in all the activities of the church in Thurso.

The stable old Rusho family, one of the oldest on the island, lived near the Danos at the lower town landing on the south shore. They were prominent and faithful members of the church but I did not know any of them well until Robert, the son of Leon and Marjorie, moved with his wife Gloria to the Turcotte farm in Thurso to run the post office there.

Constant support of the church was the tradition of the Milo Cummings family who farmed on the southwestern shore. Milo's sons Ernest and Earl and Aaron were all attractive intelligent men. Ernest became a police officer in Philadelphia. Earl, a seaman, married Mabel McRae as we have noted, and Aaron married Mildred Dano and took over the Cummings farm. Aaron and Mildred were the island's most persistanr churchgoers. From the south shore Garnseys came to church also, and the McFaddens and the Matthews family that settled on the island in the 1920's. Among the most persistent members were David and Laney Atherton—beloved by all who knew them—who lived in a little house behind the isle called Boscobel.

Far up at the west end of the island lay the old Flynn farm, which one reached by following the Baseline Road past the abandoned silver mine and through deep woods and rock ledges to the farm's gate. The name Flynn remained attached to the farm, but even in my early experience Johnny Johnson and his family were the actual proprietors. Johnny was a smiling agreeable man—a violinist as we have noticed—who had a large family of daughters who inherited their father's pleasant ways. These girls were always at church and always at the ice cream socials, filling the lawn with their merry laughter. Despite their friendliness I never became well acquainted with them. They lived too far away for familiarity, but another kind of distance was operative also. I did not learn of that factor until years later when one of the girls, by then an old lady, confessed to me that they had felt shy of this sophisticated teen-ager with his knowing big-city ways, and that they had attributed to me the glamorous attributes of a story-book prince, to be admired from a discreet distance. How flattering, even in old age, to know that one had ever—even long ago—been a feminine idol!

The Grindstone church drew immeasurable support for many years from a summer resident of the south shore, Dr. Gove Johnson. He lived with his large family on Boscobel Island, an isle near the town dock where the mail boat landed. The Johnsons came from Washington D.C., where Dr. Johnson was the pastor of the National Baptist Church. He was a small dark-haired man, swarthy, cleanshaven, with an angular face and wide cheek bones and a very long nose. His smile was quick, and he had a deep voice that cast a kind of radiance about him.

Dr. Johnson, though an arch-Baptist, faithfully attended the Sunday services in Thurso with his family, making the long trip across the island. At first they came in hay wagons, in journeys that they made into jolly outings. Later, they would arrive at the church in cars which were faster but not nearly as much fun. However they came, they always came, rain or shine. Mrs. Johnson was born a Russell. A woman of aristocratic mien, she was a bright and animated person with a crown of white hair and a merry laugh that was infectious. I have never known more hospitable people than the Johnsons. My family and I often made the long three-mile walk across the island of a summer afternoon to visit them, we youngsters swimming and canoeing while our elders talked on the broad veranda off the big white house the Russell family had built years before on Boscobel. The good times I had down through the years with the Johnson girls, Norma and Grace, are among my most treasured memories.

Dr. Johnson seemed to feel that the Methodists needed Baptist support in their effort to be heard in Heaven. Thus when a Grindstone preacher would utter a particularly cogent prayer in church, one might hear a sudden deep "amen" in the middle of it. And, when other sentiments were uttered from the pulpit which Dr. Johnson endorsed, he would back them up with resounding "yeas" and "hallelujahs." To a small boy brought up in a big city Methodist church where there was absolute silence while the pastor was speaking from the pulpit, and where any sound, even a whisper, was considered sacrilege, such interruptions were unthinkable, however sonorous. They were met with threatening scowls and warning forefingers; for they threatened to bring down a thunderbolt from heaven. But Dr. Johnson's booming "yeas" and "hallelujahs" continued, and no descending bolt ever struck him.

Dr. Johnson loved rotund words, and how fondly he would dwell on "glory" and

The Church

"doom" and "lowly" in his occasional sermons. With his arms spread wide and his wondrous smile beaming down from the pulpit upon a spellbound congregation, he could be irresistible. There was something of the old-time actor in him. With his dark romantic looks, long nose and vibrant voice, he was akin to such actors of his time as George Arliss and Walter Hampton—not handsome, but of compelling character. Dr. Johnson knew how to make effective use of his beatific smile and voice. But he was genuinely a kind and noble man who spread good will wherever he went. The islanders loved him more than they loved any person associated with the church before or since, and their affection deepened as the years went by.

The big event in the summer church calendar was the annual outdoor service at Aunt Jane's bay in August. Dr. Johnson always presided over it with unconcealed pleasure. To worship God in an amphitheater of ageless rocks overlooking Dr. Johnson's beloved river was a rare occasion and people came from all over the island, by every kind of conveyance.

The weather for the Aunt Jane's bay services was always worrisome. If the big day was clearly to be a day of outright rain, the service would be put off until the following Sunday. The days when one could not be sure whether it would rain or not were a problem. On such days, the congregation usually took its chances. People arrived with rain coats and umbrellas and held the service anyway. If the Deity tested their faith with a sudden downpour they accepted their soggy discomfort stoically. In view of another concern of the church, going on with the service was important, for not all the gains of worship at Aunt Jane's Bay were spiritual. Many well-to-do summer people who did not ordinarily attend the church were attracted by the novelty of the observance. The service always brought in, therefore, a record-breaking collection plate, in which a satisfying profusion of crisp green bills stood upright to cover the silver coins that ordinarily predominated in the church's collection basket as it passed from hand to hand. The weather made a great deal of difference.

There were two hymns that were always sung at Aunt Jane's Bay. One of the two hymns was "Rock of Ages." It had special meaning for one who was sitting on a large boulder. The other hymn was much easier to understand— "We Shall Gather at the River." With a broad shining river out beyond the Bay, the hymn's promise was very real. It was Dr. Johnson's favorite and it was mine, too.

Dr. Johnson died in 1944 and Mrs. Johnson died in 1946. Their deaths were obscured by the intense distractions of World War II. When I returned from the service, as happened so often in my absences from the Island these essential persons were both gone. The Aunt Jane's Bay services are still held, but for those of us who remember the Johnsons' role in the old services at Aunt Jane's Bay, the deep old meanings are sorely missed. They are, for me, a sort of memorial for the Johnsons.

The Gabriels presided over the Grindstone church for ten years, longer than any of their predecessors. In their retirement they still continued to come in summers to a cottage on the river at Morristown, near Ogdensburg. This warmhearted couple was so much loved on Grindstone Island that the Ladies' Aid Society *en masse* made several excursions by bus to visit them, and my own parents made a special effort to see them in St. Petersburg. Mrs. Gabriel died in the late 1950's; he lived on until 1969. They had been the creators of a notable period of vitality in the life of the island church.

After the Gabriels there followed a long succession of one-year summer pastorates. Mostly we heard the clear young voices of divinity students, candidates for the ministry under the care of the Methodist District Conference in Watertown. In some years the pulpit was occupied by members of the clergy who were summer residents on the island—members of the faculties of Yale, Princeton, Colgate, or the University of Toronto. They brought a big-city tone to the pastorate that was now quite compatible with a congregation that had changed also as the years had passed. Suave city people had gradually taken over the island and the church, while just as gradually the native parishioners had diminished in numbers. The church of the 1970's was a very different institution from the country church I had known up to the 1950's. No more did strident Elder Wrights yelp from the pulpit. The farmer's festival, the ice cream social, was no longer held on Saturday nights and there was no longer any Ladies' Aid Society to organize socials and suppers and to quilt and knit and sew. As the years passed the society lost to death such strong members as Mrs. Sturdevant and Mother Brown. Finally the deaths of Nellie Dodge, and of Grace Slate in 1962, inflicted irreparable damage and the Ladies' Aid Society dissolved—one more step in the decline of the native culture of the island. Henceforth it would be committees of the summer people, helped by a few islanders who weren't working, who would plan and serve the suppers in the parish house, more in the atmosphere of suburban Westchester than of the island of former days.

The Church

Yet these suppers, and the worship services on Sunday mornings, are still the only gatherings at which all on the island can meet and know each other. The post office and all stores are gone. If one is not a churchgoer today on Grindstone Island he lives in complete isolation as he picks up his mail at a lonely box by the roadside.

32.
My Island Sinks

In the middle of World War II Hi Marshal seemed to lose all interest in his life. His wife Eliza had already died, Flossie had departed to take up other work, his daughter Mary had married and gone to Chicago. He was left alone, broken in spirit. Complications of prostate surgery—still a very risky operation in those days—ended his life. His death, in retrospect, was the beginning of the end for the old island as well. Hi's guest house across the road—once Mort Marshall's home—thereafter went unused and untended and finally crumbled into the surrounding jungle. Hi's store was taken over by Ed Turcotte and his wife Ellen. They tried for half a dozen years to make it pay but failed utterly and quit by 1950. The building then stood empty. People blamed the bankruptcy of the store on strict new enforcement of Canada's customs laws, or on Ed's notorious lack of ambition, or, more reasonably, on his poor business sense in extending credit. But the reason for the islanders' poor credit should have been considered. Something in the island had changed.

Shortly after 1950, I returned to the island in the spring and Hi Marshall's building was gone. On its old foundations an ugly insubstantial one-story structure stood. It had just been named Dodge Hall—no doubt after Emmet Dodge, the principal perpetrator of the deed. Emmet had carried away the framing timbers of the upper story to raise them again on the shore of the old Forsyth Quarry. The act was important symbolically: the top floor of the old store soon became the materials of a summer cottage, the home of Marvin and Helen Pope. Dodge Hall underwent a similar metamorphosis in function, becoming a rallying-place for young summer people searching for folk fun with local rustics. It became a crude dance hall for Saturday night bashes where small mainland bands now play for the crowds in the rock and roll tradition. Swarming in from shores far and near, young vacationers cavort with others of their own kind, imagining all the while that they are joining in the exotic customs of the hayseeds of the island. The elders of these young revelers often come along to Dodge Hall to participate in these hee-haw antics and in the fantasy that they are quaint surviving rituals of a charming rural life. As a matter of fact the rustics of their imagining scarcely exist any more.

Forced out of the island store, the Grindstone post office moved to restricted quarters in Nellie Dodge's home, the northernmost of the old quarrymens' houses, and there, throughout most of the 50's, Nellie gave out the mail and sold stamps and—not very profitably—a few food staples and candies in a pitiful survival of the work of the onetime island store. When Nellie died in 1959, Bertha McRae, now retired from her teaching in Tuckahoe, picked up the thread of storekeeping that was in her own McRae family tradition and sold cigarettes and pop and candy, in summer only, until age overtook her. In the late 60's a marina below the marsh sold beer and bread and matches along with its gasoline but that enterprise ended soon after Bertha's.

The Grindstone Post Office, after Nellie Dodge's death, was moved to the old Turcotte farm just west of the village center. By 1959, it had become the home of David and Hildred Garnsey, and Hildred became the postmistress. David was by then a brusque eccentric old man, grizzled, toothless, persistently dressed in shabby overalls, addicted to his pipe and still given to monosyllabic conversation accented with grunts and expletives. The monotony of winter life on the island was often too much for this unstable man and for relief he committed himself to winter stays in the State Mental Hospital in Ogdensburg. He is said to have taken great pleasure in those sojourns. Hildred carried on alone during those intervals, running the post office smoothly with a pleasant tolerance. Whenever I see Carol Burnett on television in one of her family roles I am reminded of Hildred, who had something of Carol Burnett about her. Happily, Hildred had nothing in her of Carol's malice. The post office became once more a meeting place for summer people and islanders, all getting their mail and picking up candy bars, bread and a few staples. When David died in 1976, however, Hildred resigned and quit the island.

The post office remained on the Turcotte farm. It was now bought by Robert Rusho, a Robert Redfield look-alike, of the responsible old Rusho family of the south shore. Robert renovated Hildred's house and farmed the land and his wife Gloria became the efficient new postmistresses. Once again the post office functioned smoothly. Then rumors arose that the postal authorities were concerned about the losses of the Grindstone Post Office and were considering closing it. The summer people began to purchase their Christmas stamps from Gloria in summer in order to increase her sales, and such efforts to support the post office may have helped it to survive for a while.

My Island Sinks

But another trouble rose. Both Hildred and Gloria tried scrupulously to maintain the office hours that their contract with the government prescribed, and while doing so they had continuing friction with Francis Garnsey, the bringer of the mail from Clayton. Late and erratic delivery was the problem. Francis was always carrying passengers and island freight as well as the mail, and there were times when he could not easily keep to the schedule for mail deliveries at the post office. Gloria protested vigorously, and Francis, on his part, seemed able to retort in terms that found the exact incensing word. Then on days when Francis' arrival was delayed beyond the post office's official closing hour, Gloria began to lock up the post office on the dot of time. Island patrons could not get their mail until the following day—on weekends, not until the following Monday, and if Monday were a holiday, not even until Tuesday. Of course there were complaints. The authorities solved all problems in 1976 by closing the post office entirely. Francis Garnsey became the mailman of a standard R. F. D. route, dropping all mail in roadside mailboxes along one or two major roads of the island only. Thus it has been ever since. And with the closing of the post office the island lost the last vestige of an island store.

The death of the post office brought to a new low the facilities for public gathering on the island. The cheese factory, the Lower School, the general store, and now the post office with its little candy counter were closed. The nadir came in 1990 with the closing of the Upper School, the last school on the island, for lack of enough year-round pupils to justify its cost. A result of depopulation, the closing of the school became a cause of further depopulation. Year-round residence on the island has become practically impossible for families having children of primary school age.

With the disappearance of these institutions there is almost no way that anyone can earn an income on Grindstone Island, or spend it. The fortunate boy or girl who is given a dime or even a dollar, cannot buy a candy bar in all these ten square miles, nor can an adult buy a cup of coffee. Once a year, only, one can buy a meal—at the church's annual dinner. The one old island institution that has not fallen is the Grindstone Island church. To church one can still go and meet many other residents of the island.

Even the church is no longer a preserver of the old life of the island, however. It lives on because it has accepted the island's new populations and expresses their life and interests. The summer people do not know the old social world of the island and they cannot be its saviors.

It is the old island, however that has been my home. I cannot prevent its passing, or my own. I can only record its life so that a century of memorable living in this place will not slip beyond recovery by those who care. I hope those caring ones will forgive my expressing, in conclusion, the deep feelings of one who has loved the old island and must submit now, willy-nilly, to its disappearance.

Reveries at Departure

The day came when I myself had to join the flow of exiles from the island. The compulsions in my case were different but powerful—failure of eyes and other organs that called for easier living than the island could provide. While leaving, this very old man cannot refrain from comparing the island that he sees at the age of eighty-seven with the island he first knew as a boy of seven, and from reflecting on the essential changes that have occurred during a long life. Old men always lament change, and the world always discounts their protests, usually with justice, because the outcry of the aged is usually the cry of egos offended by time's bypassing of their work. But the old island was not my creation, but only my infatuation. I see objective reason for my grief at the disappearance of many a charm of the island in which I used to take delight.

Loss of vista is my first lament as I think of the island that I first knew. I came to an emerald isle of rich meadows and long views over rock and river to far places, and I leave a jungle isle. Nothing is so lovely as a tree—where there are none. But a million trees are another matter. The very tree that presents beauty blocks out beauty, and the million trees of Grindstone Island now shut off almost all of those favorite avenues of vision that delighted me with glimpses of distant fields of cattle and sparkling water. I remember the stunning beauty of the view from the veranda of the old parsonage, where one could look northwestward over river and islands and far into Canada's blue hills. The summer sunsets from that spot were breathtaking. Now scrubby woods have choked the pasture lands and deny the eye all access to the river. And thus it is throughout the island. There is no view.

For human beings places have only limited charm if they are devoid of human beings. Depopulation has stripped the island of a facet of its brightness. Today the desolation and the dullness begins a furlong from the shore. There is no post office, there is no store, no farmer in the fields, no whinnying horse at any roadside rail, no promise of companionship. How I longed, in these later days, to look down the road and see Davy

My Island Sinks

Black chatting with someone at the roadside, or spy old Mrs. Brown swinging her way homeward, managing her stiff leg deftly under her broad skirts. Now only a rare car comes by in Thurso, and it does not stop. The evening comes, and there are not even ghosts. The fairy folk, so many in Scotland and Ireland, did not emigrate with these no-nonsense people who settled Grindstone Island, and now even the night is lonely. For forty years the elders of the old farm families have had no successors on their farms. Left untended, the fields have grown up in brush. For reasons worthy of study such desertion has not occurred on the adjacent Canadian islands of Wolfe and Amherst. But the children of Grindstone families now live far away. They come back on Old Home Day with feeling for the island in their hearts but with no possibility of returning— save, sometimes as summer people, to a cottage on the shore.

Only a person of my own ripe age dares to say that much has happened to the brilliant air and transparent water of the island. My younger neighbors laugh at this lament of mine, aware only of the comparative purity, still, of the island environment. I stand my ground and repeat my charge. The summer thunderstorms that roar over the island, now, do not wash our whole world clean as once they did. After such a total deluge the following dawn was once something to be greeted with delight: "a perfect St. Lawrence River day," they'd call it. A brisk west wind blew, lacing the river with snowy whitecaps. The cool air had become pure crystal. Those thunderstorms still move up the river on hot humid summer days and beat the earth and air with their purifying excoriations but a sickness remains that is not thoroughly expunged. A yellowness remains in the air. One cannot see in sharp detail the Canadian shore. It is of course the yellowness of smog. The west wind cannot blow it away because the west wind itself brings from the west the effluents of the industrial heartlands of two nations. The loss is mercifully concealed from the young, who do not remember the days when the air was pristine and exhilarating.

A change in the quality of the water on the island shores is obvious but not yet disturbing to generations who know only how clear the St. Lawrence is still, when compared with other lakes and streams of their experience. This lament has to come from one who can recall gliding in a St. Lawrence skiff across Thurso Bay as if in an airplane flying over miles of lovely green jungle, scanning a carpet of low marine grasses above which schools of minnows darted. Occasionally one disturbed a turtle, legs splaying wildly as it scrambled to hide among the water plants, or ran alongside a water snake twisting its way, head held high, toward safety in the rocks along the shore. Today in July and August that lush carpet is no longer seen. It is overlain by an overgrowth too thick for boats or even fish to penetrate with any ease. One dips an oar into a mess of weeds and a dirty cloud spreads through a tangle of plant life. Even in the deep channels outside the bay where formerly one trolled for fish, one's line is caught at once on stringy weeds. Long strands of the same ugly stuff foul one's propellers. The cause of this change is of course pollution of the river—by industrial dumping or by reckless use upstream of fertilizers in a thousand miles of commercial farming, or by mere increase of population and its inevitable human wastes.

Pollution of the silence of the river has been a clear and gross development in the consciousness of anyone of long memory who has any appreciation of silence. The shattering of the island's serenity has mainly been the work of relatively inexpensive outboard motors, and of the development of means of bringing them to the river in great numbers. "The boating explosion" is the exact word for this catastrophe. When outboard motors first became available on the river, all islanders rejoiced. Gananoque and Clayton now became only minutes away. We could easily visit friends on distant islands, easily get a doctor, meet trains, speed departing guests, reach distant fishing grounds, and easily get supplies without dependence on the mailboat or the island stores. The development seemed wonderful. We were liberated.

Suddenly we discovered that everyone else had been liberated too. The river was filled with roaring boats. Towed over highways by automobiles, they slipped down ramps into the river in thousands. Strange boats began to proliferate in our bays, bringing families with shore dinners for cooking in our groves. Inexperienced "captains" left rubbish around their fires and excrement among the bushes where we picked huckleberries. We began to resent these intruders who invaded our once lonely coves. For the first time "No Trespassing" signs began to appear everywhere along our shores.

Then, in the 1970's came the beginning of the speedboat contamination of the sound-space of the islands. Each season faster and faster, some going fifty miles per hour, these introverted helmsmen began racing up and down our Leek Island Channel, profligate wasters of petroleum, hammering the shores with their wash, blind to the beauty they were passing. Intent on their engines, they might as well have been burning up the concrete lanes of an Indianapolis speedway. Poor old Jay Robinson, pounding the seats of a skiff on a glassy river! If he were in that place and mood today he would not be battling an imaginary enemy but fighting the swells created by these roaring monsters, throwing him about. Now, before leaving Thurso Bay for Gananoque, one has to pause at the exit from the bay as before a traffic light on a major highway, waiting for these philistine captains to flash past, eyes on nothing but their dials. A supplementary group of noisy polluters appeared with the rental houseboat crowd who were beginning to prowl slowly about the river leaving no place inviolate, anchoring within feet of one's cottage and blasting it off its foundations with rock music until the wee small hours. And there was nothing one could do about it.

Once upon a time the river was so still that one could hear and enjoy certain pleasant sounds that came far over the waters. Even across the island I could hear the whistles of the great steamboats—"the Toronto" and "the Kingston"—as they came and went from Clayton on their way down the river to Montreal, Quebec and the Saguenay. The automobile sealed their fate. It ended also the trains that contributed magic sounds to the aural experience of our quiet island. I loved to pick up the distant whistle of the morning train coming in from New York, far up the line out of Clayton, and the heavy puffing of the night train struggling upgrade in its evening departure for New York. Hardly a vestige of that railway remains now—only a weedbed running in a straight line across the fields south of Clayton, not recognizable to those who do not know that a railway once lay there. The train that ran into Gananoque is gone too. The whistle of the noon train that brought passengers to the river from the junction north of town was as sweet to me once as the song of birds—both tokens that I was at home on the island after a long winter in the din of Brooklyn. Unlike Clayton's, the railway station of Gananoque still stands—as a restaurant surrounded by parking lots and endless automobiles, selling junk food and trinkets to hordes of tourists milling about in jeans and shorts.

Just before I left Grindstone Island for the last time I steered my boat toward the head of Grindstone on a calm Sunday afternoon on my way to Clayton. I came abreast of Potter's Grove with its lovely beach, from which I had set forth with Orlando Potter long ago to fish on Tripod Shoals. Now the beach was swarming with people, splashing in the water or lying on the beach listening to their boom boxes, and the cove was crammed with a myriad of boats ranging from large cruisers to small outboards. The people who were sporting there were blameless, merely seeking their share at last in the pleasures of that once-lovely place. But it was a scene straight out of Coney Island at its worst. What a far cry from the peaceful days when the lovely Potter farmhouse stood on the bluff above a deserted beach! I felt saddened. Many more people were now enjoying the river—or its remnants—and that was good. But I did not care to return to Potter's Beach again, and I was depressed by the thought that there are now too many people in the world for any of them to know the world at its best.

I am a widower. The island that I loved has passed away. We first met when both the island and I were in our prime, and these are fortunate eyes that followed her and doted on her ways when both of us were in our bloom. But the island of my affection is lost and gone forever like Clementine, and these eyes, too, have done all that they could. So I take my leave of Grindstone and of you, my readers. It is time to say, with Walter Savage Landor,

> I warm'd both hands before the fire of Life;
> It sinks; and I am ready to depart.

Stanley Norcom

My Island Sinks

Stanley Norcom, Author, at age 90

Index

Abraham and Strauss 9
Ackert, Grace 52
Ackert, Harow 52
Ada T., the 39 75
Admiralty Group 40
Alexander Hamilton, the 155
Alexandria Bay 6 8 192
American Channel 9
Amherst Island 211
Arabella Island 75 83 85
Arawanna, the 39
Atherton, David and Laney 17 201
Aunt Jane's Bay 15 173 203
autism 18 22
automobile 45 169

Bacon, Francis MacNeil 84
Bacon, Robert Low 83
Bacon, Virginia Murray 83
bread 25 42 59
Bakewell, Alan 183f
Barber engine 39 135
Base Line ridges 30
Baseline Road 19f 147f 158f 171 201
bats 188
battle of Hickory Island 83
Bazinett, Ada ix
beavers 158
Below the Marsh 23 154 157-164
Benedict, Dr. 124
Bird, Dr. 56
birds 11 16 129 147 158 188
Black, Caroline 163
Black, Davy 2 29 50 56 65 91ff 95-101 104 141 154 159 191 195
Black, Etta Hutchinson 160
Black family 1
Black farm 160f
Black, John 160f 200
Black, Kate Kelly 154
Black, Lawrence 161
Black, Wella 161
Black's Hill 37f 40 125 159 161
Black's Point 179
blacksmith shop 30
Bloodletter Island 165
boarding house 29 90 103 107 189
boathouses 39 43 69 75 91
boating explosion 212
boatmen 75 78 81 84f 105 154 162 183
Bohlen, Charles 83
Boldt, George 9
Boldt Castle 192

Boscobel Island 17 202
Britten, Willy 47
"Britten" of Bowmanville, the 38
Brooklyn 3 13f 45f 96 140 145f
Brown, David 105
Brown, Ella 105
Brown, Elizabeth 29f 103-106 195 204
Brown, Ernest 105
Browning 9
Buck Bay 84
Bullock family 47
Burgess, Gregg 58
Buster Brown haircut 45
butchering 131f

Calhoun, Aleitha 72 179
Calhoun, Ben 65 162f
Calhoun, Maggie McIntosh 111
Calumet Island 15
Camp Frontenac 156 173
camping 46 51f
Canada 27 30 83 161 167 178 211
Canadians on Grindstone 14 29 35f 41 43 47 50 53 55 59 74f 93 113 122 142 153ff
Canadian Ship Channel 165
Canoe Point 40 169-171
Canoe Point State Park 170
canoeing 63f 158f
Cape Vincent 185f
Carnegie, Alice Garnsey 122f
Carnegie, Corbett 85 160ff
Carnegie, Dorothy Garnsey 122f 161f 179
Carnegie, Ella Brown 155
Carnegie family 1
Carnegie, James 123 160
Carnegie, Jessie Brown 28 101 105 159
Carnegie, Leslie 105 155f 160f
Carnegie, Lloyd 162 179
Carnegie, Milton ix
Carnegie, Paul 85 160
Carnegie, Robert 105
carriage shed 196
Carter, Bernard S. 85
Carter, Hope Thacher 85
catastrophies 165-168
Cement Point 84
cemeteries 1ff 27 50 95 101 143 160 189 200
Cerow, Charley 148
Cerow, Gordon 7
Charleston Lake 161

Chase, Sid 29 50 91 115
cheese factory 1 12 17 19 27 41 124 127 147-51 153 180 187
Chicage Granite Co. 89
Chicago Quarry 71 73f 89f 93 95 107f 111
chickens 127
cholera 20
Chris Hansen Junket Co. 150
church 2 22 31 71 81 97 153 179 183 186-205
church attendance 187
church suppers 47 148 209
cisterns 35 199
Chaflin, Mrs. 150
Clara, B., the 11
Clarkson University 170
Clayton 3 5ff 40f 43f 75f 82 98f 135 142 155 185f 212
Clayton band 11
Clayton Bank 43
Clayton Center 54
Clayton docks 8f 11
Clayton government 15
Clayton Guides Association 115
Clayton Museum 13
Clayton public library ix 12
Clayton railway station 8f
Cliff Cottage 105
Club Island 83 85
cobblestones 92
Columbia Hotel 6
Columbia University 85f
Conant, Florence Carnegie 156
Conant, Let 156
Corwell, Russell 191
Cook, Douglas ix x
Cook family 50
Cook, Harry 78f
Coral Island 85
Corbin, Verda ix
Cross-Island Rd. 16 18ff 24 27f 74 92
Crossman Hotel 6
Crouch, Mary 173-175
Crouch, Walter 172
Cummings, Aaron 201
Cummings, Addy 24 28 113
Cummings, Earl 185 201
Cummings, Ernest 201
Cummings, John 185
Cummings, Mabel McRae 185
Cummings, Mildred Dano 200f
Cummings, Milo 201
Cummings, Nellie 24

Cummings, Richard 186
Cummings, Shirley 185
Cummings, Walt 160
Cummings, Will 24 28 39 113 115 200
customs officers 9 47 65 115

dancing 60
Dano, Ambrose and Ardelia 200f
Dano, Elmer 18
Dano family 1 18
Davis, Dr. 56
Deathdealer Island 165f
Debby Lynn, the 156
De Laval cream separator 37
Delaney, Allie 119 170
Delaney, Bertha 119
Delaney family 169f 187
Delaney, Mrs. 119 169f
Delaney's Bay 157
Delaney, William 170
depop-and repopulation 81 188 204 209ff
dialect 14 56 70 95 103
diet 60
diphtheria 20
divinity students 204
Dodge, Cleveland E. 6 43f 75 85
Dodge, Cleveland E. Jr. 86
Dodge, Emmet 24 73 168 196 200
Dodge, Emmet and Nellie 112-116
Dodge Hall 207
Dodge, James 114
Dodge, John 114
Dodge, Nellie 189 204 208
Dodge, Pauline Morgan 85f
Dodge, Willie 114
Dorasdale 93 98
Dore, Gustav 192
Dorr, Alfred 29 70 96
drownings 56 114 168 179 184
drunkenness 52f 58 95f 156 179 191
Dumfounder Island 165
Ebersole, George x
Edwards, Lloyd x
Eisenman, Alvin ix
Edwards, Robert D. i x
Elder, Robert 145
Elder Robinson 189
electricity 128 150 193
Ellis Block 7 11
Ellis, Charles 7
Emery, Charles G. 15 43
Esley pump organ 37

family feeling 121f
farming 81 87 127-134 169 200 210
Faust, Mrs. 107
ferry 41 136
field patterns 127
Fine View 6
fire boat 117
fires 117-119 123 130 148f 178
fishing 34 76 177
fishing guides 11 28 75 11 117 178f
Fleetwing Islands 192
Flynn Bay 19 171
Flynn farm 19 201
Flynn, Joe 177
folk medicine 60 125
Forsyth dome 91
Forsyth, Jeanie 93 115
Forsyth Quarry lands 115
Forsyth, Quarry 37 89 93 95 113 207
Forsyth, Robert 91 95 98f
Fowler, Chauncey 74
French Canadians 1 74f
French Creek 101
Frontenac Hotel 5f 9 11 148

Gabriel, Azad 195
Gabriel, Rev. and Mrs. B.R. 194-199 204
Gailey, Carl 184f
Ganonoque 8 40 47 55 59 65 74 75 78 98 99 153 155 163 166ff 178 213
Gananoque Public Library ix
Ganonoque River 166
Garnsey, Alice 122 .
Garnsey, Ben 27f 97
Garnsey, Bertha 123
Garnsey, Carrie Slate 78f
Garnsey, David 13 17 75 123 208
Garnsey, Dorothy 122
Garnsey family 1
Garnsey, Francis 156 209
Garnsey, Fred 123
Garnsey, Garland 78
Garnsey, Glen 78
Garnsey, Hildred Dano 75 123 208
Garnsey, Hub 13 24 31 75 100 118 121-125 155f 160 162 187 121-125
Garnsey, "Uncle" Hubbard 3 28 74 99 141

Garnsey, John 78
Garnsey, Katy 123
Garnsey, Kenneth 27
Garnsey, Laurence 193
Garnsey, Martha 122
Garnsey, Maude Wright 193
Garnsey, Merrit 155
Garnsey, Robert 18 75 123 156 173
Garnsey, Ruby 123
Garnsey, Thornton 78
Garnsey, Will 48
Gauthier, Billy 154
Ghost Island 167
Gillespie family 9 105
glacial drumlin 170
glacial potholes 40
Goodrich, David M. 85
Gordon, Harry and Maggie 28 155
Graham, Billy 159 171
grain harvesting 130
Grand Tour of the Great Lakes 9
granite 1 28 38 81
Granite Island 93 98
Grant, Robert 73 78
Great Northern Pike 35 77
great depression 145
Grennell Island 6 75
Grindstone Island cheese 150
Grossman, Ben 200

Half-Moon Bay 40
Happ, Charley 11 44
Happ, Clara Reese 11
harness racing 70 78
Hartwell, Mr. 93
harvest dining 130
Haxall, Elizabeth Dodge ix 85
haying 129
Head of the Island 6 39 81-87
Hein, Norvin i vii x 91
Hein, Jeanne x 199f
Hen Island 85
Herald House Hotel 6
Hi Marshall's store 2 13 16 24ff 55-61 71 122 153 173 180 198
Hickory Island 83
Hicks, D.S. 85
history, local vii 182
homicide 168
horses 70 78 129 198 210
Houghton, Paul 183
houseboats 213
housemoving 69f 74
Howard-Smith, Douglas 161

Howard-Smith, Mrs. 161
Hubbard House hotel 6
Hutchinson, Claude 29f 107

ice punts 155
ice cream socials 48 154 177 197 201
ice-floes 20 155
icehouse 35
illegitimacy 57
Indian remains 78
International Hotel 98
International Rift 192
Irish 84 177 211
iron bridge 23 159
Irwin, May 85
Ivey, Mr. 15

Jazz Age 23
Jefferson County Court 90f
jetties 90f
Johnson, Dr. Gove 202-204
Johnson, Ella 162
Johnson family 17
Johnson, Grace 202
Johnson, Jane 57
Johnson, Johnny 84 201
Johnson, Mary 57
Johnson, Norma 202
Johnson, Will and Ella 154 162
Jolly Isle 34
J.P. Morgan & Co. 82

Kalaria Island 168
Kelly family 1
Kelly, Horace 73 90f 93
Kelly, Jim 95
Kelly, Kate 95
Kelly, Potter 183
Kendall, Harold i ix 76
Kendall, Harry 76
Kenney, Captain 8 155
kerosene 14 35 59 117 146
Kingston 8 83 135
Kinney, Betty 44
Kipp family 48 124 154 177f
Kittle, James 200
Koenig, Robert 173
Kufchock, Ruth Cummings x 186
Kumtuit 84 86

La Farge piano 37
Ladies' Aid Society 71 195ff
Lake Ontario 8
Lake of the Isles 192

Lake Fleet islands 165 170
Leavitt, Henry Sheldon 82 84
Leavitt, Martha 82
Leek Island 27 37 48 49 56 73 90 98 142 177
Leek Island Channel 49f 90 93 124 167 177 212
Leek Island Hospital 177f
Lember, Belva Graham 171
Les Roches 83
lightning 148 166
Long Point 157f
Lower Marsh 157 163 169
Lower School 19 171 18
lower town landing 161f
Lowville 1 12 150

MacLean, Dr. Paul 86
mail carriers 123 155f
mailboat 12 15 155f
Manichaeans 195
marina 47 142 208
Marks, Aminta and John ix
Marshall, Ed 57
Marshall, Eliza Delaney 30 47 57f 169
Marshall family 169 187
Marshall, Fred 57
Marshall, Hiram (Hi) 28 30 33 40 55 61 93 97 100 119 153 177 207
Marshall, Mary 30 170 207
Marshall, Mort 28 117-119
Marshall, Mrs. Mort 28
Martin, Barbara 170
Martin, Bertha Delaney 170
Martin, Bill 170
Martin, Junior 170
Matthews family 201
Matthews, Charles 74 200
Matthews, Ruby Garnsey 123
Maybrook 23
McAvoy, Josiah and Ida 169
McAvoy, Ruth 169
McAvoy, Si 169
McCaddy, Willie 98
McCarthy, George 21ff 188
McCarthy, Lowell 22f
McFadden, Bert 183f
McFadden, Ernest 75
McFadden family 201
McIntosh, Charlotte 29 107-111 179 187
McRae, Alexander Richard 33
McRae Beach 28

McRae, Bertha 34 39 42 115f 142 163 181-185 208
McRae, Bessie 21
McRae cabin 21
McRae, Deed Hutchinson 21 161
McRae, Dick 2 40 56 60 177
McRae, Dick and Nettie 33-42 140 141-143 187
McRae family 1 2
McRae farm 15 30 31 157 177
McRae, James 21f
McRae, Jessie 21 75
McRae, Mabel 34 142 181 185 201
McRae, Mary 21
McRae, Nettie 40ff 79 187
McRae Point 16 141 143
McRae's Cove 16 27 142
McRae, Tom 21f 42 75 130 159
Meeks, Don and Doreen ix 53
Methodist. See "church"
Mid-River Farm 83
Middle Road 19
Mix, Myrtle Dano 200
Model A Ford 142
Moneau, Duke 168 178f
Moneysunk Island 38
Montgomery Ward 153
moraines 40
Morgan, Emma Leavitt 85
Morgan family 6 43
Morgan, James Hewitt 82 84
Morgan, Lewis Henry 82 84
Morgan, Martha 84
Morgan, William Fellowes 82 84 85
motor sounds 39f 75
Murdock family 159 200
Murray family 6 78
Murray, Fanny 83
Murray, Harry Alexander 82
Murray, Dr. Harry 83
Murray Hill Island 6
Murray, Dr. Josephine x 83
Murray Bacon, Virginia 83
muskellunge 178

National Institute of Health 86
Navy Islands 170 192
Netley Island 154 162
"New Island Wanderer," the 5
New Perfection stoves 59
New York City 8 14 43 46 52 91 123 143 173 183
Newberry, Jessie Matthews vii 20
news diffusion 148
"Newsboy," the 5

newspaper, Clayton 70
"no tresspasing" signs 212
Nohawkers 83
Norcom family 25 29 69
North Shore Road 24 27 29 69 72-79 90 107 154
"notions" 92 98

Old Home Day 211
organists 189

Packard, Emma 27 73f 115 198f
paintings 132
Papoose Island 6 83 85
Parker, Patricia Bazinett ix
parish house 196
Park Hotel 6
Parmenter family 47
patent medicines 60
Pelow, Joe 8
Pettit, Alden 168
Pettit, Will 30 75 108
Pfeiffer, Gertrude ix 86
Pfeiffer, Ray and Lolita 173
Pfeiffer, Dr. Raymond 86
Phelan, Mary Marshall 30 170 207
Phelan, Stanley 170
Phelps Dodge Corporation 85
Picton Island 92 200
Picton Island quarry 92 200
pigs 38 131f 148
Point Vivian 6
pollution of air, water, sound 211ff
Pope, Beverly ix
Pope, Marvin and Helen 207
population increase 19
population loss 179f
post offices 13 24f 75 95 153-156 180 201 208f
Potter, Albert 75f
Potter, Dr. 75
Potter, Eva 76
Potter family 75ff
Potter, Hattie Kittle 76
Potter, Orlando 75ff
Potter, Walter 76
Potters' Beach 77f 213f
Printer, the Rev. Florence 194
privies 19 38 44 50 109 142 199f
Prohibition 178
Pruyn, Mrs. Frederick 85
Punts lighthouse 165
Punts, the 167

quarries 19 28f 38 89-93 95 147

quarrymen 29 87 109f
quilts 105

R.F.D. route 209
radio 148
rag rugs 105
Ratchford, Mrs. 13f
Rattray, Captain Jim 41 136 155
Red Boathouse, the 84
Reese, Chet 170
Reese, Gertrude 14 43 See "Webster"
reforestation 30 145 170 178 210
"Robert Fulton," the 3
Robinson, Alec 65f
Robinson, Jay 49-54 154 159 212
Robinson, Mrs. Jay 53 107
Rochester boarding house 6
Roman Catholics 170 187 190
Rossmassler cottage 162
Rossmassler, Peter ix 163
Round Island 5
Rouse, Joe, Korleen and Lizzie 20f
Rueckert, Dr. Frederic 86
Rueckert, Joan Dodge x 86
Rum Point 84
rumrunners 178
Rusho family 1 201
Rusho, Gloria viii 75 201 208f
Rusho, Leon i ix 201
Rusho, Marjorie ix
Rusho, Milton ix
Rusho, Robert 75 201 208
Russell, Clarence 163
Russell family 202
Russell, Florence Black 162f
Russell, Hiram 154 162f 198

saloon 104
Sampson family 47
sanitation 20 123 127 148 150 200
schoolteachers 114 142 181
Scotch Irish 1 58 110
Scotch whiskey 178
Scotland 91 95 97 211
Scots 91 98
Scudder 11
Sears Roebuck 153
Seven Pines island 73
Sharples cream separator 37 154
Sharples family 154 162
sheriff 13 168
Shorts' lot, the old 189
Shorts, Deacon Alexander 189
sickness 13 20 55f 58 117 123 143 146 169 185 193

silver mine 201
Skinner spoon 34 76f
Slate, Aleitha Calhoun 72 179
Slate, Elizabeth 160
Slate, Ellen 71 75
Slate, Erma ix x 72
Slate, Erwin ("Buck") 30
Slate, Frank 30 69-72 78 168
Slate, Grace 69 71f 204
Slate, Harry 72 78 179
Slate, Howard 70 72 78
Slate, John 155
Slate, Phrone 30 124 160
Slate shipyard 69 159f 168
Slate, Sylvester ("Van") 69
Sorrows Isle 34
Soulier, Charley 168
south shore residents 171 183
South Shore Road 16f 57
St. Lawrence skiff 177 183
St. Lawrence University 170
St. Regis Indians 170
Stanley Steamer 93
State Mental Hospital 208
stores 36 41f 142 180f 208 (See "Hi Marshall's Store.")
Sturdevant, Flossie 63-67 153f 188 207
Sturdevant, Lilla 66
Sturdevant, Sarah 64ff 204
Sturdevant, Will 30 65ff 135
sturgeon 91
summer people 87 116 154 160 188 199f 203f 207ff 211

Taylor, Chester ix
Teachers' College, Columbia U. 86
telephone 128 193
television 148
Thacher, Louise Leavitt 84
Thacher, Thomas C. Jr. 84
Thacher, Vera Morgan 84
theft 108
Thousand Island Granite Corp. 89
Thousand Islander, the 5
Thousand Island House 6
Thousand Island Park 6
threshing machine 130
Thurso Bay 28 33 37 50 63 69 89 93 96 115 189 211 213
Thurso Bay Association 115
Thurso, Scotland 91
Thurso Village 1ff 16 24ff 27-31 81 159 169f 211
Thwartway 27
Tip Camp 173

219

tobacco 15 36 47 55 58 141 160
"Toronto," the 8
tourists 7
town dock landing 16 57 75 78 171 173
Tripod Shoals 77 213
truck gardening 28 74
tuberculosis 22 63
Turcotte, Ada 75
Turcotte, Clara Fowler 74f
Turcotte, Ed 71 75 207
Turcotte, Ellen 75 207
Turcotte family 1 28 41 141 154 168
Turcotte farm 27 201
Turcotte house site 114
Turcotte, Irwin 75
Turcotte, Joseph 39 74
Turcotte, Aleatha 75
Turcotte, Verna 75
typhoid fever 20

"U-auto-go," the 156
Upper Marsh 23 27f 38 50 89 157ff
Upper School 19f 114 181 209

Van Slate shipyard 159f
Vitek, William x

"Wah Wah," the 39f 55
Walsh, Rev. W.S.B. 190f
Walton House hotel 6
Wanderer's Channel 40
Wapler, Wendell 72 78
Watch Island 6 83f
Watertown 82 142 170 184f
Webster place, the 146
Webster, Bill 33 45 140f 145
Webster family 11
Webster, Gertrude Reese 14 43ff 52 140 145
Webster, Lew 12 14f 42-48 90f 139-146
Webster Point 31 33 37 46 51ff 141 157 171
Webster, Walter Llewellyn 45
Webster's Cove 50
Wellesley Island 181 183 192
wells 20 199f
Westmoreland 193
Whiskey Island 6 83 85
"Whistler," the 39 40 44 135f 142
"Whistler II," the 142
Whiston, Leo 192
Whiston, Rev. and Mrs. Wm. A. **191ff**

White, Camilla Morgan 84
White, Dr. James C. 84
White family 6
White, Michael 84
Wickwire, Mr. 144f
Wide Waters 28 49 73 76ff 90 154
Wild Goose Island 83 85
Williams, A.L. 7
wind 14 39 135 159 166 174f 211
Wolfe, Christopher 85
Wolfe, Emma Leavitt 85
Wolfe Island 211
Wood, J. Walter 6 86
World War I 173 174 177 191
World War II 15 114 146 179f 204
Wright, Mrs. David 193
Wright, Rev. David 193

Yennek, the 8 155

Zencey, Eric x